INTERACTION
PROCESS ANALYSIS

INTERACTION
PROCESS ANALYSIS

*A Method for the Study
of Small Groups*

ROBERT F. BALES

The University of Chicago Press
Chicago and London

The University of Chicago Press, Chicago 60637
The University of Chicago Press, Ltd., London

International Standard Book Number: 0-226-03618-9
Library of Congress Catalog Card Number: 76-15042

CONTENTS

PREFACE

Interaction Process Analysis is a term which has been adopted to designate a body of methods which have been developing over the last twenty years. These methods in various forms have been invented, borrowed, and reinvented by researchers in answer to a wide variety of different needs, but they all have in common some kind of first-hand observation of social interaction in small face-to-face groups.

Similarly, the term "small group" is suggested to provide a convenient way of referring to the kinds of groups which have been or presumably can be studied by this body of methods. Concretely, these groups are very diverse in composition, character, and purpose. Included in the referent are groups such as those formed for group discussion and group therapy, for counseling, planning, training programs, and experimental teaching procedures. Policy forming committees, boards and panels, diagnostic councils in clinical work, problem-solving groups in experimental social psychology and sociology, teams and work groups, family and household groups, children's play groups, adolescent gangs, adult cliques, social and recreational clubs, and small associations of a great many kinds fall within the classification, as do groups of two, such as interviewer and interviewee, therapist and patient, teacher and pupil, and professional specialist and client, to name only a few. Groups of these kinds, ranging in number of persons involved from two to something around twenty, then, may be classed together as "small groups" on the basis of their amenability to study by a certain body of research procedures.

Whether or not this classification is of particular theoretical significance, it is nevertheless clear that direct, face-to-face interaction takes place in all of these groups and there is little reason to doubt that human interaction on a face-to-face level has at least certain formal similarities wherever we find it. Probably it will be recognized also that some more or less identical *problems* of first-hand skills and ethics in human relations are involved for the participants in all. The scientific relevance of the present procedure is based on these minimum assumptions.

There are many people who hope and believe that the most desirable solutions to these problems of ethics and basic human relations skills, in some fundamental evaluative sense, are the same for human interaction wherever we find it. This, so far as the present author is concerned, is a moot point and only in part a scientific question. It involves problems of fundamental values which in their nature are not answerable by scientific methods. However, insofar as these beliefs include assumptions as to the empirical nature of human interaction—that is, that certain types of action tend to have certain types of effects on subsequent action—the methods of science do become involved. In short, the present method, in connection with whatever set of value premises the reader may supply, may be relevant to the answering of problems of values and ethics but, in itself, the method and the assumptions which underlie it are value-neutral. The method is not based upon any particular set of values or ideology other than those which are the norms of scientific procedure.

This work in its present initial form should be regarded as a progress report, designed primarily for other researchers in the field. It is a working manual, not a finished product. Most of the data presented can be regarded only as illustrative. Insofar as the term "interaction process analysis" is accepted by other workers, it should be taken to refer to a body of closely related but changing and developing methods. As such, it has a wider referent than the particular set of categories and procedures tentatively outlined in this manual or referred to in the bibliography. The changing nature of the method is not incidental but inherent, since the method itself is intimately linked on the one hand to theory and on the other to empirical observation, each of which inherently is a growing point for modification.

There is no attempt at this point to present a fully developed and tested version of the method. It might be argued, of course, that the method is too undeveloped to justify the dignity of a special name and publication now. There is a growing demand, however, from persons who need such a method in their research or who are already contributing to its development from starting points of their own. Although the method is still in its pioneering stages, it seems to have reached a point where it can and should be made available to other researchers in the field for the broader application and critical review necessary to its further development. It is planned to revise and republish the manual as often as new developments warrant.

The initial interest which led to the development of the present method was theoretical and general rather than practical or specific. Prior to 1946 the writer had become interested in the possibility of using small groups, such as those indicated above, as a means of developing a more adequate body of theory relevant to the analysis of full-scale social systems as well as to the analysis of the small groups around which the method is primarily designed. As a part of this interest, two memoranda were drawn up in an attempt to formulate some of the basic structural characteristics and dynamic processes one would expect to find in small groups, utilizing knowledge and impressions which are generally current in sociology, social anthropology, social psychology, and psychology. Various parts of these initial documents have been reworked and restated in the sections of this manual which deal with the theoretical framework for the method and the analysis and interpretation of data. The second of these two memoranda contained a series of hypotheses concerning the relationships between various aspects of structure and process one might expect to find in small groups, proceeding according to the model provided by full-scale social systems. It was evident that in order to test this series of hypotheses, involving various kinds of known and unknown vagueness, it would be desirable to develop a method of observation which would give operational definitions of at least the main variables involved and which at the same time would be sufficiently generalized to apply to a large variety of small groups.

Thus, at the outset, it was determined that an attempt should be made to develop a general-purpose, standard set of categories for observation and analysis, rather than a series of special lists of categories, each particularly fitted for a particular kind of group or a particular hypothesis. Studies involving various kinds of process analysis of social interaction in small groups have been made in the past, and some starting points therefore are available. (See Bibliography.) The categories which have been used in these studies, however, are for the most part special sets developed for the purpose at hand. One of the difficulties of specialized lists, of course, is that they are often so tightly bound to their original research context that they can hardly be applied to other groups or, if applied, fit very poorly. A second difficulty is that there are not available norms based on large numbers of observations in terms of which one could assess the findings of a particular study. A third difficulty centers around the fact that in process analysis of this kind (especially when the observations are made directly of the original interaction rather than from sound or typewritten transcripts) extended and detailed observer training is necessary, with definitions of categories and detailed procedures clearly outlined. The fact that in previous studies the training of observers had been done only for the particular experiment made it difficult for others to apply the same set of categories with any assurance of obtaining comparable results.

In the analysis of full-scale social systems, we consider ourselves fortunate when we have roughly comparable rates of incidence of a series of phenomena—such as rates of suicide, rates of crime and delinquency, rates of commitment or mortality for given disorders, birth and death rates, marriage and divorce rates, rates of mobility, incomes, price levels, etc.—for the same social systems, for various parts of the same social system, or for a series of social systems. When these rates are based on data gathered in a comparable way and conform to standard definitions, we are able to make more definitive comparisons. This sort of analysis has been notably effective in the regions of the social sciences where such data have been available. As yet, we have very little systematic data in the form of rates of occurrence of any phenomenon whatever for small groups of any kind. It seems reasonable to expect that progress in the field of small groups will be accelerated greatly as we move nearer this goal.

Furthermore, it is exciting to realize that our attempts need not be confined simply to the production of rates of the second-best degree of relevance for theoretical purposes, which, unfortunately, is often characteristic of rates available for larger social systems. We have the opportunity to design our observations much more exactly around our theoretical needs and, moreover, to obtain *simultaneous* measures of a *system* of theoretically relevant variables.

These were some of the various considerations which led the

writer to the conclusion that there is a need for a general-purpose set of categories derived as clearly as possible from a generalized theoretical framework, with detailed definitions of categories and detailed instructions and training methods for observers. An instrument of this kind, it is felt, can find a place in many kinds of research being done at present in the field of small groups.

It is true that particular studies will often, if not usually, require the observation of particular variables which may not be included in such a general-purpose instrument, or which may be lumped with other variables. However, in the field of clinical psychology to take only a single example, a number of diagnostic tests for personality are available, with more or less standard procedures for observing, recording, and analyzing the data—projective tests, personality inventories, life history schedules, intelligence tests, and the like. In clinical practice and research no one test or procedure is expected to give all of the relevant data for the diagnosis of a given personality or difficulty. On the contrary, a number of tests are employed to give basic measures, in terms of norms wherever possible, even when the diagnostic problem is a specific or limited one, since the personality is considered to be a system or organization in which parts or aspects are so interrelated that even for comparatively restricted problems of diagnosis the clinician needs to know as much as he can find out about the state of affairs in all parts or aspects of the system.

In an analogous way, the present instrument is conceived as a general-purpose supplement to various other instruments or procedures that will be required for particular groups and for the testing of particular hypotheses. It will have the advantages that grow out of extensive use and the development of norms on large numbers of observations and will also give simultaneous measures of a basic system of conceptually relevant variables that are considered to be important aspects of the same empirical system. Indeed, it may turn out that the method will have more value as a simplified conceptual and operational model for the analysis of interaction systems, both large and small in scale, than as an auxiliary instrument in experimental studies. Ideally, it is hoped that it may have some significance in both directions.

The first steps toward the development of the instrument proper were taken in the fall of 1946 in connection with a study of the procedures of a diagnostic council, such as those commonly used in clinics and hospitals. The council in this case was composed of seven members of the Department of Social Relations who were conducting a study of several subjects at the Harvard Psychological Clinic. The observers were allowed to sit in at these conferences at one end of the room and make whatever notes they liked. A beginning was made on the strictly empirical, *ad hoc* level, by attempting to find out whether or not categories could be invented on the spur of the moment to characterize the remarks being made. Almost immediately, of course, repetitions began to occur, and so a preliminary list of categories was built up. The list was ordered according to theoretical preconceptions, and was then tried again empirically. (This weaving back and forth between theoretical formulation and empirical trial is the procedure which has been employed throughout.)

It soon became apparent that some arrangement more satisfactory than ordinary paper forms would have to be developed, for it was desired to keep separate records of the interactions of each person in the group, according to time sequence and according to a list of categories which at that time was very long. At this point, construction of the apparatus described in Chapter 1 was begun. The use of this apparatus has greatly facilitated the development of the method and simplified the mechanical problem of recording; the apparatus, however, is not an absolutely essential part of the method since the list of categories in its present form is short enough to permit the use of prepared paper forms. One year was spent in making and repeatedly revising the list of categories, using the weekly meetings of the Diagnostic Council as empirical test material. Also during this time, a number of ways of analyzing the data were explored and the more promising were developed.

At the end of this academic year, the author attended the First National Training Laboratory in Group Development at Bethel, Maine. Here the list was again revised and used by a team of observers in gathering interaction data on the Basic Skills Training Groups which were the principal work groups present. The content of discussion in these groups was considerably different from that of

the Diagnostic Council and new problems in observation were introduced. Prominent among these were problems involved when a
group uses role-playing and extensive self-evaluation as training procedures. On the basis of this more extended experience, and in anticipation of future uses, the set of categories was again revised, this
time with special reference to its possibilities for use in observing
explicitly therapeutic groups, i.e., groups ranging from two in number, in an interviewing or counseling situation, to groups of patients
up to fifteen or more, as employed for group therapy in hospitals, out-
patient clinics, etc. This new focus resulted in the elaboration of
certain categories but few changes in basic conception.

In the following academic year, the list was used for a variety of
purposes in a laboratory seminar concerned with research methods
in the study of small groups. In this seminar the list was used as a
partial basis for theoretical orientation of the members, as an observation instrument for a diagnostic role-playing test which was developed, and as a basic instrument of observation in an experiment
which involved two different styles of leadership in two groups of
subjects concerned with discussion and training in basic human relations skills. The two leader patterns were defined partly in terms of
the categories of activity which were encouraged, permitted, or pro-
hibited to the leader. The results on members were assessed partly in
terms of modifications and differentiations in interaction patterns.
This experimental use afforded valuable experience in the training of
observers, in the assessment of the reliability and validity of the categories in practical observation, and the usefulness of indices derived
from the observations, both for technical analysis and for feedback
to group members for their own evaluation and training. On the
basis of this experience the system of categories was again revised,
primarily by the lumping of certain categories in which differentiation was unreliable, and by a regrouping of the categories to make
the rationale more apparent.

This revision was used for a second year, 1948–49, in a laboratory
seminar in a similar way, and greater emphasis was placed on problems of reliability and analysis of the data. In the course of this
year, the categories were again subjected to a major revision. This
was probably the most significant simplification in the total develop-

ment of the instrument, in that it brought all of the former categories within the scope of a single problem-solving frame of reference, and revealed that a great many of the former distinctions between categories which had appeared irreducible were actually based on distinctions of time sequence. This discovery made it possible to reduce the total number of categories to twelve, within which certain finer qualitative distinctions can be recaptured by analysis of time sequences. This simplification appears to be a major step forward in the problem of how to get reliable observations without destroying theoretically significant distinctions. The system of categories presented in this manual is the result of this last revision.

The present formulation is the result, then, of a series of some eleven or twelve major revisions and a considerable amount of exploratory experience. The number of categories separately distinguished has varied from five to eighty-seven. The set of categories as it now stands is a kind of practical compromise between the demands of theoretical adequacy, the curbs introduced by the number and kinds of distinctions moderately trained observers can make in actual scoring situations, and the demand for a reasonable simplicity in the processing of data and the interpretation of results to subjects for feedback and training purposes. Although it is expected that further changes will be made, the series of revisions viewed in retrospect shows a rather convincing and consistent trend toward the essential simplicity and generality of the form as it now stands. There is perhaps some reason to feel that the system is approaching a practical optimum form for the generalized purposes it was meant to serve.

It is expected that the system of categories can be used for a great many special problems as it now stands, and for many more by simply breaking down one or more of the major categories to introduce the necessary distinctions without disturbing the other categories or relinquishing the advantages which may eventually accrue from the employment of a standard instrument with the accumulation of data and development of norms.

Besides theoretical deduction and empirical trial, one of the important sources in the development of the system of categories has been the examination and analysis of various lists of categories in one way or another similar to it. The general procedure has been to go through such lists, taking all items in any way applicable or promising, and putting each on a separate card. Each card was then classified under one of the categories in the existing framework, or new major categories were set up to take care of areas not adequately designated in the existing frame. Many items were discarded because they were on an unsuitable level of abstraction, because they were too highly specialized or idiosyncratic, because the term used was rare or obsolete, because they were longer verbal forms of items that could be more simply designated or expressed more generally, and so on. The items in each category were used in developing definitions, and the major headings for the categories were revised in line with content and empirical experience in observation.

Among the lists or observation systems used in this fashion were Murray's list of needs and press (19); Allport and Odbert's dictionary of psychological states and trait names (1); vonWiese's and Becker's list of categories in their "frame of reference for the systematics of action patterns" (29); French's categories for observers, constructed for use in his study of group disruption and cohesion (13); categories for observers, constructed by Lippitt (18), and later by Lippitt and Zander (31) for their studies of group leadership; various lists for use in analyzing counseling protocols by Rogers (23), Porter (21), Snyder (25), Covner (9), Curran (10), Raimy (22), Royer (24), and Lewis (17); Benne's and Sheat's analysis of functional roles of group members (6); Deutche's list of functional roles of group members (11); Anderson's list for observation of teacher-pupil relations (2); Steinzor's list for analysis of verbal interaction in groups (26); observation and analysis procedures employed by Frank and associates in investigations of therapy groups (12); observation and analysis procedures employed by Thelen and associates at the University of Chicago (27) including Withall's Social-Emotional Climate Index (30); observation and analysis procedures employed by Guetzkow and associates at the University of Michigan (14), by Carr in his pioneering study at the University of Michigan (7), by Thomas and associates in their early work at Columbia University (28), by Hader and Lindeman of the New York School of Social Work (15). As this goes to press, the system of Joël and Shapiro (16), developed for recording what goes on in group psychotherapy, has just come to the author's attention.

The debt of the present writer to these various sources will be apparent to those familiar with them. Interaction process analysis, as we propose to use the term, is by no means a new technique. It is still in its bare beginnings, however, in respect to refinement of the method, generalization of the method to apply to many sorts of small groups, methods of analyzing the data, and recognition of its potentialities as an independent growing point of systematic theory. Many, though not all, of the researchers mentioned above have been acquainted both with the work of each other and with the work of the present writer, and have benefited by communication with each other. Nevertheless, within the last few years in various research centers there has been a series of spontaneous and independent developments leading toward a common focus on the process analysis of social interaction in small groups. There is no doubt in the writer's mind that a new empirical field of investigation is crystallizing. This new field cuts across former disciplinary lines in the social sciences, particularly those of clinical psychology, social psychology, sociology, and social anthropology. The study of small groups in their many aspects is quite properly the concern of all of these fields. It has substantial theoretical roots in each of them, and promises to be an important point of articulation between them.

A review of the works cited above will reveal a number of the difficulties inherent in the development of a generalized instrument such as that proposed here. This review may also lead to the conclusion which is that of the present writer—that the development of such an instrument, in spite of obvious difficulties, is a logical next step in a rapidly growing field of research. The general development and use of such an instrument might go far toward making research in the field of small groups a cumulative growth, so that the data obtained by one researcher would be an immediate aid to other researchers who had gathered data in the same terms. The comments and criticisms of all those who may be interested in research in the field of small groups are solicited, and the writer will attempt to aid in any way he can those who would like to use the present method or some modification of it in their own research.

It is a pleasure to acknowledge the support and facilities provided for the development of the method by the Laboratory of Social Relations at Harvard University and especially to thank Professor

Samuel Stouffer, the Director, who has been a staunch supporter and instigator of the project from the first. The Laboratory has constructed and equipped the experimental room in which the research is being done, and has made research time and assistance available to the author for the past three years. The graduate students in the laboratory seminar, Research Methods in the Study of Small Groups, have been willing subjects, observers, experimenters, critics, and to a certain degree, co-authors of the present book. I regret that the decision to omit the citation of historical and theoretical sources of the theoretical framework presented in Chapter 2 prevents me from properly acknowledging my more general intellectual debts. However, I cannot refrain from mentioning and thanking at least two of my mentors: Professor Samuel H. Jameson, my first teacher in sociology, who aroused my initial interest in problems of measuring social interaction, and Professor Talcott Parsons, who, probably more than any other single person, has influenced my thinking in the analysis of social action and social systems.

Special thanks are due to Mr. Fred Strodtbeck, Laboratory Research Assistant, who has played a very considerable part in the technical development of the method, and is the author of Chapter 4.

Robert F. Bales
Laboratory of Social Relations
Harvard University

July 1949

CHAPTER 1

DESCRIPTION OF THE METHOD

The purpose of this chapter is to give a simple, non-technical description of the method as it is used in the laboratory. This is an overview within which the discussions to follow can be fitted.

The observation situation. Illustration 1, page 2, shows two observers seated in the observation room. An intercommunication amplifier and an Interaction Recorder are visible in the foreground. The observers appear to be looking through windows; in reality, these are a row of three one-way mirrors. In the room on the other side of the glass is a group of people engaged in solving a chess problem. They know that they are being observed; that is, they have been told that the mirrors are transparent from the other side and that the observers there have sound recording equipment. The observers, however, are not visible to the subjects. When the subjects look, they simply see themselves reflected.

Illustration 2, page 2, shows the mirrors as they appear to a group engaged in discussion. The background knowledge that observations are being taken probably has some effect on the subjects' behavior, but most of them seem to accept the mirrors as a part of the conventional boundaries of their situation and go on about their business very much as usual. It appears that the knowledge of observation is not a particularly disrupting factor, possibly because we are all used to being observed in social situations, at least in an informal sense. It is disturbing, however, to suspect that one may be under observation, without actually knowing. It is our general practice, therefore, to make the situation clear in a matter-of-fact way. On occasion, the design may specifically require that the subjects do not know they are under observation. In such cases they are taken into the observation room after the meeting; they are shown the equipment and are allowed to listen to the sound recording of themselves until the novelty has worn off. They are also asked whether they have any objections to the specific use the observers wish to make of the data. Thus far, there have been no refusals or negative reactions.

There are two microphones in ceiling baskets in the experimental

Illustration 1. Discussion group from observers' vantage point.

Illustration 2. Discussion group from participants' vantage point.

room where the subjects meet. These microphones are connected to preamplifying equipment in the observation room. This prepares the signal for sound recording either on wire or on plastic discs. (Wire is used when high fidelity and temporary storage is desired; the plastic discs are used when lower fidelity is acceptable and ease of handling and storage is more important.) The signal is also fed into a power amplifier and so to a monitoring speaker for the observers. The volume does not have to be kept low since both rooms are sound treated and the connecting mirrors are backed with a second clear pane to further insulate the rooms from each other. The observers therefore can confer with each other in low tones without being heard in the experimental room. This is a very great advantage in training and complicated observation, since as many as six observers can be accommodated for different kinds of tasks. A team of observers of this size could hardly operate in the same room with the subjects. In general, two interaction observers are used in order to have a check on reliability. Two Interaction Recorders are available. Usually numbers on holders are placed in front of the subjects, for the convenience of the interaction observers who use the numbers to identify the subjects.

Illustration 3, page 4, is a picture of the Interaction Recorder. This apparatus consists essentially of a case containing a driving mechanism for a wide paper tape upon which scores can be written. A detachable glass plate containing the list of categories fits on the top of the case. At the right side of the list, in proper position for marking down scores or checks, the moving tape is exposed. As each score is put down, it moves with the tape under the check list and disappears, leaving the entire space following the list of categories free for writing again. Inside the case, a marker puts an inked mark across the tape at the end of each minute, and a counter on the switch panel shows the number of minutes that have been recorded. The panel also contains a small ruby light which flashes on momentarily once each minute as a signal to the observer to canvass the group for expressive tension behavior which he might otherwise miss in following the more overt interaction. Mechanical details of the Interaction Recorder and directions for construction have previously been published (5).

The arrangement described above is ideal for many sorts of problems. It requires fairly complicated and expensive laboratory facilities, however, and assumes that the subjects can be brought to the laboratory without destroying those features of their interaction which are desired for observation. Many sorts of variations in observational conditions may fall short of the experimental room ideal in one way or another without destroying the essential features of the method.

Ideally, the method is designed for use in the original observation of interaction as it occurs. There is no doubt that a certain loss of content results when the observer attempts to depend upon sound recording alone, and still another loss as the sound record is converted into a written transcript. Even sound motion pictures are

Illustration 3. Interaction recorder.

inferior to the original interaction, to say nothing of their almost prohibitive cost. However, there are many sorts of problems for which an analysis of the sound recording or written transcript should prove quite adequate.

Again, the isolation of the two observers by one-way mirrors appears to be an ideal arrangement, because it involves the least possible disturbance of the subjects. There are, of course, many situations in which this is impossible. The method can be used with the observer sitting at the table with the participants or at a table nearby, providing the subjects have accepted his role as an observer. Situations where subjects are in overt movement rather than seated around a table have not been explored, but there is no reason in principle to suppose that an observer with suitable preparation could not operate while standing or in moderate movement.

The Interaction Recorder is a convenience, but not a necessity. It permits the scores to be retained in their original sequence and simplifies the coordination of scores with the sound recording. Some programs of analysis do not require this refinement, however, and the method may be used with paper forms or the scores may be recorded in a variety of other ways. We have tried dictating the number of the category and the who-to-whom designation to a second sound recording coordinated with the first; while this is possible, it is difficult, since it involves speaking at the same time one is listening, and requires a sound-proof observation room. Listening and writing seems to be a more natural procedure, but further exploration of the possibilities of dictation on the spot is indicated.

Similarly, the sound recording is not an absolute necessity. It is highly desirable as a sort of "insurance" against accidental loss and is necessary to a complete study of reliability. If there is sufficient reason to accept the scores of a trained observer, however, the sound recording can be dispensed with. The absolute minimum necessity in the application of the method is a single trained observer with some way of recording scores. By memorizing the categories and the numbers he assigns to subjects, such an observer might even dispense with prepared forms and require only a pencil and paper.

In brief, the heart of the method is a way of classifying direct, face-to-face interaction as it takes place, act by act, and a series of ways of summarizing and analyzing the resulting data so that they yield useful information. There are a great number of variations in the kinds of concrete situations in which this may be done, various degrees of completeness in the access of the observer to the original interaction, various degrees of completeness in the record he may take, and various degrees of completeness in the analysis he may make of the data. For purposes of exposition we will ignore these many variations and assume the ideal observation and recording arrangements.

The observer's job. How does the observer go about his job? He has the Interaction Recorder in front of him, and on it is the list of categories into which he classifies every item of behavior he can observe and interpret. The classification which he makes is clearly and unequivocally a matter of interpretation; that is, it involves the imputation of meaning, the "reading in" of content, the inference that the behavior has function(s), either by intent or by effect. Strenuous efforts are made to clarify the bases upon which these inferences are made, to cancel out the effects of value judgments from the observer's own particular point of view, to standardize the process of inference, and to determine whether the operation is reliable. However, the essential operation is still one of inference as to the meaningful or functional content of behavior. This feature specifically and radically differentiates the present method from all methods of analyzing interaction on the basis of purely spacio-temporal characteristics, such as that of Chapple (8) or various types of time and motion studies.

The observer, then, has the set of categories before him and is familiar with its ramifications in great detail. He knows the central theoretical meanings of the variables or categories and he also knows the great range of variations of concrete behavior included within each of the categories. He has practiced and developed certain sensitivities and a facility in making rapid decisions and putting down scores. Like a skilled typist or telegrapher, he can work a certain distance "behind." As the people in the other room talk to each other, he breaks their behavior down into the smallest meaningful units he can distinguish, and records the scores by putting down beside the proper category the number of the person speaking and the number of the person spoken to. Thus, if Subject 1 begins, "Oh, by the way, John," the observer writes down the symbol "1–2" (i.e., "Subject 1 to Subject 2") just opposite Category 6, "Gives orientation, etc.," on the moving tape. When John looks up or says "Yes," the observer writes down another score, "2–1," opposite Category 3, "Agrees, shows passive acceptance, understands, etc." These scores written down on the moving tape then pass under the plate containing the categories and leave the space clear for further scores. The observer follows the interaction continuously in this microscopic manner, attempting to keep the scores in the sequence in which they actually occur, and to omit no item of behavior. All kinds of behavior —overt skeletal, verbal, gestural, expressive—are included, provided that the observer can assign a meaning to the behavior in terms of the categories. The problem of determining what constitutes a unit to be scored is discussed in the next chapter.

When the two observers working in this manner have completed the scoring of a meeting, they take the tapes out of the Interaction Recorders. They then have two records which they hope will be sufficiently alike to be accepted as reliable observations. More specifically, they will want to know in most cases whether the variation due to some experimental variable introduced in the middle of the meeting, let us say, is greater than the variation between them as observers.

They can make a rough immediate estimate of reliability by simply placing their tapes side by side, connecting the scores on each in temporal sequence, and looking to see whether the shapes of their line charts are similar. A small segment of such a line chart is shown in Illustration 3, page 4. Connecting lines have been drawn in on the tape in the machine to demonstrate this technique. Such lines, of course, cannot be drawn for real scores until the tape has been taken out of the machine, since the scores move out of sight as fast as they are put down. The drawing of line charts is only a crude preliminary approach to reliability which may be useful in training observers because they can form a quick immediate estimate of the ways in which they differ. Problems of training and of testing reliability for various purposes are discussed in Chapters 3 and 4.

It may be that the primary interest of the investigators is in the microscopic act-to-act sequences as they combine into larger temporal patterns. In this case, the initial analysis may be carried out directly with the tape. Sequential analysis is of particular interest in the development of the method, since it is on the assumption of a kind of idealized sequence, or perhaps several similar kinds, that the categories are arranged in their present order.

The interaction categories. The twelve major categories in terms of which the scoring is done are shown in Chart 1. Since the whole theoretical rationale of the method is involved one way or another in the categories and their content and arrangement, it is not possible in this brief introduction to point out more than a few of the significant features of the system. The theoretical rationale is discussed in detail in Chapter 2 and each category is defined in detail, with examples, in the Appendix.

Perhaps the simplest way to conceive an idealized problem-solving sequence is in terms of the four sections of the chart, labeled A, B, C, and D. Section C constitutes a group of activities which can be characterized very generally as Questions. Section B constitutes a group of Attempted Answers. Section A contains several varieties of Positive Reactions, and Section D contains a similar group of Negative Reactions. Using this conception, one might hypothesize that the interaction process consists of Questions, followed by Attempted Answers, followed by either Negative or Positive Reactions. This, however, is an idealized conception which is largely formal in nature and ignores most of the important empirical characteristics of interaction in which we are interested.

Another way of describing the relations of the categories to each other is to regard the middle area of the system, Sections B and C, as constituting an area of Task Problems, while the terminal sections, A and D, constitute an area of Social-Emotional Problems. The idealized interaction process would then be described as one of alternating emphasis on the two types of problems. When attention is given to the task, strains are created in the social and emotional relations of the members of the group, and attention then turns to the solution of these problems. So long as the group devotes its activity simply to social-emotional activity, however, the task is not getting done, and attention would be expected to turn again to the task area.

Chart 1. The system of categories used in observation and their major relations.

Social-Emotional Area: Positive	A	1 **Shows solidarity**, raises other's status, gives help, reward:
		2 **Shows tension release**, jokes, laughs, shows satisfaction:
		3 **Agrees**, shows passive acceptance, understands, concurs, complies:
Task Area: Neutral	B	4 **Gives suggestion**, direction, implying autonomy for other:
		5 **Gives opinion**, evaluation, analysis, expresses feeling, wish:
		6 **Gives orientation**, information, repeats, clarifies, confirms:
	C	7 **Asks for orientation**, information, repetition, confirmation:
		8 **Asks for opinion**, evaluation, analysis, expression of feeling:
		9 **Asks for suggestion**, direction, possible ways of action:
Social-Emotional Area: Negative	D	10 **Disagrees**, shows passive rejection, formality, withholds help:
		11 **Shows tension**, asks for help, withdraws out of field:
		12 **Shows antagonism**, deflates other's status, defends or asserts self:

a b c d e f

KEY:

a Problems of Communication
b Problems of Evaluation
c Problems of Control
d Problems of Decision
e Problems of Tension Reduction
f Problems of Reintegration

A Positive Reactions
B Attempted Answers
C Questions
D Negative Reactions

A somewhat more abstract way of describing this alternation is to regard the problems in the task area as primarily Adaptive-Instrumental in significance, while the problems in the social-emotional area are primarily Integrative-Expressive in significance. With this terminology one can hypothesize that the necessity of adaptation to the outer situation leads to instrumentally oriented activity, which in turn tends to create strains in the existing integration of the group. When these strains grow acute enough, activity turns to the expression of emotional tensions and the reintegration of the group. While reintegration is being achieved, however, the demands of adaptation wait, and activity eventually turns again to the adaptive-instrumental task. This is still a very generalized and abstract way of conceiving the problem-solving nature of social interaction, but, we believe, one of very great theoretical relevance and power.

A more concrete and differentiated conception of the problem-solving sequence which appears to be at a strategic level of abstraction may be outlined in terms of pairs of categories. It will be noticed that there is a symmetrical relation between the top half and the bottom half of the list of categories, with the middle line between Categories 6 and 7 taken as the starting point. To illustrate, Category 7 is concerned with activities which indicate a need for factual orientation of some kind and Category 6, its companion category above, is concerned with activities which appear to be intended to answer needs of this kind. Similarly, Category 8, asking for opinion, etc., is answered by Category 5, giving opinion, etc. The other categories have a similar relation. For each category below the line there is a companion category above the line, in a position symmetrical with it as to distance removed from the middle line.

Each pair of categories can be regarded as concerned with a particular aspect or phase of the complete problem-solving process. The successful transition through any particular phase may be regarded as one of the functional prerequisites to the maintenance of the interaction system in a kind of equilibrium. By equilibrium, we mean a turnover of the continuing process in a more or less regular pattern and emphasis of phases. For present purposes these functional prerequisites may be formulated positively and given one-word designations which indicate roughly their kind of relevance to the successful and complete problem-solving sequence. In these one-word terms, Categories 7 and 6 are concerned with the functional problem of communication. The next pair, 8 and 5, are concerned with problems of evaluation, and following in order, Categories 9 and 4 with problems of control, 10 and 3 with problems of decision, 11 and 2 with problems of tension reduction, and 12 and 1 are concerned with problems of reintegration.

In conceiving the problem-solving process according to this model, then, we assume that there is a general tendency toward equilibrium; that is, a more or less regular turnover of phases back to a steady-state. In order to maintain or regain the moving steady-state, problems of communication must be solved as they arise, and so must also problems of evaluation, control, decision, tension reduction, and reintegration. It may be that through time there is a differing emphasis on each of these types of functional problems, so that there is an actual temporal order of "agenda topics," as it were, in the course of a group meeting.

To illustrate, it is not hard to imagine that in a small group of, say, five persons meeting for an hour, dealing with a single major topical problem, and coming to a successful conclusion, the order of events might follow something like this order: The first phase of the meeting might be devoted largely to getting an initial factual or cognitive orientation to the problem as the group faces it. This might be followed by a phase of analyzing and diagnosing the situation in the light of the values, needs, and desires of the members of the group, and the formulation of a general common goal. The next phase might be devoted to finding ways and means of controlling the factors in the situation, including the activities of the members, in order to bring about the desired state of affairs which is the goal. On nearing completion of this sub-phase, a sub-phase of actual decision or crystallization of intent might then appear, with further last-minute articulation of the earlier steps. Then a period of laughing and joking might appear as a penultimate phase, releasing and dissipating the various tensions created in the process up to that point. Finally, a short phase of reward, praise, and encouragement of the members by each other would knit the group together again and bring the meeting to a close. In brief, the functional problems of communication, evaluation, control, decision, tension reduction, and reintegration, have been separated out, enlarged into informal "agenda topics," and made to form the skeleton order of major events of the meeting.

This is a highly idealized and schematized conception of the process as we actually observe it. Actually, of course, all of the functional problems are potential at any given point in time, and interaction may turn momentarily to any one of them. For any given period of time within the total span of the meeting, all types of activity may be found occurring. The agenda topics, insofar as they exist, exist only as a matter of relative emphasis. In addition to these complications, which must be taken into account even in the most highly idealized conception, there are many subtle problems of overlapping, unsuccessful completion of phases, turning back, recapitulation, and the like.

Some of these problems are discussed in Chapter 2, since they are involved in setting up the system of categories for observation, and again more empirically in Chapter 5, since in the final analysis we are interested in knowing how interaction actually does proceed under various kinds of conditions, and not simply in how we can conceive of it in some idealized fashion. By "idealized" in this connection we mean conceptually simplified. One should not confuse this meaning with the meaning it may also have as "the way we should like things to go," or "the way we should try to make them go." This distinction has not been clear in many discussions of group process. Very often sentiments as to "how it should go" have been presented as hypotheses as to "how it actually does go," and vice versa. Although both of these problems are relevant to decision in practice or application, they should be kept clearly distinguished from each other in research. We are concerned with how it actually does go under various conditions, and so the idealized conceptions presented above actually are hypotheses meant to be tested by observation. They are incomplete, however, because we have not specified the conditions under which we expect them to hold true.

The testing of hypotheses about process requires a working back and forth from empirical observation to the most general theoretical conceptions we can construct. It involves, among other things, a constant process of redefinition of the concrete activities we class in a particular category as we think we have new insights into their functional significance, and then testing through observation to see whether we can find in our observations more regular uniformities which in turn we can rationalize in terms of our conceptual scheme. Underlying the present set of categories and their arrangement is an assumption that all of the activities which appear in a group, no matter how trivial or apparently irrelevant, can be meaningfully or functionally related to an overarching idea of a problem-solving sequence. If this idea has been conveyed, that is sufficient for present purposes.

How the observations are analyzed. Usually, except for training purposes, the observers or experimenters will want to make a systematic study of their data from several points of view. Extensive processing of the data is facilitated by transferring all scores on the tapes to I.B.M. punch cards, one card per score. A holder upon which the tape may be placed is available. A key on the holder fits over the paper tape in such a way that the category numbers fall in the same place as on the Interaction Recorder. The punch card operator can then read off directly for each score its component characteristics: the number of the category in which the act was classified, followed by the number of the person in the group initiating the act, followed by the number of the person who was the object or target of the act. Tabulations can then be made with the focus of interest on the meeting or group as a whole, the individual members, particular sub-periods within the meeting, act-to-act sequences, and so on.

Up to the present time we have explored only a few of the most obvious of the many types of tabulations and indices which can be derived from the data produced by the method. We hope that in time the method can be standardized so that data which have been tested for reliability can be processed repeatedly for testing new hypotheses for which indices are developed subsequent to the original observation; in this way new hypotheses could be tested in some cases without having to run new experiments. In short, we hope that by standardization the data can be made cumulative. A few of the kinds of indices which have been used and might become more or less standard are described in Chapter 5. Certain results of the use

Chart 2. Counselor's rates of activity in Categories 6, 5, and 8, by ten-minute periods through four interviews with student.*

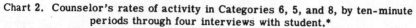

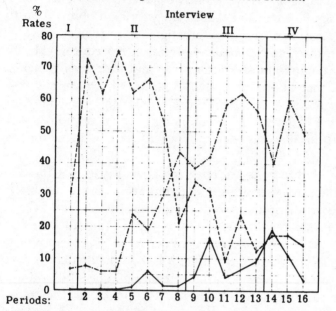

*
Counselor, Mr. William Perry, Harvard Bureau of Study Counsel; student, "Mr. Strand." Scored from typewritten protocol. Rate for each period represented as the proportion of activity in the given category for given period to all counselor activity for same period.

- - - - Category 6 (Gives orientation, information, repeats, clarifies, confirms.)

— · — Category 5 (Gives opinion, evaluation, analysis, expresses feeling, wish.)

——— Category 8 (Asks for opinion, evaluation, analysis, expression of feeling.)

of the version of the method as used at the First National Training Laboratory for Group Development have been reported by Back (3) and Norfleet (20).

Before concluding this introductory discussion it may be helpful to give a few samples of the kinds of problems and analysis for which the method may be used. Chart 2 shows an example from the field of counseling. Mr. William Perry of the Harvard Bureau of Study Counsel has developed a hypothesis which, roughly, is this: If the counselor takes an essentially non-directive role in this type of student counseling for a period averaging somewhere around forty minutes, a relationship can often be established such that the student ceases to expect the counselor to take the initiative and responsibility for solving his problems, but rather undertakes initiative and responsibility himself. Once this relationship is established, the counselor can then begin to introduce interpretations and otherwise play a more active role in hastening the achievement of the ends of the counseling, with a minimum of that impairment of client integrity and freedom which so often accompanies counselor activity.

In testing a hypothesis of this sort, a rather skillful and sensitively timed change of role is required of the counselor. Mr. Perry has been conducting interviews with this hypothesis in mind, and desires first of all to know if he has been doing what he thinks he has been doing. The problem is to delineate the balance between the non-directive role and the more active or interpretive role in various periods of the interviews. The investigator selects a sample protocol from regular practice and subjects it to an interaction process analysis. Chart 2 shows the counselor's rates of activity in three categories immediately relevant to the hypothesis. Category 6 (particularly section c of this category, see Appendix) is the non-directive type of activity par excellence. On the chart it may be seen that this type of activity formed a very large proportion of the counselor's total activity until very near the end of the second interview. (The first interview was a very brief conversation to arrange a meeting.) It begins a general decline at about the forty-minute mark and continues to decline thereafter. On the other hand, Category 5, in this case the interpretation and analysis of the student's problem, remains at the desired very low level until the forty-minute mark, and continues thereafter to increase. Its companion category, 8, in this case asking the student to make an interpretation or analysis of some part of his problem, remains at zero until the fifty-minute mark, when it shows a slight rise just before the counselor's rate of interpretation rises. This sequence—asking the student to interpret before offering to interpret—occurs again in the third interview and in general the rate rises with its companion category. From this analysis, it can be said that insofar as the desired features of the counselor's role can be represented by rates of these particular categories, he succeeded in maintaining the required role for the required time and thereafter modified it slowly to a very different type of role, as required to test the hypothesis.

Chart 3 shows three aspects of the student's activity which are of some interest. Perhaps the most striking change is in his rates of activity in Category 11, which consists of various tension symptoms and either explicit or implicit requests for help. This rate is comparatively very high at the beginning, but declines rapidly to a low point by the forty-minute mark. Thereafter it varies up and down within a narrow range, the high points coinciding with periods in which the subject expressed aggression or antagonism (Category 12), in this case not against the counselor, but against the father who was involved, as it turned out, in the subject's study problems. The expression of this aggression, however, did not begin until after the forty-minute mark, by which time the tension had reached a low point. Another interesting feature is the subject's rate of activity in Category 2 (shows tension release, laughs, jokes, etc.). This rate is comparatively high in the beginning of the series, when tension symptoms are also high. It then drops, and thereafter shows a pattern of alternation with tension symptoms until toward the end of the series, when it again reaches a high. In our experience with various types of interaction, we have come to expect the rate of tension release to be higher at the beginning and end of sessions than in the middle.

This example will give some idea, perhaps, as to the use of the method to check whether or not an experimental variable required by a hypothesis has actually been injected into the interaction, and also the possibilities of tracing in a temporal way the changes in interaction which follow. It also foreshadows the possibilities of studying the concomitant variation of different types of activities—that is, a study of the natural features and internal dimensions of the interaction process—in addition to the more usual study of "before and after" measures. Some of these implications will be illustrated in Chapter 5.

Chart 4 shows another way of arranging data, namely, in terms of "profiles." Profiles for a meeting or a series of meetings, or for individual members within any given period, can be obtained by making a breakdown of the total activity to show the percentage of the total

Chart 3. Student's rates of activity in Categories 2, 11, and 12, by ten-minute periods through four interviews with counselor.*

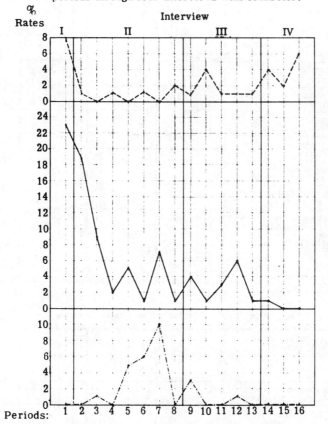

*Counselor, Mr. William Perry, Harvard Bureau of Study Counsel; student, "Mr. Strand." Scored from typewritten protocol. Rate for each period represented as the proportion of activity in the given category for given period to all student activity for same period.

---- Category 2 (Shows tension release, jokes, laughs, shows satisfaction.)

——— Category 11 (Shows tension, asks for help, withdraws out of field.)

—·—·· Category 12 (Shows antagonism, deflates other's status, defends or asserts self.)

Chart 4. Interaction profile of leader in nondirective role.

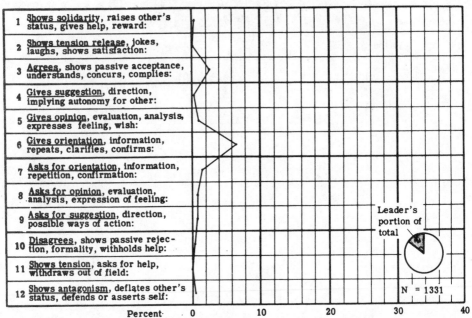

1	<u>Shows solidarity</u>, raises other's status, gives help, reward:	
2	<u>Shows tension release</u>, jokes, laughs, shows satisfaction:	
3	<u>Agrees</u>, shows passive acceptance, understands, concurs, complies:	
4	<u>Gives suggestion</u>, direction, implying autonomy for other:	
5	<u>Gives opinion</u>, evaluation, analysis, expresses feeling, wish:	
6	<u>Gives orientation</u>, information, repeats, clarifies, confirms:	
7	<u>Asks for orientation</u>, information, repetition, confirmation:	
8	<u>Asks for opinion</u>, evaluation, analysis, expression of feeling:	
9	<u>Asks for suggestion</u>, direction, possible ways of action:	
10	<u>Disagrees</u>, shows passive rejection, formality, withholds help:	
11	<u>Shows tension</u>, asks for help, withdraws out of field:	
12	<u>Shows antagonism</u>, deflates other's status, defends or asserts self:	

Leader's portion of total

N = 1331

Percent   0   10   20   30   40

Chart 5. Interaction profile of leader in democratic-directive role.

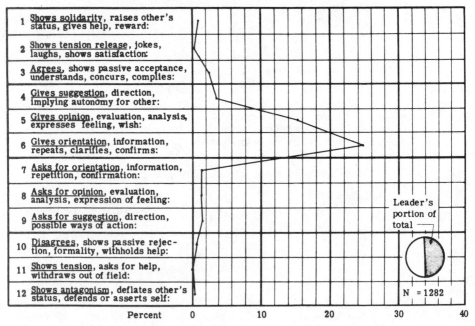

1	<u>Shows solidarity</u>, raises other's status, gives help, reward:	
2	<u>Shows tension release</u>, jokes, laughs, shows satisfaction:	
3	<u>Agrees</u>, shows passive acceptance, understands, concurs, complies:	
4	<u>Gives suggestion</u>, direction, implying autonomy for other:	
5	<u>Gives opinion</u>, evaluation, analysis, expresses feeling, wish:	
6	<u>Gives orientation</u>, information, repeats, clarifies, confirms:	
7	<u>Asks for orientation</u>, information, repetition, confirmation:	
8	<u>Asks for opinion</u>, evaluation, analysis, expression of feeling:	
9	<u>Asks for suggestion</u>, direction, possible ways of action:	
10	<u>Disagrees</u>, shows passive rejection, formality, withholds help:	
11	<u>Shows tension</u>, asks for help, withdraws out of field:	
12	<u>Shows antagonism</u>, deflates other's status, defends or asserts self:	

Leader's portion of total

N = 1282

Percent   0   10   20   30   40

falling in each category of activity. These percentages we speak of as "rates." A plotting of these rates as a frequency polygon attached to the system of categories, as in Chart 4, will show by inspection whether the rate of agreement exceeds the rate of disagreement, whether the rate of integrative status behavior exceeds the rate of malintegrative status behavior, and similar items of interest for technical analysis, feedback to group members, and training.

In a recent exploratory study, two different roles which the leader was required to take in two similar training groups were defined explicitly in terms of the categories of activity permitted and activity denied to him in each. His success in preserving the required role in each group was checked and controlled by the interaction profile through the course of the study. The results were made known to him after each meeting. Chart 4 shows the profile of the leader's activity in one group where he was supposed to maintain a role similar to that taken by a non-directive therapist, as nearly as that can be approximated in a group leadership situation. Chart 5 shows the profile of the same leader's activity in a second group where he was supposed to take a more directive (though definitely not an "autocratic") role.

Perhaps the most striking difference is in the gross amount of leader activity. In the "non-directive" training group, the leader accounted for only about 14% of the total activity. In the "directive" training group the leader alone accounted for about 52% of the total activity. Furthermore, the quality of activity differed. In his non-directive role, the leader had very low rates in all categories except Category 6 and Category 3, both of which were permitted to him as strictly consonant with his defined role. In his directive role, although Category 6 is still his most frequent type of activity, he is relatively much higher in Categories 5 and 4, both defined as consonant with his role, and somewhat higher in Categories 8, 9, and 1, all of which were permitted. In neither role did the leader disagree or display the negative types of social-emotional activity with any significant frequency.

The activities of the members in each group are shown in Charts 6 and 7. The members of the non-directive group, of course, show a fuller profile, since the leader took up less of the total time. The total

Chart 6. Interaction profile of members in group with nondirective leader.

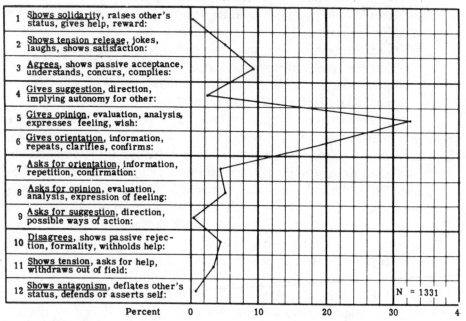

Chart 7. Interaction profile of members in group with democratically-directive leader.

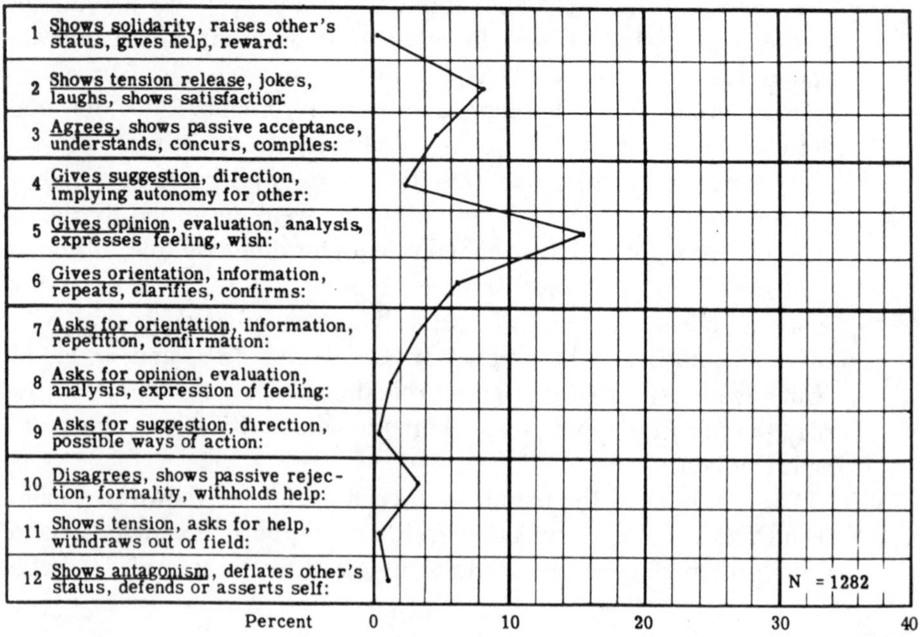

time for the two groups was approximately the same, about an hour and a half, and the total number of scores including both leader and members was roughly comparable, with 1331 for the non-directive group, and 1282 for the directive group. There is then, a real difference in the amount of member participation between the two groups. There are several interesting differences in the two profiles. It will be noticed that, relatively speaking, the rate of showing agreement in the non-directive group is higher, but so also is the rate of showing tension symptoms. In the directive group, the rate of tension symptoms is lower but the rate of showing tension release, joking and laughing, is higher. In the non-directive the members carry more of the discussion in the task area and in particular show a relative nonsymmetrical increase in Category 8, asking for opinion and evaluation. Since in maintaining his role the non-directive leader avoided giving opinion and evaluation, even though asked, this function was taken over by the members, perhaps with some increase in tension, which was not so fully released as in the directive group. There are several reasons for emphasizing that these profiles are suggestive only. In the first place only two groups are shown, each for one meeting, and we cannot at present provide data on a sufficient number of similar groups to say with confidence that these results would appear again. Despite the care we exercised in attempting to match the members of these groups, drawing two groups of six from around eighty volunteers, we learned from observation that there were major differences in the personalities of members of matched pairs. Our interpretation of the differences in terms of our experience thus far is of the nature of hypothesis for further testing and should be recognized as such. Some of the general problems of interpretation are discussed in Chapter 5.

The profiles do suggest, however, that a partial characterization of the kind of social situation a given person is creating and reacting to can be obtained by the analysis of individual profiles. In this particular study the role of the leader was treated as the experimental variable and was conceived to represent a part of the social situation to which the members of the group as a whole were reacting. The behavior of the members was thus treated as a dependent variable. However, the data produced by the technique are such that there is the possibility in analysis of taking the behavior of each member in turn as the independent or dependent variable, and perhaps eventually arriving at rough empirical generalizations as to what types of behavior under given conditions generally provoke other types. Such generalizations in all likelihood would go beyond those we assume in the construction of our system on the idea of "sequences."

The profiles of groups will differ according to many factors. Certainly one would expect variations according to the personalities of the participants, the social organization and culture that has developed in the interaction, and the type of situation and problem the group faces. Several profiles which follow are suggestive in these respects.

Chart 8 is a profile of interaction among pre-school children in a play situation. This chart will also serve as an illustration of the use of the method with protocol material, since it was scored from the written descriptive observations made by Beaver, one of the co-workers of Dorothy S. Thomas in her early work on techniques of observation of social behavior (28). The reader may have access to this published protocol, and so may check his impression of it with the profile presented here. As compared with the profiles which follow, this profile is quite atypical. In general, the proportion of interaction in the social-emotional area as compared with the task area is very much larger than in adult profiles, particularly as to the rates of Categories 1 and 12. The children's social-emotional behavior, both positive and negative, is relatively uninhibited and uncontrolled. Within the task area the highest rate is that of Category 4, direct suggestion, almost entirely unsupported by any preliminary or accompanying analysis, inference, or persuasion. The technique of control among these children is crude in the extreme. Most of the activity in Category 6 is simply a running report about the self and what the self is doing, although in some instances these reports seem to be equivalent to suggestions to the other to join in and do the same.

Chart 9 is a total profile of group discussion among five four-person groups of ninth-grade boys. These groups were presented with two- or three-sentence "stories" of some social situation and then

Chart 8. Interaction profile of a preschool gang.*

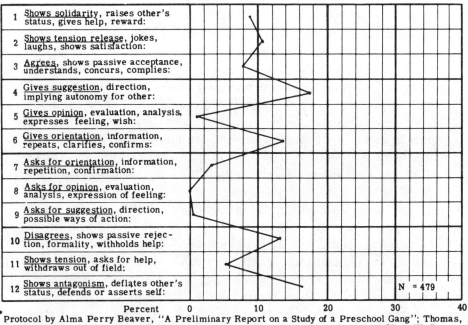

| | | Percent | 0 | 10 | 20 | 30 | 40 |

1 <u>Shows solidarity</u>, raises other's status, gives help, reward:

2 <u>Shows tension release</u>, jokes, laughs, shows satisfaction:

3 <u>Agrees</u>, shows passive acceptance, understands, concurs, complies:

4 <u>Gives suggestion</u>, direction, implying autonomy for other:

5 <u>Gives opinion</u>, evaluation, analysis, expresses feeling, wish:

6 <u>Gives orientation</u>, information, repeats, clarifies, confirms:

7 <u>Asks for orientation</u>, information, repetition, confirmation:

8 <u>Asks for opinion</u>, evaluation, analysis, expression of feeling:

9 <u>Asks for suggestion</u>, direction, possible ways of action:

10 <u>Disagrees</u>, shows passive rejection, formality, withholds help:

11 <u>Shows tension</u>, asks for help, withdraws out of field:

12 <u>Shows antagonism</u>, deflates other's status, defends or asserts self:

N = 479

* Protocol by Alma Perry Beaver, "A Preliminary Report on a Study of a Preschool Gang"; Thomas, Dorothy Swain, and associates, Some New Techniques for Studying Social Behavior, Chap. VI, Bureau of Publications, Teacher's College, Columbia University, New York, N. Y., 1929, 99-117.

Chart 9. Pooled interaction profile for five four-person groups of 9th grade boys.

1 <u>Shows solidarity</u>, raises other's status, gives help, reward:

2 <u>Shows tension release</u>, jokes, laughs, shows satisfaction:

3 <u>Agrees</u>, shows passive acceptance, understands, concurs, complies:

4 <u>Gives suggestion</u>, direction, implying autonomy for other:

5 <u>Gives opinion</u>, evaluation, analysis, expresses feeling, wish:

6 <u>Gives orientation</u>, information, repeats, clarifies, confirms:

7 <u>Asks for orientation</u>, information, repetition, confirmation:

8 <u>Asks for opinion</u>, evaluation, analysis, expression of feeling:

9 <u>Asks for suggestion</u>, direction, possible ways of action:

10 <u>Disagrees</u>, shows passive rejection, formality, withholds help:

11 <u>Shows tension</u>, asks for help, withdraws out of field:

12 <u>Shows antagonism</u>, deflates other's status, defends or asserts self:

N = 1870

Percent   0   10   20   30   40

were asked to choose which one of two "explanations" of the behavior of the person in the story was most "likely and true to life."
In this profile the proportion of interaction in the social-emotional
area is still marked, but the extremely high rates of showing solidarity and antagonism seen in the children's records are not present
here. Apparently there is somewhat greater control over emotional
expression. However, one notes high rates of showing tension symptoms in Category 11, and of showing tension release, laughing, joking, "horsing around," etc. in Category 2. In profiles of adult discussion groups we do not ordinarily find the rate of joking, laughing,
etc. to be higher than the rate of agreement as it is here.

Chart 10 shows a total profile of a similar kind of discussion among
five separate married couples—i.e., groups of two. The husband and
the wife each filled out a short individual questionnaire in which
they made judgments about which of three other couples they had
picked out for discussion "furnished their home most comfortably,"
"did the best job of raising their children," and the like. The husband
and wife were then asked to come to a joint decision about those
judgments on which they disagreed in their individual question-
naires. The profile is the result of pooling of scores on these five discussions. In this profile there are at least two interesting things. The
rate of activity in Category 6, giving information, etc., exceeds that
of Category 5, which is not usual for other types of groups we have
observed. Second, the rate of antagonism, although not as high as
that of the children, is still much higher than that of most adult
groups. The high rate of Category 6 may be in part due to the fact
that the couples had to keep track of a somewhat complicated set of
answers on three different sheets of paper, but also is probably in
part a function of the degree of efficiency in communication that had
been built up in past interaction. It was only necessary for the wife
to recall to her husband "how the Jones' basement looked" that time
they were there, in order for the implication to be clear to him. The
opinion and analysis which might otherwise have been made overt,
were apparently in many cases simply "understood." As to the amount
of antagonism, three factors at least may have been operating. First,
this was one of the few instances in which the subjects were not
aware that they were being observed, and may have interacted some-

Chart 10. Pooled interaction profile for five married couples.

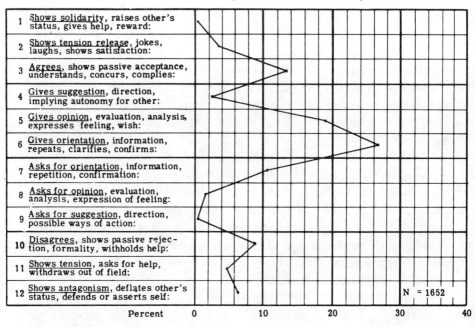

| | Percent | 0 | 10 | 20 | 30 | 40 |

1 Shows solidarity, raises other's status, gives help, reward:
2 Shows tension release, jokes, laughs, shows satisfaction:
3 Agrees, shows passive acceptance, understands, concurs, complies:
4 Gives suggestion, direction, implying autonomy for other:
5 Gives opinion, evaluation, analysis, expresses feeling, wish:
6 Gives orientation, information, repeats, clarifies, confirms:
7 Asks for orientation, information, repetition, confirmation:
8 Asks for opinion, evaluation, analysis, expression of feeling:
9 Asks for suggestion, direction, possible ways of action:
10 Disagrees, shows passive rejection, formality, withholds help:
11 Shows tension, asks for help, withdraws out of field:
12 Shows antagonism, deflates other's status, defends or asserts self:

N = 1652

Chart 11. Interaction profile for thesis discussion group (The Group Mind).

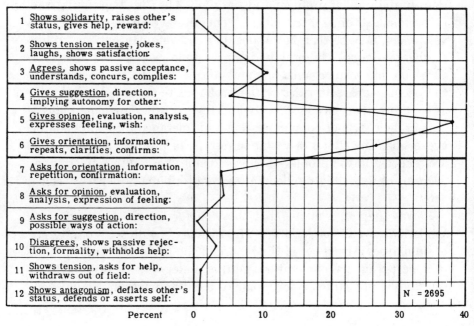

1 Shows solidarity, raises other's status, gives help, reward:
2 Shows tension release, jokes, laughs, shows satisfaction:
3 Agrees, shows passive acceptance, understands, concurs, complies:
4 Gives suggestion, direction, implying autonomy for other:
5 Gives opinion, evaluation, analysis, expresses feeling, wish:
6 Gives orientation, information, repeats, clarifies, confirms:
7 Asks for orientation, information, repetition, confirmation:
8 Asks for opinion, evaluation, analysis, expression of feeling:
9 Asks for suggestion, direction, possible ways of action:
10 Disagrees, shows passive rejection, formality, withholds help:
11 Shows tension, asks for help, withdraws out of field:
12 Shows antagonism, deflates other's status, defends or asserts self:

N = 2695

| | Percent | 0 | 10 | 20 | 30 | 40 |

what more freely than they would have otherwise. Second, the amount of antagonism in the marital relationship may generally be more marked than in the more temporary segmental relationships we usually observe. Third, it may be that the basic solidarity of the bond between the two persons in the marital relationship is generally enough to permit rather free and abrupt display of antagonism without endangering the relationship. There may be more inhibition of aggression in the more fragile relationships than in those which are more durable.

Chart 11 shows a profile of an academic discussion group of six persons, four staff members and two graduate students, meeting for three hours to discuss the thesis plans of one of the students. As compared to the profiles just examined, the amount of negative social-emotional behavior is at a bare minimum, and the rates of activity dealing with information and analysis are unusually high. In most ways, this profile is about as far removed from the profile of the pre-school children as one could imagine.

In these profiles then, we see suggestive traces of the four major sources of variation mentioned: (1) variations in personality, (2) variations in social organization and (3) culture, and (4) variations in the type of problem and situation. The effects of variations in personality, or at least of the general stage in personality development, may be seen in the peculiar characteristics of the profile of the pre-school children and ninth-grade boys. The effects of variations of social organization and culture may be seen perhaps in the peculiar characteristics of the profile of the married couples if, as we think, their basic solidarity and their private language plays a part in their style of communication and tolerance for expression of aggression. The effects of variation in type of problem and situation are reflected in the profiles of the academic thesis discussion group, in terms of its highly intellectualized and minimally negative character.

It was suggested above that these factors might be sources of similarity as well as of variation. This idea may be illustrated in terms of similarities arising out of the nature of the problem situation. One of the experimental explorations getting under way as this is written is a study designed to explore some of the differences in group inter-

Chart 12. Interaction profile, standard chess situation, two-person group.

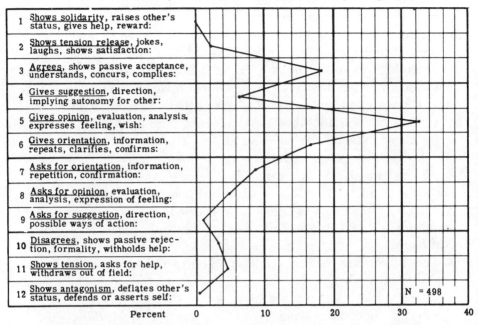

Chart 13. Interaction profile, standard chess situation, four-person group.

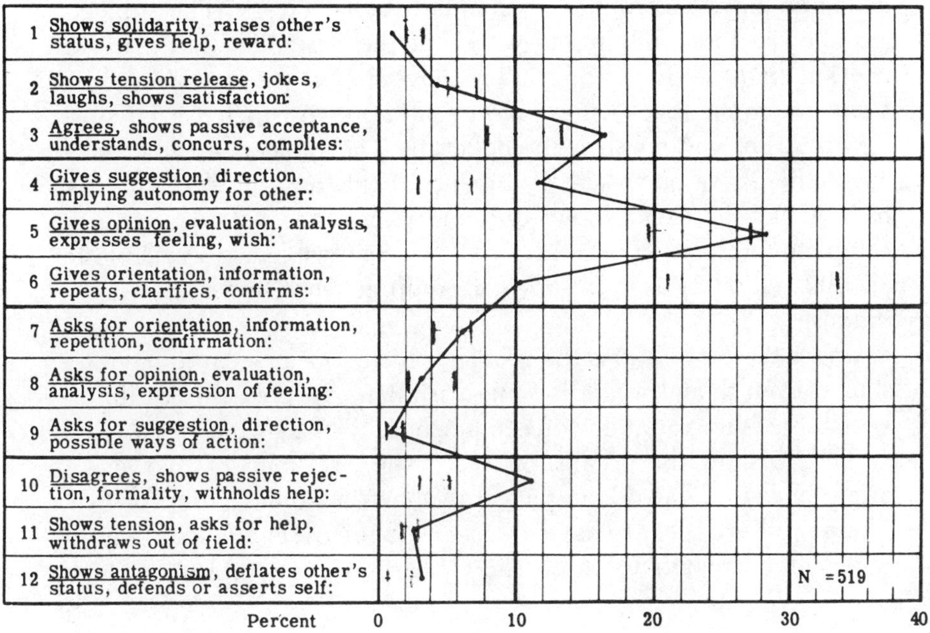

action connected with differences in the size of group. The different sizes to be studied will range from two to ten. In order to reveal the effect of changes in the variable of size, it is desired to hold other factors as constant as possible, or to randomize their incidence. In order to hold the problem situation as constant as possible a large chess board and a standard chess problem involving only four different types of pieces has been devised. Only persons who have never played chess are taken as subjects. An hour in advance of the experimental session the subjects are each given a short manual which describes very simply the moves of the pieces and the few minimum essentials of the game they need to know to be able to solve the problem. This they read in one-half hour. They are then given a short test on what they have learned, the test functioning both as a review and as a test of "chess aptitude." This takes one half hour.

The subjects are then conducted to the experimental room, introduced to each other, and to the problem they are to solve. The subjects are to play as a group against one of the experimenters, and are to plan their stategy and decide as a group on each move they are to make. The experimenter has only one piece, the Black King, which he plays according to a standard best strategy. The subjects are allowed forty minutes to work out the best plan they can for checkmating the Black King. Each move they make is answered by a move from the Black King. This is a situation in which it is possible for groups of various sizes to cooperate. The subjects do not know each other, have no special sentiments about the problem situation, have about the same knowledge and experience with it, and the complete information necessary to solve the problem is available to all. Illustration 1, page 2, shows a group at work under these conditions.

Under these conditions the profiles which appear seem to be quite similar even though there is some variation expected due to difference in size and variations due to personality of participants. Charts 12 and 13 show the profiles of two groups, a group of two and a group of four. Chart 27 on page 149 shows a similar group of five. These profiles appear to have at least a "family resemblance" to each other, as compared to those shown earlier—a resemblance which reasonably may be attributed to the similarity of the problem situation faced by subjects.

The effects of variations of group size in themselves form a range of extremely interesting and practically significant problems. However the observations may contribute to a still more general purpose. If they are stable and reliable we will have the first empirical norms for a standard problem situation. Within the framework of a standard problem like the chess problem and a given size of group, it should be possible to introduce experimental variables of almost unlimited diversity—variations in the problem, in the composition of personality types within the groups, in the social organization of members —with some prospect of being able to detect the resulting variations in interaction. The combination of a standard frame-problem and a standard method of observing and analyzing interaction, with the development of norms, should constitute a new and very powerful experimental instrument in our field.

CHAPTER 2

THEORETICAL FRAMEWORK

Introduction. The purpose of this chapter is to set forth as clearly
and concisely as possible the thinking which has gone into the construction of the present set of categories. It is believed that this general orientation, in addition to the detailed scoring procedures, will
be of help to observers using the method and may form a basis for
subsequent criticism, evaluation, and modification of the method.
The procedures and the set of categories rest upon a state of theory
which is necessarily incomplete; as the theory improves, the method
necessarily will undergo further modification. Similarly, it is recognized that the articulation between the body of theory and the scoring procedures, as well as the actual content and arrangement of the
categories, is imperfect. An attempt to give the main outlines of the
more general theory, therefore, should help to point out the imperfections and lead to further rectification of the method. From the other
side—that is, the inductive side—the use of the categories for
various purposes of observation may lead to empirical insights
which will necessitate modifications in the more general body
of theory, the definitions, the methodological assumptions, and
the principles of classification. For this purpose also it is desirable to have the theory and procedures formulated as explicitly
as possible in each stage, so that their imperfections may be seen
more clearly and may be more readily rectified.

In order to avoid at least some of the problems about the ontologi-
cal or metaphysical status of the body of theory, the whole discussion which follows may be regarded as a set of extended directions
or suggested conventions for the orientation of the observer in the
use of the present method. In keeping with this mode of exposition,
the more general orientation suggestions lead directly into detailed
scoring procedures wherever appropriate. Furthermore, there will be
no attempt to trace the historical and theoretical sources of the point
of view presented here, for it would be impossible to do justice to
this problem without an extensive treatment. The sources are many
and the debt is great.

Concepts and empirical generalizations. It is assumed that the goal of the social scientist is to discover "empirical generalizations" about human behavior and to show that these observed uniformities are special cases or special combinations of more abstract and more general propositions. Generalizations can be made only in terms of regularities of "something" with regard to "something else." If these "somethings" are ideas or symbols, our generalization is simply a kind of assumption, definition, or syntactical statement. It is a generalization or, more exactly, a syntactical proposition about our theory, and not a generalization about what we observe. On the other hand, if the "somethings" are phenomena which can be observed directly or indirectly, the statement of their connection with each other is called an empirical generalization.

The ultimate stuff or empirical phenomena which the social scientist can observe, record, interpret, and arrange in many ways may be thought of under two heads: (1) action or interaction, i.e., the overt behavior of concrete human individuals, and (2) situation. Those things to which action is addressed—the self, other individuals, physical objects, etc.—may be said to comprise the concrete situation of action for the acting individual. All of our relevant empirical generalizations must refer sooner or later to some aspect(s) of concrete action(s) or the situation(s) of action(s). This is true whether the generalizations are made about personality, social system, or culture. Generalizations about any of these three types of systems or structures are at least one step removed (by abstraction) from the more complex and ultimate stuff we can all observe: activity addressed to persons and things. The observation of social interaction and its situation is the common starting ground for all of the social sciences.

In order to arrive at empirical generalizations about human behavior or the situation in which it takes place, it is necessary to break down action and situation into component parts, or to abstract from them analytically. This may be done in an infinite number of ways, depending upon the purpose of the scientist. The social sciences differ from each other in terms of the way they break down this ultimate material or abstract from it. For example, certain selected regularities in the action of a given human individual may be collected to yield generalizations about his personality structure. On the other hand, certain selected regularities in the distribution of types of interaction between separate human individuals in a group may be collected to yield generalizations about the social structure of the group. Again, certain selected regularities in interaction which survive over time and even in spite of complete replacement of particular members may be collected to yield generalizations about the culture of the group.

One type of selection and description is no more primary than the other, and none of the three directions of abstraction mentioned takes account of everything that might be observed about the action and the situation which form the ultimate stuff of observation. When we define just what part or aspect of action and situation we are going to observe, record, interpret, etc., in order to arrive at some generalizations we think will be useful for our purpose, whatever it may be, and give this part or aspect a name, we are defining a concept.

Empirical generalizations can be made only in terms of observation of some kind, and observation can be made only in terms of concepts of some kind. There is no choice as to whether one should or should not use concepts in observation. It is impossible to make a statement of any kind without using some kind of concept. Observers do not differ in that some use concepts and some do not; observers do differ in that some use certain concepts and some use certain other concepts and hence they may observe different things about the same ultimate stuff. It is a commonplace that in scientific procedure it is necessary to examine and define as carefully as possible the concepts which one uses, instead of simply taking them for granted. It is a specific part of the intention of the scientist that his concepts be modified, redefined, or discarded and replaced as his investigation and search for empirical generalizations proceeds.

Definition of a small group. The categories in the present system are designed for use in the observation of social interaction in small groups. The definition as to what constitutes a small group is a minimum arbitrary definition constructed for purposes of the present method, although it might possibly have other uses. The immediate purposes of the definition are to determine the kind of group to which the present technique logically may be applied, and to identify the kind of group to which the theoretical parts of the discussion are meant to apply.

A small group is defined as any number of persons engaged in interaction with each other in a single face-to-face meeting or a series of such meetings, in which each member receives some impression or perception of each other member distinct enough so that he can, either at the time or in later questioning, give some reaction to each of the others as an individual person, even though it be only to recall that the other was present.

According to this definition, a number of persons who have never interacted with each other do not constitute a small group. A number of persons who may be physically present at the same event (such as a lecture) but do not interact with each other enough for each to be able to form any distinct impression of every other, or for the observers to produce some data concerning the relation of each member to every other, do not constitute a small group in the present sense. A number of persons so large or scattered that they interact with each other only indirectly as unknown members of sub-groups or through intermediary persons or impersonal means of communication (such as an industrial organization as a whole) is too large, too complex and indistinct to fall within the definition. Some collections of people which initially appear to fall within the definition may prove, when techniques are applied, to fall outside the definition as a total group because one or several of the members may prove not to have been aware in any discernible way of the presence of one or more of the others. In this case, only that nucleus of persons, each of whom recognizes or remembers each of the others, and is in turn recognized or remembered by each of the others, constitutes the small group.

Kind of content formulated by the categories. The present set of categories is meant to be a general-purpose framework for observation which can be used to obtain a series of standard indices regarding the structure and dynamics of interaction in any small group as defined in the preceding section. It is considered desirable to have such descriptive indices in order to be able to compare different small groups with each other or the same small group with itself at different points in its development, as, for example, before and after the introduction of some experimental variable. In addition to the use of descriptive indices for comparative analysis of this kind, it is desirable to have indices to explore hypotheses concerning "uniformities of coexistence"; that is, hypotheses which seek to formulate regular relationships between different aspects of structure or dynamics within the same group, so that if one has information concerning certain characteristics of the group or its situation, he can predict that certain other characteristics will or will not appear.

In order to be applied for these purposes, the set of categories must be concerned with aspects of interaction so general that they will appear in communication between the members of any small group, regardless of the idiosyncratic content of the topic of their discussion or the kind of concrete problems or subjects with which they may be dealing. In addition to the formulation of behavior that always appears, the list must be concerned with certain variations of behavior which may not be frequent in certain groups but which potentially can and do appear under certain conditions, regardless of idiosyncratic content. The idiosyncratic or "topical content" of discussion or activity is not formulated in the present set of categories. It is assumed that in most experiments or observations topical content will have to be recorded in some way, either by an observer who takes notes as a secretary does in recording the minutes of a meeting, or by sound recording for later analysis or reference, but the systematic treatment of topical content is a different problem from that attacked here. It is hardly necessary to add that the interpretation of rates and other indices obtained from the present method will nearly always require a broader knowledge of the idiosyncratic content.

The present set of categories is concerned with what we call interaction content or process content as distinguished from topical content. In other words, it is concerned with content which it is assumed can be detected by the observer in the process of interaction in any small group. The observer assumes that all small groups are similar in that they involve a plurality of persons who have certain common task problems arising out of their relation to an outer situation, and certain problems of social and emotional relationships arising out of their contact with each other. The possibility of a generalized set of categories like that presented here rests upon this assumption. Another important assumption involved is that each act of each individual in the group can be analyzed with regard to its bearing on these problems. This kind of abstract analysis we call interaction process analysis. The present set of categories is an attempt to provide a systematic framework in terms of which this kind of analysis can be made.

At its own level of abstraction, the type of analysis described here may be called inclusive and continuous. The set of categories is meant to be completely inclusive in the sense that every act which can be observed can be classified in one positively defined category. The method is continuous in that it requires the observer to make a classification of every act he can observe, as it occurs in sequence, so that his work of classification and scoring for any given period of observation is continuous. No observed acts in a given period are omitted from classification except by error.

The condition of continuous scoring itself imposes certain limitations on the kind of content which can be included in the categories. The units fitting the categories are very small. This means that the observer is at all times very busy keeping up with what is going on at the present moment. He does not have time for long or complicated inferences. In a sense, he must work more or less on the surface meaning of activity, and forego involved depth interpretations. The context which can be kept in mind is more or less confined to the "present." The observer is not able, for example, to keep track of all of the vicissitudes a particular proposal has undergone. Suppose that one subject in the group makes a proposal. Another member of the group disagrees, and presents his reasoning. The observer can keep enough of the context in mind to note this as a disagreement. Suppose now, however, that the first person answers with a remark. It may be difficult for the observer to remember back far enough to tell whether this first person is sticking precisely to his first proposal or modifying it in some way. To avoid having the observer try to follow the threads of the argument, the present method requires the observer to drop that earlier part of the context and simply make a judgment as to whether the first person is now agreeing, or disagreeing with what the second person has said. In general, the observer is not required to keep in mind a logical context of argument which embraces more than the contribution of the last person, or the anticipated reaction of the next person. Indeed, the method makes a virtue of this limitation by using restriction of context as a device for resolving certain classification conflicts. This is discussed further in Chapter 3.

It has been taken as a general principle in the construction of the set of categories that all of the categories included should assume essentially the same time span; that is, they should all refer to single acts of communication or expression. This is not to deny that there are significant categories of analysis which require longer contexts for application. Quite the contrary, the burden of proof is probably on the present method to show that it is not excessively atomistic in the size of unit chosen. This particular requirement, nevertheless, has been extremely useful in exposing the shift in level of abstraction which so often takes place in our thinking without explicit awareness. This shift can prevent us from making out the bare skeleton of interaction because of the inclusion of too many levels of analysis at once. With regard to significant categories of analysis which require longer contexts for application, one might wish to know whether a particular idea being expressed is a new idea in the group discussion, for example, or whether a given individual is regularly the person who presents new ideas. This kind of judgment, however, requires that the observer be able to think back and remember whether the idea has been expressed before in the group, and this kind of characterization of an act is therefore suppressed in the present set of categories. As another example, one might want to know whether a particular contribution is relevant or effective according to some logical criterion. Again, this judgment requires a larger context; in some cases the judgment could not be made until after the meeting had been completed and one could trace back and find out whether this particular statement had actually solved a difficulty or changed the course of events in some significant way. As a somewhat different kind of example, one might want to know how rigid, persistent, or perseverative a particular person had been in maintaining an opinion. However, these concepts refer to the way in which a series of acts relate to each other, and hence involve a context which rules them out of the present set of categories. Still other possible categories of analysis require an evaluative frame of reference or context. One might want to know, for example, who makes good suggestions and who makes poor suggestions, from some preconceived point of view. Even if the standards for such judgments were made explicit, the process of inference necessary to arrive at a judgment or classification would often be so long that the observer working on the interaction level could not apply them easily.

In summary, categories have been omitted which do not apply on the level of the single act, which require the observer to be evaluative in the moral, ethical sense, which require him to make judgments of logical relevance, validity, rigor, etc., or which are not readable in themselves or in a minimum context.

The unit to be scored. The unit to be scored is the smallest discriminable segment of verbal or nonverbal behavior to which the observer, using the present set of categories after appropriate training, can assign a classification under conditions of continuous serial scoring. This unit may be called an act, or more properly, a single interaction, since all acts in the present scheme are regarded as interactions. The unit as defined here has also been called the single item of thought or the single item of behavior.

Often the unit will be a single simple sentence expressing or conveying a complete simple thought. Usually there will be a subject and predicate, though sometimes one of these elements will only be implied. As an example, if the actor in a conversation says "What?", the observer translates "What was that?" or "I do not understand you" or "Would you repeat that?", thus filling out both subject and predicate. Complex sentences always involve more than one score. Dependent clauses are separately scored. If a series of predicates are asserted of a single subject, a separate score is given for each additional predicate on the reasoning that each one constitutes a new item of information or opinion. Compound sentences joined by "and," "but," etc., are broken down into their component simple parts, each of which is given a score. As an example of the foregoing points, the following sentence would be analyzed into four units: "This problem which we talked about for three hours yesterday/ impresses me as very complicated/ difficult/ and perhaps beyond our power to solve./" (End of units are indicated by the diagonal.)

In addition to speech centered around the issue being discussed, interaction includes facial expressions, gestures, bodily attitudes, emotional signs, or nonverbal acts of various kinds, either expressive and nonfocal, or more definitely directed toward other people. These expressions and gestures can be detected by the observer, given an interpretation in terms of the categories, and recorded. The observer should remain as alert as possible; keeping his eyes on the group constantly, he should canvass the separate members for nonobtrusive expressive reactions at least once each minute and put down a score each time he can make a discrimination. The Interaction Recorder is equipped with a warning light which flashes on once each minute as a signal for the observer to canvass the entire group for nonobtrusive and nonfocal expressive reactions, such as out of field symptoms. This kind of activity, which tends to be continuous and unlike speech does not break up naturally into units, is broken into units arbitrarily by the one-minute signal. If the observer notes the beginning of such continuous activity in the period between lights, he should record it when it starts and add a score each time the light goes on, for as long as the behavior continues.

In order for an observer to record without missing units he must have a high degree of training along with a full understanding of the rationale which underlies the categories. He also must have well developed position habits on the categories and must clearly establish in his mind the identification numbers of the members. Such an observer will have time to look around the group as he goes along, scoring certain things more or less automatically and when sudden bursts of interaction occur, can fall four or five scores behind without becoming confused. Needless to say, the observer should not permit himself to "fall asleep" or to skip over little things which he might think are out of context or unimportant. Inexperienced observers typically fail to look up, and so miss many scores they should obtain. The experienced observer may have more than twice as many scores recorded as the inexperienced, and it is probable that the observer with fewer scores is missing units he should be scoring. (In practice it appears that a properly trained observer on leisurely adult interaction in groups of six or seven persons engaged in group discussion will obtain from ten to fifteen scores per minute.) Reliability of unitizing depends very heavily, then, on the training of the observers and on the development in joint training sessions of certain minor conventions which help to adapt the method to the particular scoring situation.

The observer's point of view. The observer attempts to take the "role of the generalized other" with regard to the actor at any given moment. That is, the observer tries to think of himself as a generalized group member, or, insofar as he can, as the specific other to whom the actor is talking, or toward whom the actor's behavior is directed, or by whom the actor's behavior is perceived. The observer then endeavors to classify the act of the actor according to its instrumental or expressive significance to that other group member. In other words, the observer attempts to put himself in the shoes of the person the actor is acting toward and then asks himself: "If this fellow (the actor) were acting toward me (a group member) in this way, what would his act mean to me? That is, what is he trying to do, either for himself or for us jointly (i.e., what is the instrumental significance of his act) or what does his act reveal to me about him or his present emotional or psychological state (i.e., what is the expressive significance of his act)?"

The observer assumes that in any given interaction the group member to whom the actor is talking is trying to put himself in the actor's shoes, and that by this process the group member helps himself to arrive at an understanding of what the actor is trying to do or what he is feeling. In other words, the observer assumes that the other, or group member, is attempting to empathize with the actor and, at the same time, is testing his own reaction to what he perceives—all of this as a basic process in communication. The observer carries the complication one step further by trying to empathize with the other or group member as the group member perceives the actor. All categories are described in terms which assume the point of view of the group member toward whom the action is directed. The actor as described in the following section is the actor as seen by the other, as seen in turn by the observer. Although this point of view is theoretically complicated, in practice there seems to be little confusion about it, apparently because it is so similar to the point of view from which we ordinarily apprehend action when we are one of the participants. As a matter of experience, observers have been able to use the list without ever having explicitly raised the question of the point of view. The point of view of the observer is intentionally different from that of a participant only insofar as the framework provided by the categories may give him a somewhat more selective, generalized, abstract, and possibly more articulate mental set, and also, perhaps, an added sensitivity to certain content implications.

The question arises as to how much the observer is to depend upon any knowledge he may have about the personalities of the members in the group, their mannerisms, their ulterior purposes, etc., prior to their entrance into the small group observed. A similar question arises as to how much the observer is to depend upon his knowledge of the common culture of the particular small group, its norms and definitions of the situation which, in spite of the limitations of context described later, may operate to fill out or attenuate the meaning of every act which occurs. The answer is implied above. The observer tries to put himself in the shoes of the other or group member in reacting to each act of the actor and to apply the frame of reference he feels the other to have. If the observer has prior knowledge of the actor which the other does not have, the observer should try to ignore his prior knowledge and see the actor as he thinks the other does. By the same rule, the observer should try to go as deep or to utilize as much of the context as he feels the other does. In therapy situations, when the other is the therapist, this may be a cut below the ordinary level of meaning given to social interaction. With regard to the culture of the group, the observer is to take the common small group culture into account in his interpretation to the extent he feels the other takes it into account. In groups formed under observation and observed continuously through their development, the observer is likely to be acculturated to approximately the same extent as all the other regular members and the problem is thus simplified somewhat. (There may be some reason to believe that even in this case the observer will be less well acculturated than the members since in the busy work of observing unit by unit, he often misses the larger implications of some things being done and after the meeting is not able to give a very coherent account of what went on.) In some situations the observer may be a relative stranger, and in these cases, he simply has to do the best he can in attempting to feel into the cultural overtones. In cases where the observer knows some or perhaps each of the participants more thoroughly than they are known to each other, he attempts to attenuate the fuller overtones he may detect because of his special knowledge and to strike the approximate level of the other in each case, on the basis of his guess as to the knowledge the other would be expected to have through participating in the interaction. In general, it is probably preferable that the observer should not have such special knowledge and that he be able to observe the group continuously from its original formation.

To put the matter in other words, the content of the common culture of the small group serves as the norm or baseline from which present interactions are to be interpreted, whenever possible. This point of view is opposed to one which includes a larger frame of reference peculiarly the observer's own, with respect particularly to what he may know about personalities outside the contemporary group setting. In the application of the present method, the observer is concerned not so much with what the basic personality characteristics of the individual may be, but with the way the individual is reacting here and now in the light of the common small group culture, its expectations, and definitions of the situation. Changes in behavior are expected to occur in response to changes in the situation of each given individual, and the present method of observation is meant to pick up these changes as they occur on the microscopic level. The application of preconceived notions or stereotypes as to what the individual is like in general tends to obscure these momentary reactive changes, because of a kind of constancy tendency in social perception; hence, such application should be avoided insofar as possible. The observer may test his orientation at any point with the rule of thumb question: "If this fellow (the actor) were acting toward me (a group member) in this way, what would his act mean to me?" If the observer finds that his answer is in terms of the fact that the present act reminds him of something he already knows about the actor from outside sources, he knows that his orientation is not that required for the proper application of the method.

Actor and situation as a frame of reference. In the present conceptual frame, every action is treated as an interaction. The action is regarded as an interaction because it is conceived to fall between, to connect, or to relate a subject to some aspect of situation or object. Usually, but not necessarily, the observed interaction will involve at least two separate biological individuals in addition to the observer. We assume that because of the ability to manipulate symbols which is characteristic of socialized human beings, any given person may be an object to himself. That is, in his capacity as a thinker, evaluator, or actor, he can think about himself, have emotional reactions or evaluate judgments about himself, and act in one way toward another part of himself which is tending to act in a contrary way. As examples, we often speak of a person as talking to himself, feeling ashamed of himself, expressing himself, trying to talk himself into something, as agreeing with himself, disagreeing with himself, etc. In cases of this kind, under the present scheme, the self is regarded as a situational focus or object, and that part or aspect of the same concrete individual which is taking the momentary reflexive role is regarded as the subject or actor. A single biological individual in a room working at a problem, talking to himself or thinking out loud, is thus technically regarded as engaged in interaction, and insofar as the interaction is with the self—a social object— the actor is regarded as engaged in social interaction.

The personality, then, in the present conceptual frame, is not treated as an irreducible unit, but is conceived by the observer as a complex of sub-parts or sub-aspects not all of which are in overt action at once. The conception of the actor as only a part (the presently managing aspect of the personality) implies that the actor is not coextensive with the biological individual we observe. It is thus impossible to locate in any exact physical sense the author of the acts we observe. The author or actor involved in any present act is, for conceptual purposes, only a point of reference adopted for the analysis of that particular act. If the observer demands a more concrete way of looking at the problem, he may think of the author of a given act as that part of the person, or that coalition of parts, which for the moment is in command and is managing the motor apparatus. For technical purposes it is probably more satisfactory to say that the actor is simply the subjective or internal aspect of the present act itself, but this way of conceptualizing brings the referent of the term actor almost to the vanishing point and seems to be unnecessarily refined or rarified for the observer in his practical job of recording. The postulation of an actor in a somewhat more substantive sense is a conceptual convention adopted by the observer in order to allow him to think of each act as having an author which is somehow not quite identical with the overt act he sees. This author or actor stands behind the overt act, persists through it, and ties the present act to acts which have gone before and to acts which are to come, but it is nevertheless not identical with the more extended self seen as object by the actor.

When the standpoint of the actor is taken as the point of reference for a given act, everything else relevant to that act becomes, for conceptual purposes, a part of the situation. Actor and situation thus constitute the two poles of a major conceptual dichotomy. The actor, as the subject pole of the dichotomy, is treated as an irreducible point of reference (although the categories on the interaction list constitute a classification of things which the actor does). The situation, however, as the other or object pole of the dichotomy, is differentiated into a set of major foci. These foci (or target objects as they will be called later) are considered to group into two major target areas, which may be called the inner situation and the outer situation. The target objects in the inner situation include the self, and the other(s) or in-group. The target objects in the outer situation include the other(s) not present or belonging to the out-group, and all of the residual physical objects, spatial and temporal relationships, etc., which may be relevant to action but which are not subjectively identified by the actor as a part or aspect of self or in-group.

Before presenting a diagram which may help to make these relations clearer, we have to consider the fact that the process of action itself, regarded as a chain or progression of activities, past, present, and anticipated future, may be viewed as object from the point of view of actor—this as another result of the ability of the socialized human being to manipulate symbols. Some assumptions about the nature of this process will be presented in a later section; just now we are concerned merely with making a place for it in our conceptual

Chart 14. Actor and situation as a frame of reference.

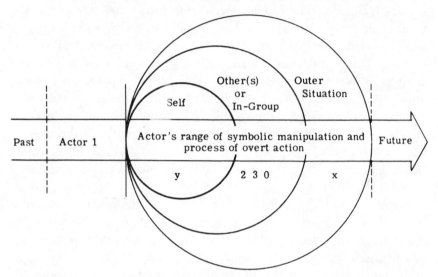

framework. Since the process of action in itself is intrinsically time-involved and transitive, it cuts across the subject-object dichotomy which is the primitive basis for all of the above distinctions. In other words, from the point of view of the actor, the process of action may be felt subjectively to be peculiarly a part or aspect of self; or a part or aspect of the other or in-group; or a somewhat external affair which, so far as subjective involvement is concerned, is a part of the outer situation.

The diagram presented in Chart 14 is a crude representation of the relationship of the various aspects of the actor-situation frame of reference.

It does not seem possible to represent all of the relationships properly on a two-dimensional diagram. The diagram is meant to be only roughly illustrative of certain assumptions and may very well imply things that are not meant. The essential things it is meant to represent, however, are these:

The observer does not appear on the diagram, since we cannot state in general whether the actor will be aware of his presence at all or, if so, whether the actor will see him as a part of the outer situation, as a part of the in-group, or as a part of the self (as he would in the case where the observer is participating as a member of the in-group and is scoring his own present activity). The reader of the diagram is taking the point of view the observer takes as he analyzes a given momentary act.

The actor, designated by the number 1 in this particular case, is given a special place on the diagram in an attempt to represent the fact that he is conceived as separated from the situation proper. However, we also wish to represent him as having no determinate position in the time dimension, or rather, as having a range through it by symbolic manipulation and overt action. Aside from the position designated actor, all the rest of the diagram represents the other side of the dichotomy, i.e., the situation. The time dimension as perceived by the actor reads from left to right, from past, through present, to future. Only the present is drawn in as actual. It is desired to represent the assumption that the past and the future can be reached (i.e., constructed or reconstructed) by the actor only through the channel of symbolic manipulation, which in itself is present activity. Similarly, the actor can only reach (i.e., perceive, evaluate, or change through overt action) the various foci in the situation through the channel provided by the process of action itself, which includes both symbolic activity and overt action. The process of action itself is represented as cutting through past, present, and future situations and is transitive in nature, passing from subject pole to object pole as indicated by the arrow-like form. The process of action is the generalized means through which the various factors influencing action are related to each other by the actor. The situation is represented by three progressively inclusive circles, with the innermost circle representing the self, the next innermost the other or in-group, and the outermost representing the bounds of the outer situation.

Thus, from the point of view provided by the concept "actor," the situation includes not only the outer situation—past, present, and future, external to the group as a whole, which we ordinarily think of when we say the word "situation"—but also all other persons of the in-group—and their past, present, and potential future activity, which is the inner, peculiarly social part of the actor's situation—and finally, the self, which includes the effects left in the personality by past actions, the memories, the desires, all the more permanent structure of the personality formed through genetic endowment and past experience, and the future possible actions which the actor regards in the present moment as object. The total situation, then, embraces the outer situation, all other persons of the in-group, and the self.

The rough similarity of these concepts to certain basic psycho-analytic concepts is evident: The similarity of actor to ego; of outer situation to reality; of inner or social situation to super-ego and ego-ideal; and of the self, regarded as object, to the id. However, the present writer is not prepared to say how far this similarity goes. It is his impression that the cognate psychoanalytic concepts are similar in logical origin but are designed for a somewhat different purpose, are ordinarily used in a more substantive sense, and carry with them assumptions about the genetic sources, the particular kind of content, and the semipermanent character of parts of the personality which imply a stability of reference to the terms which are not characteristic of the present concepts. The terms actor and situation in the present conceptual scheme do not have stable refer-ents through a time span of any length. At best, the observer can point to their concrete referents only for a given momentary act which he chooses to isolate for analysis. In the next act of the same person, another part or aspect or balance of forces may be uppermost in the personality, in the sense of steering action, and what the observer a moment ago regarded as actor now becomes object or a part of the self. Furthermore, a second source of instability of referent consists in the fact that when another person speaks or acts in rela-tion to the first, the referents of actor and situation reverse as the observer changes to a point of view in which the second person now in action is actor, and the first person and his now past activities become a part of the situation. In other words, actor and situation, as the observer uses the terms, are two poles of a conceptual frame-work which the observer uses to characterize certain aspects of each act as it comes along. The referents of these concepts change both as action proceeds with the same person acting and also as the observer changes his point of view to a new person. For the observer, the act itself is the center of attention; the actor and the situation are descriptive aspects of the act.

There is a further source of instability of referent of the concepts.

This consists in the fact that the actor in a given momentary act, even in the abstract sense described, may be acting with regard to the outer situation in one or both of two different capacities. The actor, regarded as the executive agent of the self, may at the same time be acting as the momentary executive agent of the other or in-group. The first instability of referent mentioned above arises out of the fact that the present act (which is identified with the actor) in the next moment may become a part of the self seen as object. The present instability of referent arises out of the fact that the actor is capable of regarding the object—group or other person— as a part of the self or as extensions of the self. For example, when the actor "asks for help" (Category 11), he may be acting primarily as the agent of the self vis-à-vis the other. However, when he "suggests a course of action" (Category 4), he may be acting as an agent both of the self and of the other or in-group vis-à-vis the outer situation, since he envisages cooperative action. The observer regards the actor as capable of identifying himself with the other group members in such a way that a larger psychological unit is formed, and this larger unit vis-à-vis the outer situation may constitute the psychologically relevant subject-object polarity. This last fact does not present any additional difficulty in scoring "who to whom" since the number assigned to the person is used to designate the actor, whether the actor is acting on behalf of the self only, or on behalf of both the self and the other.

The problem of scoring "who to whom" as a part of the present method is a matter essentially of identifying the actor and the target object for a given act. The target object may be defined as that area or focus in the situation (i.e., self, other or in-group, or outer situation) which the actor aims to affect or change, or which is affecting and changing him, and to which he is therefore giving primary attention in the present momentary act. To return to the diagram in Chart 14, the reader can represent a single act or interaction by drawing an arrow, beginning at the point designated actor, signified by the number 1, passing by way of the process of action, and ending in any one of the three target objects. For example, if the act under analysis were the question "I wonder where I put my glasses?" asked by the actor of himself, an arrow passing from "1" to "y" would locate the act. The act would be recorded on the Interaction Recorder or on a paper form by putting the symbols 1–y (read one to y) following Category 7 on the list of categories. In later reconstruction we would be able to say what preceded and followed this act, whose act it was, and that it was a question asked by this person of himself, asking for some kind of information or report; in short, that he was trying to remember something. The topical content—the fact that it was his glasses he was trying to remember—we could get only by checking through the sound recording or written transcription.

The method employs conventional symbols to stand for the actor and the various foci in the situation. Each individual in the group is assigned an identification number by the observer. These, and the symbols O, x, and y (to be explained below) are chosen to fit in with the positions on the columns of IBM punch cards, so that they can be punched in directly without an intermediate coding. Thus, the IBM punch card code and, at the same time, the key to the symbols on Chart 14, is as follows:

The *actor* is designated by his assigned number, 1, 2, 3, etc.

The *self* is designated by the letter "y."

The *other* is designated by his assigned number, 1, 2, 3, etc.

The *in-group* as a whole is designated by a zero.

The *other(s) not present and in the out-group,*
    the *outer situation,* and
    the *observer* are all designated by the letter "x."

The *process of action itself* is designated according to its psychological location, as a part of self, other, or in-group, using the same symbols as above, generally as "y."

Thus, an interaction recorded 1–y, 2–y, etc. is identified as some interaction addressed by the actor to himself. An interaction recorded as 1–2, 2–3, etc. is identified as some interaction addressed by a given actor to some other specific person in the group, that is, the in-group. An interaction recorded as 1–0, 2–0, etc. is identified as some interaction addressed generally to several members or the in-group as a whole. An interaction recorded as 1–x, 2–x, etc. is identified as some interaction by the given actor addressed to or directed toward some other person not physically present in the in-group, but only recalled or symbolically represented.

The problem-solving sequence as a frame of reference. The preceding section presented a set of concepts dealing with certain aspects of the context within which any given act takes place and in terms of which the act may be located and scored. The concepts in that section are all derived from the subject-object polarity which we assume to be a descriptive characteristic of any human interaction. One of the target objects within this frame of reference was called the process of action itself. The purpose of the present section is to carry the analysis of the content of action a step further by introducing further assumptions about the process of action and by presenting further concepts in terms of which the observer can think about the process of action not simply as a target object, but as a *differentiated* target area. As a differentiated area, the total process of action in itself becomes a context within which a given act may be placed or located in a way similar to that in which the act is located in the subject-object polarity, as described in the preceding section.

The observer assumes that the total process of action is complex in a variety of ways. In this section we are concerned with three aspects of this complexity. First, we think of the process as complex in that it involves a distribution of phases, or parts, or aspects in the time dimension. This assumption made, we find that we have to think of the process as having an internal complexity at any given point in time. Finally, we find that the process is complex in that it involves a distribution of parts or phases between persons. All three of these assumptions are interlocking, and in certain respects identical.

With regard to time involvement, the total process of action as a system of acts is conceived as proceeding from a beginning toward an end, from a felt need or problem toward a solution, from a state of tension toward tension reduction, from a state of heightened motivation toward motivation reduction, or in an instrumentally oriented or meaningful way which may be described in terms similar to these. Action is conceived to have a sense or direction such that any given act is relevant, either logically or causally or both, to what has gone before or what the actor expects to come or both. A given act is thus regarded as a part of a larger context which is distributed in the time or process dimension, and the act is given its character in certain measure by its particular location in this context.

This forward and backward reference of action in the time dimension is assumed to rest largely on the ability of the normally socialized human animal to deal with his situation by the manipulation of symbols. This ability, we postulate, makes it possible to remember the consequences of his past action and to foresee the consequences of his present activity, or rather, to build up expectations as to what the consequences will be. In human action, we assume, both the remembered consequences and the expected consequences can become a part of the effective causation of action. The manipulation of symbols is conceived to be not simply an epiphenomenon, but an aspect of action as "real" as any other in its causal role. The manipulation of symbols, we assume, can operate to steer the ongoing act; it is through the manipulation of symbols that the present act can bear a *meaningful* as well as a causal relation to what has gone before, and that the anticipated future can play a *causal* as well as a meaningful role in the present. In short, the manipulation of symbols or the imputation of meaning on the part of the actor is, insofar as it is present, a part or an aspect of the causal process.

We thus assume that every act has important ties at least to what has gone before and usually to what the actor expects will come. As a remark about our conceptual scheme, we recognize that in postulating an actor who is the author of an act and momentarily differentiated from the self, we implicitly make the assumption that *all* behavior we observe has important ties in the forward and backward directions through the concurrent manipulation of symbols, since in a technical sense the referent of the concept "actor" is the present process of symbol manipulation. This is a heuristic assumption. We do not fully accept it, even within our conceptual scheme, recognizing that some of the behavior items we score (as examples, some of those in Category 11) may be almost entirely without symbolic content for the actor. We choose nevertheless to retain the terminology in which we attribute every behavior item to an actor as if the act had symbolic content, and we make the exception explicitly in those few instances where it is necessary.

When we wish to make a distinction regarding a predominant

weight of emphasis on the backward or forward reference of action, we shall use the terms "expressive" and "instrumental," respectively, to designate the proper weight of emphasis. If the act is judged by the observer to be steered by cognitive orientation primarily to the past, or if it is felt to be caused in a nonmeaningful manner by some existing state of emotion or motivational tension in the self, and if the results which follow it are judged not to have been specifically anticipated by symbolic manipulation, we shall speak of the act as primarily expressive. On the other hand, if the act is judged to be steered by a cognitive orientation to the future as well as the past and to be caused in part by the anticipation of future consequences, we shall speak of the act as instrumental. This distinction is recognized in our everyday habits of speech: in what we have called primarily expressive activity, the individual is said to act "because" of some immediate pressure, tension, or emotion. In the instrumental act, the individual is said to act "in order to" realize certain ends. Thus, we might drum our fingers on the table *because* we are nervous or tense, or we might raise our eyebrows *in order to* summon the waiter. The difference lies in the degree to which anticipated consequences enter in as a steering factor. All instrumental activity is also expressive, as we view it, but not all expressive activity is necessarily instrumental. All behavior is considered to be at least expressive, as viewed by the other and as apprehended and scored by the observer.

The point was made that in addition to its reference forward and backward in time, the total process of action is conceived as involving an internal complexity in a given period or at a given point of time. According to our conception of the matter, the reference forward and backward would be impossible without the internal complexity of symbolic manipulation and, conversely, the internal complexity of symbolic manipulation is intrinsically (i.e., both genetically and logically) bound up with the forward and backward reference.

The internal complexity of any given act at a given time can be conceived by the observer in terms of elements or aspects of the action process which are traditionally designated as the cognitive, affective, and conative modes of orientation. As we shall use the term "cognitive" aspects, it will subsume a range of "adaptive" variations of behavior which emphasize the manipulation of sym-. bols. These variations include perception, apperception, memory and recall, observation of and inference about the object, and communication with social objects. By the term "affective" aspects, we will understand a range of "expressive" variations, including emotional and optative reactions of all kinds to the object and evaluation —liking, disliking, approval, disapproval, etc.—of social objects. Finally, by the term "conative" aspects, we shall designate a range including decision about the object and active, overt, goal-oriented or instrumental attempts to withdraw from, adapt to, change, or control the object, including the potential activities of social objects. The socially oriented referents of the above terms are not generally given in their traditional definitions. The reasons for adding them will be apparent shortly.

It seems clear that individual acts differ in the degree of emphasis they place on one or another of these aspects; it is also clear that there is a variation in time. But no act is clearly made up of just one aspect and there seems to be no sure uniformity with which the variations in emphasis may appear in time. The most satisfactory assumption seems to be that *every act* involves some characteristics which we can abstract and call cognitive or symbolic, some characteristics we can abstract and call affective, and some we can abstract and call conative. (For certain other purposes these analytical characteristics can be designated by a cognate trio of terms: adaptive, expressive, and instrumental.) The ongoing process of action is assumed to require description in terms of all three aspects and is conceived to be responsive to deficiencies in the articulation or "support" of any of the three aspects or to surpluses, especially of an affective sort. Thus, as we shall think of the matter, when the articulation of any of these aspects fails for any reason to be adequate to maintain or support the ongoing process as a total stream or where affect is sufficiently strong, there is a sudden modification of the cognitive-affective-conative stream or process directed toward a mending or further development of the deficient aspects or an expression of the surplus affect. This deficiency or surplus removed, the stream modifies to mend another deficiency or to overcome another barrier to its free flow. The acts which we conceptually isolate and observe are these sudden modifications of the total stream, and our classification of them is in terms of the deficiency or surplus we judge to be present, or the kind of support to the ongoing process which they offer, or the kind of barrier they remove (not in terms of what they "are").

Although it seems impossible to make a direct deduction from the categories cognitive, affective, and conative, in the traditional sense, to a series of categories which formulate phases in the problem-solving process, the assumptions which we have made just above about the nature of the process, along with certain other assumptions about the social and cultural nature of the process, do give us a base from which deductions can be made. If we assume that the process of action which we are trying to describe takes place in a social context, and if we assume that implicitly or explicitly it is divided among persons and is shared by them, we can derive a fundamental sequence which will serve our purpose. As we conceive it, the process of action, from its genesis in the personality of any given individual and in its very nature, logically and ontologically, is a *social* process. Under these assumptions, we conclude that in the interaction of any small group the problem of maintaining adequate cognitive support or articulation of the total process of action is a problem of joint or shared cognitive orientation to or articulation of the problem elements (or target areas). Similarly, the problem of maintaining an adequate affective support of articulation of the total process is a problem of a *joint* or *shared* evaluation of the problem elements or target areas. And finally, the problem of maintaining an adequate conative support or articulation of the total process is a problem of *joint* or *shared* decision or consensus about the direction of instrumental activity.

From these assumptions about the social—i.e., the joint, shared nature of interaction—we can derive a set of categories which will describe the verbalized and overt problem-solving activities of a single individual, but we are unable to reverse the procedure. That is, we are unable to derive a set of categories that will describe adequately the problem-solving activities of either a single individual or a small group if we start simply from the categories of cognition, affection, and conation in their most general sense as a deductive

base. It appears that the concepts of cognition, affection, and conation are relatively high order abstractions from the concrete matrix
of interaction and are to be derived from more generic process-
related concepts of interaction, rather than vice versa. They are abstracted in such a way as to ignore the fact that the processes to
which they refer are essentially social, and distributed between persons in the interaction process.

From the assumption that the process of action is a process which
goes on *between* social objects (actor and other where more than one
individual is involved, or actor and self in the case of the single individual) we conclude that *communication* between the two foci is
an indispensable feature of the process if it is to proceed in other
than an expressive way. Communication between the two or more
foci, however, as we view it, is in itself an achievement, i.e., it is a
result of interaction and requires interaction if it is to be maintained
or sustained. This seems to imply that at least in some sense, interaction is prior to communication. This indeed is what we do imply,
along the lines suggested by George H. Mead, but this is an area of
problems which we can by-pass by assumptions for the present.

If we by-pass for the moment the problem of how communication
is achieved, and assume that at some given time it has been achieved
and that action is proceeding in a small group as a joint or shared
process, we also assume that insofar as communication does exist,
the essential elements of the process are reproduced, repeated, or
represented symbolically, separately in the minds of each of the participants. We also assume that each person proceeds with an awareness, or at least an assumption, that the process is being shared with
the other. The "sense" (i.e., the intuition of appropriate cognitive, expressive, or instrumental consonance) of the activity of each of the
participants, both from his own point of view and the point of view
of each of the others, depends upon the way the present act fits into
the total shared process. Insofar as the process is shared or is felt
to require a sharing by each of the participants, any failure of
sufficiently exact reproduction in the mind of any *one* of the participants (as to the thinking, feeling, or intention of the others) may be
felt by him and by the others to constitute an impairment of the
integrity of the total process and may constitute the occasion for one

of the sudden modifications of the total process, as mentioned above, in an effort to restore its shared integrity.

Such repairs as we observe them empirically seem to involve at least three separable acts or interactions. The observer can distinguish an "initial act" which signals at least to him (the observer) and often to the other participants that the impairment is present. Such an act is sometimes primarily expressive (such as a startled or bewildered expression on the face of one of the participants) but often is an act which is apparently *meant* by the actor to signal a difficulty or need, such as a question, a disagreement, a request for repetition, or the like. If the signal is noted by another participant, the next act is often a kind of attempted answer to the problem indicated by the signal. This attempted answer we shall call a "medial act." Again, the "medial act" may be primarily expressive, but often is an instrumental act which has a problem-solving relevance to the problem signaled by the initial act; examples of such instrumental acts would be an answer to a question or the giving of a requested repetition. Following the medial act, the first participant usually gives a signal as to whether the attempted answer of the other has or has not solved the problem signaled by the initial act and this permits the other to determine whether the process is again integrally shared. This third act we shall call the "terminal act." It is conceived to be terminal simply in a logical or communicative sense, not necessarily (in fact, we believe, usually not) terminal in an empirical sense; i.e., there are few impairments of process which are repaired to the satisfaction of all in a simple three-act sequence. A nod of understanding or an agreement might be terminal in both a logical and an empirical sense. A disagreement following an initial act and medial act would be logically terminal with regard to the two prior acts but it might at the same time empirically constitute the initial act of a new three-phase sequence. The terminal act, as we define it, may be either positive or negative. In any sequence we shall call a terminal act positive if it signals that the actor apprehends the attempted answer of the other as a successful solution to the problem raised by the initial act; we shall call it negative if it signals that the actor apprehends the attempted answer of the other as an unsuccessful solution to his own problem. Chart 15 shows the categories arranged in a problem solving sequence according to this conception.

In applying the method, the observer should keep in mind this idealized three-phase sequence as a logical context which will help him to locate and classify the act. The sequence will often be observed to follow through empirically as described but this does not always occur. Sometimes initial acts are ignored. Often medial acts continue autonomously and are interrupted by an initial act of an-

Chart 15. The problem-solving sequence as a frame of reference.

Initial acts	Medial acts	Terminal acts		
7	6	10	3	
8	5	11	2	Future
9	4	12	1	
Questions	Attempted Answers	Negative Reactions	Positive Reactions	
Forward reference	Forward and Backward reference	Backward reference	Backward reference	

The numbers are the numbers of the twelve categories. For detailed definitions, see Appendix. For category titles, see Chart 16.

other logical sequence from another participant before terminated by the first actor. Sometimes no discernible terminal act is given. When the terminal act is negative, the sequence necessarily becomes more extensive and complicated, overlapping with the next.

The problem-solving sequence—initial act, medial act, and terminal act—is presented here not as a characterization of the way interaction always goes but as a specification of the *minimal* number of interactions logically necessary to restore the integrity of the total process of action when a single impairment has appeared in interaction between the minimal two participants. These three phases may be thought of as a conceptualization by the observer of a problem-solving sequence at a minimal degree of articulation. As such, the three concepts taken as a sequence constitute a "context" in terms of which we can classify or locate any given empirical act. Stated another way, the three concepts taken as a sequence constitute one of the conceptual dimensions which we shall use to generate or deduce, or rationalize the set of categories in terms of which observations are made in the present method. This dimension, it may be repeated, is deduced not simply from the general assumptions that the process of action has cognitive, affective and conative aspects, (which we retain as an additional specification) but rather it is deduced from probably more essential or basic assumptions about the social, joint, or shared nature of the action process as we observe it and about its distribution in time. The logically minimal distribution in time and the logically minimal distribution between actors is merged into the one conceptual sequence: initial act, medial act, and terminal act. The frame of reference is thus applicable even though we are observing the verbalized problem-solving activities of a single individual.

The recognition that we are dealing with interaction and not simply with solipsistic acts of conceptually isolated individuals involves the recognition that there are certain fundamental characteristics of action which we cannot deduce from the conception of action in terms of cognitive, affective, and conative aspects. The idea that an act is a part of an *interaction system* which is distributed both in time and between members is a fundamental idea and must be accepted as axiomatic. It is not a conclusion that can be deduced logically from more elementary principles or properties of action. These *are* the most elementary properties, as we view the matter, and can be observed or at least apprehended or grasped from first-hand observation.

To make this idea more concrete and to extend it a bit beyond the three-act sequence, let us suggest an experiment. First we would have to accept provisionally the system of categories and observation method as the set of concepts in terms of which our observations were to be made. Suppose then we set up a standard problem like the chess problem described in the preceding chapter. We obtain a number of groups of a given size, say five people each, and observe each of them according to standard procedures until they complete the problem. Suppose we then found that for each group taken as a whole the profiles were very similar.

Then suppose that for one group we were to break down the total period they required to solve the problem into six or eight sub-periods, and made a profile for each sub-period. Suppose we found these sub-periods were very different from each other. If the profiles for these sub-periods differed from each other more than the total profiles of the series of groups differed from each other, we would have some justification for saying that there is a system-influence which is distributed in time, so that one discovers the pattern of the system only by observing through a complete "cycle of operations". and not by smaller samples.

Now suppose we were to take a total profile for one of our groups again and, instead of a time breakdown, we make a breakdown to show the profile of each individual member. Suppose these profiles turned out to be very different from each other and yet fitted together to make a total group profile just like the other total group profiles. If the profiles for these individual members differed from each other more than the total profiles for the series of groups differed from each other, we would have some justification for saying that there is a system-influence which is distributed between members, so that one discovers the pattern of the system only by looking at the total activity of all members put together over the total time or, in other terminology, by looking at the social system and not simply at the individual roles.

This is a concrete illustration of one meaning of the proposition that each act is a part of an *interaction system,* distributed in time and between members. We do not have immediately available data which were gathered to test these hypotheses but the illustrative material presented in Chapter 5, together with that in Chapter 1, bears quite directly on the problem.

Chart 16, which should be compared with Chart 15, illustrates the positions of the twelve categories in the problem-solving sequence conceived in this way. The problem-solving sequence is visualized as a system of interaction distributed in time and between members,

Chart 16. The system of categories used in observation and their major relations.

Social-Emotional Area: Positive	A	1	Shows solidarity, raises other's status, gives help, reward:
		2	Shows tension release, jokes, laughs, shows satisfaction:
		3	Agrees, shows passive acceptance, understands, concurs, complies:
Task Area: Neutral	B	4	Gives suggestion, direction, implying autonomy for other:
		5	Gives opinion, evaluation, analysis, expresses feeling, wish:
		6	Gives orientation, information, repeats, clarifies, confirms:
	C	7	Asks for orientation, information, repetition, confirmation:
		8	Asks for opinion, evaluation, analysis, expression of feeling:
		9	Asks for suggestion, direction, possible ways of action:
Social-Emotional Area: Negative	D	10	Disagrees, shows passive rejection, formality, withholds help:
		11	Shows tension, asks for help, withdraws out of field:
		12	Shows antagonism, deflates other's status, defends or asserts self:

a b c d e f

KEY:

a Problems of Communication
b Problems of Evaluation
c Problems of Control
d Problems of Decision
e Problems of Tension Reduction
f Problems of Reintegration

A Positive Reactions
B Attempted Answers
C Questions
D Negative Reactions

with a general tendency to move from an initial state in which some problem is recognized to a terminal state in which the problem is solved. By abstracting in one way we can visualize certain problems as growing out of the relation of the members of the system to a situation that impinges on their adjustment. We can designate these problems in the traditional way as problems of cognitive orientation —"what is it?"; problems of affective orientation—"how does it affect us?"; and problems of conative orientation—"what shall we do about it?".

These three types of problems may be said to arise quite directly out of the nature of the relationship between the interaction system and the outer situation. These are problems of "foreign policy" or external relations. But the interaction system has an "internal extensity" also—its distribution in time and between members—and this internal extensity gives a different twist to the problems just mentioned.

With regard to the problem of cognitive orientation, one recognizes that there is a temporal dimension ranging from the appearance of a cognitive lack of some kind to the appearance of a solution in terms of understanding, and a "social" dimension (member to member) which makes the problem one of *communication* leading to decision, and not simply one of perception.

So far as the problem of affective orientation is concerned, again there is a temporal dimension leading from tension to tension reduction in some sense, as well as a social dimension which makes the problem one of *evaluation* leading to decision in a more social, rounded sense and not simply one of diffuse emotional reaction of isolated individuals.

Similarly, for the problem of conation there is both a temporal and a social dimension ranging from vaguely stirring impulse through communication, evaluation, *decision*, and the *control* of overt action calculated in turn to control the situation and result in tension reduction.

Each of the problems mentioned above—roughly in order, the problems of communication, evaluation, control, decision, and tension reduction—is "nested" into the next, as shown in Chart 16, by the nesting brackets on the right. That is, the solution of problems of evaluation assumes an ongoing successful solution to the problem of communication; the solution of the problem of control assumes an ongoing successful solution of both the problems of communication and evaluation; and so on. The solution of each problem in turn can be regarded as a functional prerequisite to the solution of the next. In this sense, each in turn becomes a more complicated or higher order problem than the last, since each involves all of those preceding and something more. Finally, all of the preceding problems are nested into the problem of social integration or reintegration.

This last point requires more comment than we have prepared the ground for to this point. However, a few things can be said in anticipation of the next section. We start with the recognition that the interaction system is distributed in time and between persons, and is in contact with a situation which is a constant source of problems. We recognize tension reduction and reintegration as the state of affairs toward which the system tends but also as a state of affairs which demands the intermediary solution of a nesting series of sub-problems which may fail of solution at any point and for any number of reasons external to the system as such. If there is a failure of solution of any of the sub-problems we assume there is by so much a failure of tension reduction, and the integration of the system is threatened. Even in cases of successful solution of the sub-problems we assume that there is a "wear and tear" involved in the solution of sub-problems which demands periodic activity oriented more or less directly to the problem of distributing the rewards accruing from productive activity back to individual members of the system and re-establishing their feeling of solidarity or integration with it. In particular we believe that the necessities of control or modification of activity in order to control the outer situation productively is likely to put the existing integration of the system under strain, no matter how successful the attack on the situational problem may eventually be. In order to show more fully why the effort to adapt to the outer situation creates tendencies toward malintegration, it will be necessary to give a more complete treatment of interaction as constituting a social system. This we will do in the next section.

To sum up certain aspects of the point of view presented here, one can say that the process of problem-solving in a group involves a series of social processes. Conversely, those phenomena in social systems referred to as social processes are or should be regarded as problem-solving processes. One can go further and say that what we usually regard as individual problem-solving, or the process of individual thought, is essentially in form and in genesis a social process; thinking is a re-enactment by the individual of the problem-solving process as he originally went through it with other individuals. It can probably be maintained with considerable success that the best model we have for understanding what goes on *inside* the individual personality is the model of what goes on *between* individuals in the problem-solving process. The component parts—acts in a system of interaction—are identical.

In short, the idea of an interaction system is a key theoretical starting point. From it one can derive the ideas of personality, social system, and culture as particular sub-types of systems, distinguishable by abstracting in different directions from the same concrete observable phenomena: interaction. On the other hand, the characteristics of interaction as we observe it cannot be deduced from even our most general ideas about any one of the sub-systems—personality, social system, or culture. Nor can the characteristics of interaction systems be entirely deduced from our most general ideas as to the characteristics of the single act in any isolated sense. This starting point, however, is more general than the others. Although it may not be entirely clear from the short exposition here, the writer is convinced from his attempts to solve the theoretical problems posed by the present method of observation that the idea of an interaction system is a generic concept toward which we shall be forced as we attempt to integrate our theory concerning personality, social systems, and culture. Apparently there is no single logical criterion or axiomatic base from which we can deduce its properties, although the properties we assign to it must be consonant with what we observe at first hand and with what we believe theoretically about personality, social systems, and culture.

The total set of categories used for observation thus expresses a conception of the various elements in interaction systems as we observe them on a relatively low level of abstraction. The categories fit together so that, even without theoretical explanation, they can be grasped and held in mind as a *gestalt* or "total map." The distinctions between the categories can be gauged almost by feel and one does not have to memorize literally the maze of detailed definitions in order to classify interaction as it occurs, although the trained observer should have read them repeatedly.

These qualities, insofar as they exist constitute the attainment of one of the objectives of the present system. It was desired from the first to have the categories constitute a system such that as a whole they would constitute a *context* within which each component category gained its principal meaning by its particular position in the context. In other words, each category is meant to gain its central meaning from its position in the set of categories. The placing of a category in a particular position with regard to the other categories is the most important part of its definition. Even in the practical busy job of observing and recording, we believe, the categories cannot be defined properly and distinguished from each other simply in terms of the more empirical characteristics and varieties as given in the detailed definitions of the categories in the appendix. The present aspect of the definitions is considered to be more important and critical in deciding where to classify a given empirical act than the more detailed empirical definitions listed under each category. This aspect, moreover, takes precedence in all cases where the significance or place of a particular act in the total process indicates a category different from that indicated by the empirical form of that act. Thus, whereas the term "laughs" appears nominally in Category 2, as a tension release which is equated with showing relief or satisfaction, it is quite possible that the laugh may have quite a different significance in the total interaction process. It may constitute a deflation of the other's status, for example, and in this case its more definitive function in the problem-solving sequence takes precedence and it would thus be classed in Category 12.

If the most critical part of the definition of each category is conceived to be its relation to the total set of categories, it is evident, theoretically at least, that if one omits or does not understand a part of the total set of categories in the observation instrument, he probably changes to some degree the definition of each of the categories he retains, and so the way he uses them. Thus the comprehensiveness and the arrangement of the total list of categories is not a matter of indifference. This is the logical basis for making the use of the *total set* of categories an integral part of the present standard method. It is the writer's belief that observers can do a better job of classification (or that two or more observers are more likely to agree with each other in their classifications) if they have in their minds and visually before them the total *gestalt* of the full set of categories rather than an abbreviated list of selected categories or sections from the set. If the job of classifying is a job of "locating" a given act on a "map" or in a total context, it seems reasonable to expect that the observer can do the job better with a map of what he assumes to be the *complete* territory before him, however much the map may lack in finer detail, than if he has to locate what happens with only a fragment of the map or a collection of fragments put together in a haphazard or mechanical way.

The use of the total set of categories as the *gestalt* within which the classification is made is thus viewed as an integral part of the standard method, as are also the requirements of continuous scoring, and the requirement that all the persons in the observed group should be observed and scored by the same observer. When more than one observer is to be used—and this is recommended—strict adherence to the present standard method requires that each do a complete job. The labor should not be divided between the two. Their jobs are parallel repetitions of each other rather than interdependent parts of the total job. The idea is likely to occur to those who begin to use the method that preliminary training can be facilitated by dividing the labor so that a given observer scores only on selected portions of the list, or for short periods of observation, or observes only one person in the small group under analysis. In the present writer's opinion, however, results obtained by this kind of division of labor cannot legitimately be expected to agree closely with the result of the standard procedure. Division of labor may be preferable in some respects, as well as inferior in others—we have no very substantial grounds for opinion on this as yet—but there seems to be sufficient *a priori* reason for expecting that the results will be different and, in a strict sense, not comparable.

The assumptions about the importance of the total *gestalt* provided by the set of categories and the major frames of reference are in part responsible for the effort which has been expended in attempting to put the categories together in logical groups so that they can be grasped as a kind of gestalt, or closed system, or a total map in the mind of the observer. This effort has probably not been completely successful, as further use may show. As a matter of principle, complete success can hardly be expected at this point since the set of categories and their arrangement is like a crude and partly hypothetical map a group of explorers might use in an expedition which had as a part of its purpose a better mapping of the territory. An important part of our purpose is to arrive at a better and clearer picture of the basic structure, anatomy, or main dimensions and outlines of human interaction—i.e., what categories we need to describe it. Many of the things we may learn by the use of the instrument will change the instrument, for the instrument is in itself an extended set of hypotheses about the basic structure of interaction.

The social structure of the group as an aspect of the interaction system. Within the actor-situation frame one of the major target areas distinguished was that composed of the other(s) or in-group. Here we shall be concerned primarily with internal differentiations within this target area and with the self in relation to it. A target object was defined as that area or focus in the situation (i.e., self, other or in-group, or outer situation, or the process of action itself) which the actor aims to affect or change, or which is affecting and changing him, and to which he is therefore giving primary attention in the present momentary act.

The actions of other individuals in the situation are always relevant to the problems of tension reduction of any given individual, since the action of others may aid or interfere or modify his own activity in various ways. It is to the advantage of every individual in a group to stabilize the potential activity of others toward him, favorably if possible, but in any case in such a way that he can predict it. All of the individuals in the group are in the same boat so far as this problem is concerned. All of them, even those who may wish to exploit the others, have some interest in bringing about stability. A basic assumption here is that what we call the "social structure" of groups can be understood primarily as a system of solutions to the functional problems of interaction which become institutionalized in order to reduce the tensions growing out of uncertainty and unpredictability in the actions of others. The "culture" of groups similarly is to be understood as a system of solutions to the functional problems of interaction, but in this case the emphasis is on the problems arising out of the relation of the system to its outer situation in semi-abstraction from its internal relations. It is emphasized that the differentiation between social structure and the rest of culture is only a differentiation in direction of abstraction from the same concrete interaction system.

Although the social structure of the group and its culture both arise out of interaction and are formed by it, once formed, they constitute a part of the framework within which further interaction proceeds. In a similar way the personality arises out of interaction and is formed by it, but once formed, in however small a respect, it becomes a part of the framework within which further changes take place. In order to understand a great many of the nuances of interaction one must know the existing "structure" or "shape" of the personalities involved in the group, the relations they have established with each other, and the culture which they hold in common, vis-à-vis the outer situation which they all confront. Interaction as we observe it concretely seems to take all of these "structured influences" into account.

"Motivation" is a term we often use to designate the subjective combination within a given individual of these various structured influences on interaction. It is a term which we can use very handily to "stop the action" at a point which is advantageous for analysis. In this sense motivation can be regarded as the total state of the individual in relation to his total situation which is presumed to exist before and during any given act and which impels him to do what he is doing. Even the very simplest treatment of motivation must recognize a distinction between those aspects of the complete motive which simply impel the actor to "do something," and those which orient the action in a particular instrumental and adaptive way. The more adequate treatment of motivation is one in which the motivational elements are regarded as present "inner" surrogates of the structured influences of factors which also are, or once were, "outer."

Motivation is not directly observed. It is "reconstructed" by the observer from the action of the individual before, during, and after the given act, and from the situation; from both those aspects which can be directly observed and those aspects which the actor is presumed to impute to the situation from his own subjective point of view. The *relevant* situation thus is not only directly observed by the observer from his own point of view but is also reconstructed from the action (including, of course, the verbalization, which is also interpreted) of the individual under observation before, during, and after any given act. Although motivation-reduction, or tension-reduction, or satisfaction in some very broad sense is assumed to be the aim, sense, or function (not necessarily in a conscious or premeditated way) of all action, and action is "explained" or "interpreted" by referring it back to motivation, this is only a conceptual device which allows us to leave certain things unexplained while we go on to analyze other things. For many purposes motivation itself requires explanation, and this we do by referring it *in part* to the situation as the acting individual is presumed to be oriented to it and *in part* to still historically prior motivation which the individual brings to this particular situation. If the part we are interested in is the part that refers to the structure of the present situation, we have converted our conception of an "inner motivational factor" into an "outer factor" which we can deal with more easily. However, if the part we are interested in is to be referred to the historically prior motivation the individual brings to the situation, then we must continue with a life historical analysis until we come to the place where we can see how the "inner surrogate" factor was established by experience in an outer situation.

The full interpretation of action thus always sooner or later involves analysis of the life historical dimension as well as the immediate present dimension. If the analysis is followed back far enough by the tracing of the interaction between prior motivation and situation of action, there is an eventual segregation of two fundamental variables: original biological equipment and experience in situation. For some problems of analysis it is necessary to reconstruct this historical process very far back to earlier experiences in particularly crucial situations or perhaps completely back to original biological equipment and environment. For other problems of analysis it may be sufficient to make certain assumptions about both original biological equipment and prior experience in situation and then center the analysis on the structure of the situation in which the individual is oriented at present. For still other problems it may be necessary to make a historical reconstruction on the situational side to find out how the situation came to be what it is in the present. In any case, regularities in motivation on the adult level are to be understood quite as much in terms of stable features of the situation of action, both present and past, as in terms of stable features in original biological equipment. In a systematic and even in a historical sense, one is not more primary than the other. In understanding the content of adult human motivation or any motivation which is in part a product of "experience" or "learning," both have to be taken into account.

In this section we are concerned primarily with those features of the situation of action which consist of the system of social relationships of the participants. The way in which the orientation of the actor to the main dimensions of his social relationships can be used as a key to some of the main dimensions of his motivation will perhaps become clearer in the course of this section. This section attempts also to clarify the logic by which the sub-varieties of interaction are listed under each of the major categories. It is an attempt to explain how it is that we can apparently ignore so many important distinctions, and be willing to accept a set of only twelve major categories.

A great many of the qualitative distinctions we feel in the observation of interaction, and the verbal terms by which we designate these distinctions, rest essentially on our conception of the nature of the established social relationship between the participants. For example, approximately the same kind of concrete behavior might be called "rewarding the other" if the status of the actor is assumed to be higher, or "congratulating the other" if the status is assumed to be equal, or "admiring the other" if the status of the actor is assumed to be lower. Other distinctions are based on a combination of this kind of assumption plus an assumption about the nature of the preceding act, that is, on temporal sequence. For example, a given kind of concrete behavior might be called "submission" if it follows an aggressive attack by the other, or "agreement" if it follows a tentative proposal. As the detailed definitions of the categories in the appendix will show, for major types of interaction there seems to be a tendency for a special term to appear for every major variation in social position or temporal vantage point. In order to arrive at a basic language of interaction which could be used as a set of categories for observation in all sorts of situations it was necessary to pierce through this maze of words and terms, which, after all, are the concepts in terms of which we make our observations. It was impossible in the early stages of the research to make a short list that was in any way satisfactory. The available words or concepts made a great number of distinctions, and many of the distinctions involved kinds of information about the social relationships that were regarded as indispensable.

The solution came in an unexpected way and for a practical reason—the need for greater reliability in scoring. The simplification leading to the present twelve major types of interaction was accomplished by deliberately omitting all distinctions based on a judgment or assumption on the observer's part of the nature of the social relationships of the participants, and all distinctions based on combinations of these assumptions with temporal sequence. As examples, the variations "rewarding," "congratulating," and "admiring" are all included within Category 1 in spite of their different implications about the status of the participants. Similarly, "submission" and "agreement" are both included within Category 3 in spite of their different implications about the nature of the preceding act.

These "omissions" were not easy to make. They were difficult for two reasons. First, they were actually eliminations by inclusion; in other words, the distinctions had to be isolated and seen in their full outlines before they could be included with others under a major category which grasped a generic similarity. Second, the last simplifying step was difficult because it seemed to involve destroying the very information we hoped to get through the use of the method. How can we learn anything about the status of the members of a group if we destroy in the categories all qualitative distinctions which refer to status differences? The answer cannot be given in a few words, nor are we perfectly sure at this point that we have a satisfactory answer. Very briefly, we can construct indices of the ways in which various types of activity are *distributed between persons*. These indices promise to give back to us in operational and quantitative terms the kind of information we thought we would have to relinquish by giving up certain qualitative distinctions. The actual construction of these indices is discussed in Chapter 5. The theoretical dimensions and distinctions which we believe to be important and out of which the idea for constructing the indices came are now to be discussed.

Neither the self nor the other(s) or in-group as a target area is a simple homogeneous object. We assume that in the course of time both the self and the other(s) or in-group differentiate in a number of important ways. When this takes place the relationship of the self to the in-group becomes more complicated than simply one of "inclusion" as illustrated on the diagram showing the actor-situation frame of reference (Chart 14) or one of more or less molar cognitive identification with the group as a whole. When the self or the group as a whole or some specific other in the group becomes the object of affective and conative activity, the units in the problem-solving sequence suddenly involve more than simply anonymous "acts" in an expressive and instrumental relationship to each other. It becomes evident that it is not simply "an act" more or less indifferent as to point of origin which is instrumental in reaching a goal or is expressive of or provocative of emotional tensions. Rather it is "an act of a *specific differentiated person*" (self or other) as a concrete entity or as a semi-autonomous "center and author of activity." In short, the actor behaves (at least in many instances) as if he were reacting to a *person* as a whole and not simply to an anonymous disembodied momentary act, which fits or does not fit neatly into a sequence leading to satisfaction.

In the process of action, then, persons as concrete entities tend to become related to each other in affective and instrumental relationships, so that one person expresses what the other person would like to express, the activity of one person becomes a stimulus to or object of affective reactions of the other person, or one person becomes a means to ends of the other person. Although these concrete individuals may interact in sequences of initial act, medial act, and terminal act, and in part receive their "significance" or "importance" for each other in terms of their present part of "function" in the problem-solving sequence, there seems to be a human tendency to "generalize" the significance of persons as concrete units or centers of activity in such a way that as a stimulus object or target object a given person calls much more to mind than is given in the momentary present part he is playing in a given present sequence. His past actions and identity are remembered, including what he "has done" prior to his entrance into the group and what he "is" outside the present in-group, and are attributed to him in the present as a part of his total significance. His actions and identity cling to him through a time span which transcends not only present sequences but the present small group as well. Furthermore, his total significance tends to be projected into the future in such a way that other persons build up expectations as to the parts he will play in future sequences and, in a more molar way, as to what kind of person he will be and how he will be related to the self.

We assume that in general "stability of reaction" or "predictability" of *all* aspects of the situation (not only the activities of the self and other(s)) is important to a successful steering of the process of action so that it actually brings satisfactions to the participants. As a converse of this, we assume that when expectations of stability are disappointed or upset for any reason, the process of action is suddenly perceived by the actors as less efficient, more uncertain and frustration threatening, more wasteful of time and energy; we also assume that the persons participating in such a process of action are more likely to develop tensions of anxiety and aggression which persist as "surpluses" in the action process and press for expression in some way, often against the object which is "behaving" unpredictably. These various malintegrative effects of instability and unpredictability, we assume, tend to create pressures toward the stabilization of expectations with regard to the situation at every point which is amenable to such stabilization, either by "actual" or by "symbolic" means. The relationship of persons to each other, including the relationships growing out of their parts or functions in immediate problem-solving sequences and in the subject-object polarity, constitutes one very important area of the situation in which this stabilization of expectations can be achieved through interaction. In any group, the observer expects at least pressures toward or attempts to realize such a stabilization, even though the attempts are unsuccessful in some cases. We shall speak of a relationship between persons as "institutionalized" when their patterns of behavior and the expectations of each with regard to the other have reached such a degree of stability (with or without explicit discussion and agreement as to their respective roles) that departures from these expectations arouse aggression or hostility on the part not only of the disappointed person but also of the deviant person toward himself as he identifies with the other, in the form of anxiety, shame, or guilt. We shall call the expectations which have this quality the "legitimate expectations" which each has of the other; the content of these definitely structured expectations we shall refer to as "rights" and "duties," according to whether they are felt as a freedom or constraint by a particular person.

To summarize, we assume that in any small group engaged in a process of interaction an internal differentiation between persons as concrete units exists initially or tends to develop. The most general kinds of differentiation we assume grow directly out of differential kinds of participation in problem-solving sequences and in the degree of identification with the in-group. As interaction proceeds, these differentiations tend to become "stabilized" in terms of "generalizations" based on past activity of the person and "expectations" based on the projection of these generalizations to future activity or on explicit discussion and agreement as to the expected roles of each. Since this stabilization is so important emotionally, there is a tendency for certain aspects of these expectations to become more explicit as to content and "legitimized" in such a way as to exert pressures against deviance from the norms so developed. Patterns of activity of persons toward each other which are defined by the persons in terms of legitimate expectations of this kind we shall call "institutionalized patterns."

At this point we have to recognize explicitly that all of the small groups we are theorizing about (see the technical definition) are made up of persons who come into the group with abilities of symbolizing and communicating already formed. They have had experience in social interaction before, and presumably come into the group with certain generalized ideas or stereotypes as to the kinds of relationships persons can have with each other, or as to the kinds of roles which they can play, or would like to play, or feel they should play. In short, we assume, they bring with them a frame of reference, however diffuse, about the main dimensions of social relationships; they tend to fit their activity into this frame of reference and to conceive of themselves as having or seeking a position in a differentiated range of possible positions and relationships from the very first, even before their interaction together in this particular group has become definitely institutionalized. We recognize these relationships in their concrete totality are to a certain extent, ideosyncratic from group to group and culture to culture, but we assume that there are certain features of the process of action and the situation so general as always to find their reflection in the way social relationships become arranged or structured. It is these most general and universal features or dimensions that we wish to formulate.

What we need according to our assumptions, then, is a specification of the most general or universal kinds of differentiations which exist or develop between persons as concrete units in small groups. These most general dimensions, we assume, grow out of the differential functional roles or significances of persons with regard to each other in problem-solving sequences with cognitive, affective, and conative aspects, and in the subject-object polarity. According to our analysis, four dimensions or kinds of differentiation between persons are generated in this manner. We shall describe these as: (1) the dimension of differential degree of access to resources, (2) the dimension of differential degree of control over persons, (3) the dimension of differential degree of status in a stratified scale of "importance" or prestige, and (4) the dimension of differential degree of solidarity or identification with the group as a whole as constituting a "subject" in-group as over against an "object" out-group or outer situation. The dimensions so described may be derived from the distinctions already made in the preceding frameworks, in the following fashion.

(1) **The dimension of differential degree of access to resources.** Insofar as the process of interaction in the group is conative and instrumental in character and involves the utilization of external means to anticipated ends, these means may be directly available or accessible only to particular members of the group because of their particular kind of relation to the outer-situation or particular personal characteristics or skills, and only indirectly available to other members in the group through the actions, positive help, or permission of those who have direct access. In other words, persons may have different positions with regard to each other growing out of differential advantages in the possession of resources by certain persons to which others, either as a matter of fact or as a matter of rights and duties, do not have immediate access. The observer thus expects that in any group in which the process of interaction and its fruits or results in terms of satisfaction or motivation reduction are subject to a sharing between persons, certain sequences of activity will appear in which the aim of one or the other person is to change or maintain these differential advantages between persons. These relationships or relative positions, and the activity which takes place within the context of this differentiation, tend to become institutionalized, i.e., stabilized and legitimized, and in larger social systems are referred to as the structure of property relations.

The institutionalization of property relations as it is found in larger social systems has no very obvious counterpart in many small groups, where physical goods or resources are not involved prominently. Nevertheless, for any given actor in the group there are features of the situation which have the essential character of resources for the satisfaction of wants or the maintenance of an integrated unfolding of the process of action. Freedom from control, the possession of time, physical objects, and specific services are all either resources to further goals or goals in themselves which are possessed in varying degrees by members of the group and which can be given or withheld by given persons with regard to others. Any resource which is not unlimited, or which may be divided between persons, or which in its nature is such that as one person has more another automatically has less, may require the stabilization of activity related to its distribution in order to prevent insecurity or deprivation on the part of the disadvantaged members. In general we may say that given the facts that action takes placed in a social situation and that the cooperation of others in various respects is needed for successful problem solving, under these conditions the giving of help or services, the assurance of non-interference or freedom, the granting of time, or the distribution of other resources which can be divided between persons are types of activity which if unstable or unpredictable may create tensions, and in time will tend to create pressures toward the stabilization of rights and duties with regard to this distribution. The fact that there is an initial unequal distribution of certain resources among individuals plus the fact that there is a constantly changing balance of command of or access to them by specific individuals creates an asymmetrical relationship between the person , in a position of advantage—who can give help—and the person in a position of disadvantage—who needs help. This relationship, whether momentary or institutionalized, or the total structure of such relationships in the group is a part of the context within which interaction proceeds.

(2) **The dimension of differential degree of control over persons.** The instrumental or conative character of the process of action, along with the fact that the activity of others may be means to ends, the ends either of particular persons or of the group as a whole, makes it more or less inevitable that persons should try to influence, guide, or control the activity of each other by direct request or fiat. It is one of the brute facts of the social situation as the actor faces it that other individuals in the group, either singly or in combination, do possess or can possess superior physical power over him and may force him to act as they desire. They may prevent him from attaining his individual goals by suitable combination with each other or may force him to act in such a way as to attain their own goals. Since this possibility is present, it is to the advantage of all individuals in the group to come to some stable legitimate expectation as to the way in which their potential power over each other will be exercised. This is one source of pressure toward the institutionalization of direct control of persons over each other. There is also another important source of this pressure. Insofar as the reaching of

goals requires cooperative effort, the complication of the outer situation is often such as to require a complicated division of labor as a feature of the cooperation. Whenever a division of labor appears in an effort to cope with an outer situation, the need for coordination of the various efforts in various places and various times becomes apparent. Unless these efforts are coordinated, they are subject to failure. One obvious way to coordinate them is by coming to an agreement that some person or persons shall be given a right to control the activities of those persons who are addressing their efforts directly to the task. This necessity of coordination makes the control of certain persons over others an advantageous and often a necessary part of the instrumental process or the process of reaching goals. So both from the fact that persons *can* control each other by force or coercion and from the fact that they *need* to control each other because of complicated divisions of labor addressed to problem solution arise pressures for some kind of regularization or institutionalization of the control relations between persons. In every group the observer expects to find at least *pressures* toward a stabilization of control of persons over others. This order of control, once established, and the nature and extent of this control become a part of the framework within which any given actor must operate in the problem-solving process. This framework, when institutionalized as to the rights and duties involved, may be called the structure of authority. With regard to this dimension, as with regard to the dimension of property, at least two positions must be distinguished: the position of the person exercising control and the position of the person subjected to attempted or successful control. This relationship, or the total structure of such relationships within the group, whether momentary or institutionalized, is a part of the context within which interaction proceeds.

(3) **The dimension of differential degree of status in a stratified scale of importance or prestige.** The stratification of persons with regard to each other, in a more generalized sense than that implied simply by superiority of access to resources or by superiority of control, can be derived from a consideration of the evaluative elements involved in the problem-solving process and from a consideration of the tendency toward "generalization" discussed above.

We have assumed that individuals are oriented to a multiplicity of goals, and that they evaluate the factors in their situation with regard to whether or not those factors are conducive to or threaten their need satisfaction and their expectations. If we recall that other persons and their conformity to institutionalized norms of behavior can play this role, we must conclude that it is more or less inevitable that individuals should evaluate not only impersonal objects in the outer situation, but also each other as persons or concrete entities. Every individual, whether acting for himself alone or acting on behalf of the group, who is concerned with the reaching of goals will be impelled to evaluate other persons in terms of how they relate to the achievement of these goals and in terms of whether their activity tends to maintain or destroy the norms upon which emotional safety depends.

This evaluation is not necessarily an all-or-none classification as "good" or "bad," but rather the situation in most instances is such that it is possible to make a kind of rating of other individuals as units with regard to the *degree* to which they contribute to the reaching of a goal or the degree to which they conform or fail to conform to an ideal institutionalized norm. The stratification of persons, their relative prestige with regard to each other, is an outcome of the process of evaluation or affective judgment as a general aspect of the problem-solving process, as applied to persons in a "generalized," nonspecific way. It is a critical problem for the group to reach basic consensus with regard not only to the major values they hold, the goals they wish to reach, and the means permitted or required to reach them, but also with regard to the relative stratification of persons as units on the basis of their contribution or lack of contribution to the total process of action, including the realization of ideal norms. Just as disagreement over major values may produce frustration of the problem-solving process, so also may disagreements about or uncertainty about the relative value or prestige of persons produce frustration, anxiety, aggression, or perhaps make cooperation impossible.

If and when a basic consensus as to the proper status order of persons is established in the group, the group may be said to be stratified. The group may be said to possess a stratification if this stabilization as to generalized status has taken place, even though in some exceptional case all members are regarded as having essentially the same equal status. In this extreme or polar case it may be said that the participants visualize a hierarchy of positions which constitute the scale but that all individuals fall in the same place on the scale, with the positions above and below unoccupied. Incidentally, when claims as to the absolutely equal status of all members are made by the members, the observer may suspect that the expressed "ideology" of equality does not preclude the possibility that persons do in practice treat each other to some extent in terms of status distinctions. There is a kind of emotional opposition between the maintaining of a strong solidarity between persons and the making of wide status distinctions between them. That is, one may expect that as the over-all solidarity of the group is more heavily emphasized, the tendency to deny status differences within it will increase. On the other hand, if status differences increase for any reason, such as an increase of differences between persons in degrees of property and authority, these differentials between persons will tend to conflict with their basic solidarity. This is a general theorem with regard to the nature of group structure and dynamics which requires more explicit formulation and further evidence. However, if established, this theorem without doubt is a key factor in the dynamics not only of small groups but of social systems of any kind, since both differentiation and integration have obvious and strong advantages in the total problem-solving process.

With regard to the dimension of status, as with regard to property and authority, at least two positions must be distinguished: the position of the person with the higher status and the position of the person with the lower status. This relationship, or the total structure of such relationships within the group, whether momentary or institutionalized, is a part of the context within which interaction proceeds.

(4) **The dimension of differential degree of solidarity or identification with the group as a whole as constituting a "subject" in-group as over against an "object" out-group or outer situation.** If we assume that individuals live together in an outer situation which makes at least some demands that no individual person can meet without help

from others, if we assume, in short, that the fullest extent of need satisfaction requires the cooperation of people, then we would expect to find in every group the attempt to institutionalize the obligation of cooperation or the obligation to subordinate individual goals and interests to the goals and interests common to the members of the in-group. If the instrumental task demands cooperation it is to the ultimate advantage of every person in the group to have the obligation to cooperate and to subordinate individualized interests made explicit and a matter of legitimate expectation. The observer thus expects to find either a spontaneous identification of the persons of the in-group with each other, or pressures toward the development of obligations that each individual shall regard himself as a part of a larger whole which includes the other. Solidarity in its institutionalized aspects, as we define it, consists in an obligation and a right: the obligation to identify one's self cognitively, affectively, and conatively with the other, to perceive one's self as a part of a larger whole, to feel the other's concerns as one's own, to cooperate with the other, to share the other's fate; and the right to expect these attitudes and actions from the others. These claims which individuals establish over one another may be called the institutionalized solidarity of the two or of the group. Solidarity, as an *existing* kind of relationship between two or more people, of course involves aspects other than those structured as rights and obligations. There are many factors of group life which operate to strengthen or produce a kind of spontaneous solidarity, such as the possession of a common language, the sharing of a common thought process, common problems with regard to the outer situation and common definitions of its significance, the possession of definite modes and channels of communication, the opportunity or fact of frequent association, etc., but the heart of solidarity in the institutionalized sense is the stabilized mutual responsibility of each toward the other to regard himself as a part of the other, as the sharer of a common fate, and as a person who is under obligation to cooperate with the other in the satisfaction of the other's individual needs as if they were one's own. Solidarity in certain of its aspects is a quality of social relationships which tends to arise spontaneously. It does not necessarily arise *because* it has an instrumental value in the problem-solving process for each—it is in part an unpremeditated result of the expression of affect toward others and inclusion in an in-group—but the fact that it exists has an instrumental value for each, and the preserving and maintaining of it has an instrumental as well as an expressive value.

With regard to the dimension of solidarity, as with regard to property, authority, and status, at least two positions must be distinguished: the position of the person as he identifies with the other or tries to bring about a solidary relationship between himself and the other; and the position of the person as he regards the other as a foreign object, and rejects or tries to break the solidary bond, if any. This dimension, however, unlike the others, does not necessarily assume an asymmetrical relation between the two; both may accept or both may reject. The relation may assume an asymmetrical form when one accepts and the other rejects. This relationship or the total structure of such relationships within the group, whether momentary or institutionalized, is a part of the context within which interaction proceeds.

The four dimensions discussed above express what we believe to be the most generalized ways in which persons as concrete entities relate themselves to each other. These dimensions arise more or less directly out of the most generalized features of the process of action as it goes on in a subject-object polarity. Although the position of a person on these various dimensions, as well as the dimensions themselves, are considered to grow out of problem-solving interaction, either empirically or logically, or both, once the social structure of the group has become established, it thereafter constitutes a part of the framework within which all activity continues. When this framework has been established in a particular group, the action patterns of the members with regard to each other become more predictable. The existence of these predictable patterns gives a certain stability to the situation of action of each individual, and this stability of situation in terms of expectations becomes an important part of the "content" (i.e., orientation) of motivation as it is felt by the individual. The "structure" and "functioning" of the social system, hence of the situation of action for each individual, gives shape and content to the motivation of each individual. Conformance to or violation of expectations becomes a means of managing anxiety and aggression; the orientation of the individual to the main structural dimensions of social relationships gives rise to a functionally autonomous constellation of motives.

We assume that at the time of any given act, the actor conceives of the self as having a kind of generalized position in each of these dimensions insofar as they have become stabilized in the group as a whole. Thus we might speak of one person as entertaining the implicit or explicit assumption that he is generally in a position to command certain resources valuable to the group (perhaps he is expert in certain skills they require); in a position to control the activities of other persons (as an executive agent or leader with certain legitimate authority); as having a high generalized status; and as being a fully solidary member with legitimate obligations to regard the interest of others as his own. We might speak of another person as entertaining the implicit or explicit assumption that he lacks command over resources valuable to the group (he has no special knowledge, skills, or possessions); that he is generally required to subject himself to the authority of the first; that he has a low generalized status; and that he is a peripheral member of the group with individualized aims and interests which differ widely from those of the other members of the group and which he is not willing to relinquish. These two persons would have extreme positions with regard to each of the four dimensions described. There are, of course, intermediate positions, and positions which are anomalous in that they combine extremes of certain dimensions with opposite extremes of other dimensions.

In these illustrations we have been speaking of the kind of generalized positions which persons in the group tend to achieve and have ascribed to them as the process of stabilization of expectations proceeds. To an important extent, however, any such position is unstable in that it is in a constant process of being created, validated, or renewed; it is unstable also in the sense that the exigencies of the process of action, as it changes in response to instrumental or expressive needs, constantly confronts persons with the necessity of action which may not be consonant with their former position. A change in the outer situation and its demands, a gradual or sudden change in major values or goals of the group, a change in ideal norms of behavior, a change in the expectations of other persons or their willingness to accept and maintain their former positions—various changes, momentary or more permanent, may create strains in the position of the self, and may produce or call for action which leads to a change in the social position of the self. Thus, a person generally in command of resources valuable to the group may find himself lacking in those things needed as the group confronts a new problem. He may then find himself in a position of having to ask for help from some other in the group who has before been regarded as having a lower status. Or as a person generally with authority, he may have to submit in some present act to control from another person who before was in an inferior position.

In fact, we assume that in *every act* the position of the self in these various dimensions of social relationships is potentially at stake, in the sense that the act may conform with the expectations of others and reinforce or confirm the present position, or help make it, or may deviate either in a positive or negative way from expectations and lead toward a change in position. In the extreme case the individual may actually have "examined" the implication of his nascent act in relation to each of these dimensions. That is, he may have actually considered (although perhaps in a foggy and incoherent way), how such an act would affect his command over resources in relation to the other(s), his control over other persons or their control over him, his status, and his solidarity with the group. In less explicit cases, the nascent act may not have been examined explicitly and consciously but may nevertheless have been guided and steered by implicit emotional processes and sentiments oriented to these various implications for social position. In extreme cases of an opposite kind, the act may have as its main implicit (i.e., disguised or "unconscious") content or meaning, an emotional reaction to or tendency to change the relationship of the self to others. This we assume often to be the case in neurotic and near neurotic behavior. For example, compulsive stealing may have conscious meaning of gaining access to needed resources, but at the same time unconscious meaning of aggression against authority, the acquisition of status, and the gaining of love and acceptance. A systematic theory regarding the main features of social relationships should thus add a much needed element of system to our conceptual treatment of motivation.

So far as the system of categories is concerned, the assumption that *every* act has at least in germ, implications for social position, gives the key to the final simplification of the set of categories. Whether implicit or explicit we assume that any given act may have at least a "momentary positional implication" to the other in a relationship, as an expression of an emotional reaction to the position of the self with regard to the other, or as an instrumental attempt to change the relationship, or both, or as an attempt to work within the bounds of a defined position, or as an attempt to maintain, strengthen, or reintegrate the relationship. It is true that certain interactions only imply or assume the relationship, but have as their main object of interest some functional problem concerned with the outer situation, while others are concerned with the social relationship as the main object of interest. Once this distinction is recognized, however, we simplify our conceptual scheme by systematically ignoring it.

What we have done in simplifying the categories is to "telescope" or "overlap" this distinction as to whether the act only "assumes" a given relationship or is concerned with the social relationship as the main object of interest. For example: we do not distinguish between, on the one hand, a tentative suggestion by a member of a group who is apparently concerned only with the problem facing the group, and not at all with the problem of authority, and, on the other hand, a mild and neutral but nevertheless firm request by a member of the group who "assumes" himself to be in authority. These are both scored under Category 4, "Gives suggestion, direction, implying autonomy for other." We do not distinguish between a neutral exchange of objects for primarily instrumental purposes, where a social relationship of solidarity is only assumed, and an amorous advance of male to female, where the social relationship of the two is very much the object of interest. These are both scored under Category 1, "Shows solidarity, raises other's status, gives help, reward."

Thus in scoring we systematically ignore qualitative distinctions we know to be important. This we do in order to pierce through to more elementary similarities regarding the functions of acts in the problem-solving sequence. We hope that by obtaining reliable observations of these elementary characteristics and by noting the way in which these few major types of activity are *distributed between persons* we can reconstruct the main dimensions of the relationships between the participants: their relative access to resources, their relative control over each other, their relative status with regard to each other, and their relative solidarity. There are perhaps two basic reasons for hoping that this may work: first, because we assume that in some fairly concrete way the social relationships are "expressed" in the different roles and positions assumed in the problem-solving process and second, or conversely, because we assume that genetically the social relationships are products or structural results of the different roles and positions assumed in the problem-solving process. The construction of the proposed indices is discussed in Chapter 5.

CHAPTER 3

TRAINING OBSERVERS

Introduction. In this chapter certain practical and methodological aspects of observer training are considered. The practical discussion will be of interest mainly to those readers who plan actual use of the method. Some of the methodological aspects, however, are probably relevant to other sorts of observation situations in which interpretive inferences are made by observers. The discussion is organized loosely in terms of the problems as they are encountered in the course of training. This results in a mixed presentation of scoring conventions which are an integral part of the method, rules of thumb which we have found convenient, and fragmentary remarks on methodological aspects of the observer situation.

In our earlier experience in training observers, there arose a set of difficulties which became a very real point of development for the present procedure. Working with a much more complicated set of categories, we found that some trainees resisted the necessity of developing the stenographic type of skill required to record observations; others resisted the analytic assumptions which were required in "taking the role of the other" and making a classification. These resistances, coupled with the complexity of the set of categories then employed, slowed training and contributed to an unsatisfactory correspondence between observers. These difficulties were among those pressures which led to the simplification of the categories to the present twelve. This simplification appeared to permit the trainees to rechannel their energies and to devote greater effort to the mechanical aspects of scoring. From this time on they seemed much less frustrated by the nuances of interpretation.

It would be a mistake, however, to underestimate the difficulty of the present task. It still requires long practice and frequent retraining to perform consistently. We have found it instructive to study introspective reports from some of the better scorers. They report in every case that they remember very little about the meeting as a whole. They often work several scores behind the interaction and they learn to pick up a series of responses as a sort of rhythmic sequential pattern. It is by holding this expected sequential rhythm of acts in the back of their thinking that they are able to spread a burst of interaction out into separate acts. A big advance in the scoring process comes when they learn not to get frustrated when they have missed or misclassified an act. One secret of progress seems to be the acquiring of an ability to inhibit all but the present context of acts, and to avoid jamming incoming stimuli with internal reflections.

Initial Training Procedure. After a study of the rationale of the method and the possible applications, attention should be directed to the specific content of the categories. The more extended definition of each category should be read and the trainee should develop both a theoretical understanding and a "feel" for the placement of the categories on the scoring form. The definition of the unit to be scored must also be considered at this time, for the notion of the unit provides the boundaries within which the category is determined. The concepts are inseparable. When these preliminaries have been completed work can start on a written protocol. The group therapy protocol at the end of this chapter illustrates the notations we employ. The analysis of protocols is an excellent way to learn the basic steps of the procedure, since there is plenty of time to consider problems of interpretation, look up definitions, etc., without working under the necessity of immediate decision. We feel that care should be exercised, however, not to use written protocols too far beyond the original familiarization period because the development of dependence upon a written script tends to defeat the primary training objective of mastering *live* material.

In the transition phase from written protocols, recordings have been found to be of great assistance. At first the trainees listen while the instructor taps each time he recognizes a unit. The selection is then replayed and all trainees plus the instructor tap together. Stragglers easily recognize their deviance without having an issue made of it. The next step is for the trainees to put down individual tallies, unitizing the interaction, but neglecting the category classification or the person speaking. Trainees are frequently surprised to discover the ease with which they can learn to unitize consistently. Whether or not the total number of scores of different scorers is acceptably similar can be tested graphically by using the binomial probability paper described in the next chapter. The next logical step is to continue with the recorded material, classifying the interaction by category, but ignoring the who-to-whom designation. As before, reliability is tested until satisfactory results begin to appear. At this stage many preliminary conventions are developed. For example, laughter provides a troublesome problem in unitization. The question is: how many units are there in a burst of laughter? We have adopted an arbitrary convention. Whenever the person laughing has to take an additional breath we score this as an additional unit. Thus the units of laughter are roughly proportional to the duration of laughter. Many of these problems have been anticipated in the formal definitions of the categories.

The trainees may now be ready to score live material of some kind. The who-to-whom designation can be satisfactorily scored only with live material. In beginning the training with live material, it may be easier to omit the target of the act and score at first only the initiator; later the target can be added. There are, then, a series of easy stages by which the complete scoring procedure can be developed. A convenient procedure for providing live material is to have two or three members of the training team set up a role-playing situation which emphasizes certain combinations of categories. For example, they may role-play a therapy session in which the objective is to demonstrate that a nondirective therapist may stay in Category 5 despite the attempt of the patient to force him into an interpretive position. By talking slowly the role players relate the categories to actual interaction experiences and the observers are provided with an interesting training opportunity.

In this stage of training, the operation proceeds most smoothly if all members of the group score on individual pads. ° These can be

---

° Interaction Scoring Forms similar to those used for Chart 6 are available from the publisher of this book. (250-sheet package, 50 sheets per pad, $2.50.) These forms may be used both for original scoring and for the presentation of data in terms of profiles. When scoring, it is customary to enter three scores per box, one under the other. The dash between the two numbers in the score may be omitted to save space. Each row of boxes is filled out solidly from the starting line on the left side and a new sheet is used when the boxes for any one category are completely filled. This system will result in sheets containing about 100 scores each.

produced locally. The short category descriptions may be placed at the left of the scoring pad as in the charts showing interaction profiles (e.g. Chart 4). Trainees appreciate frequent breaks so that they can compare performance, get a fresh start, or discuss their most recent difficulty. The trainer should take care not to let the discussion run along in a diffuse way too long, however, since not all of the aspects of good scoring procedure can be easily verbalized. A great deal is to be learned by simply continuing to score. The periods of unbroken scoring should be gradually increased, since the ultimate objective is to be able to score live material through periods which may continue for one or more hours.

Use of impersonal criterion. In the early phases of learning to categorize, interesting individual differences arise concerning the degree to which acts will be classified in Section D (Negative Reactions) or in other particular categories. It appears that there may be certain emotional biases which make it difficult for certain persons to recognize or score certain types of interaction. We find that it is desirable to have the training sessions carried on in a very permissive atmosphere, for individuals feel about their ability to judge the actions of others somewhat as they do about their common sense. People may cheerfully agree that others may have a better education or be more intelligent, but they are very reluctant to agree that someone else may have more common sense. The ability to interpret the meaning of acts is regarded by many as the equivalent of common sense. They tend to feel, "My interpretation is as good as theirs." For this reason it is valuable sometimes to emphasize that the criterion for correctness is an impersonal one, based upon some previously agreed-upon written criterion.

In our training we have referred all questions of interpretation to an earlier manual from which this book has been produced. The question of reconciling the interpretations of observers thus becomes a question of: (1) what does the manual say? and (2) what modifications of the manual are required to anticipate issues of this nature in the future? The last point is important both as a desirable definition of the training situation and as a growing-point of the method. The formal printing and binding of the present conventions in book form will probably retard the rate of modification but, as we have explained elsewhere, it is our intention to publish revisions of the method as experience dictates. Critical reports from readers and training teams will be invaluable in this connection.

Scoring "who-to-whom." The number of persons participating and the number of foci of interaction constitute additional dimensions along which the complexity of the scoring task may vary. In general, a cocktail party or an informal luncheon is impossibly difficult for one observer because the number of foci of interaction are so great. Single-focus meetings dominated by one lecturer or resource person are easy to score even though there may be a large number of persons present.

In the more complicated observation situations dilemmas frequently arise in recording "who-to-whom." When the target is another person, the eyes of the speaker sometimes provide the source of identification. Sometimes the speaker may use the name of the person addressed. In a large number of cases the person addressed will be the person who last spoke, whose speech provides the stimulus for the present response. There will be cases where the initiator will be responding to the speech of one person, perhaps objecting to what he said, but will actually be looking at somebody else, from whom he expects the next response. In this case, the practice is to charge the objection to the first person, then add an additional request for approval or opinion from the actor to the second person.

There are other instances in which the speaker may look particular individuals in the eye while apparently talking to the group; the content of the remarks helps to determine whether the particular individual or the group is the target in these cases. Whenever the act seems to be addressed to no particular other, or to more than one other, the symbol "0" is used to designate the target. In cases where more than two persons act at once, as when all laugh together, or shout together, or agree or object at once, the symbol "0" is used to designate the actor. Thus, a general laugh would be scored 0–0 (all to all). A general nodding of heads to Actor 1 would be scored 0–1 (all to one).

Wherever the fact that something is being communicated is secondary or incidental to the act, its primary ultimate or terminal target should be recorded rather than the person who receives the communication. Thus, if the actor is giving his attention primarily to the situation, actually observing or puzzling about it—i.e., the outer situation—the act is recorded 1-x, even though he may be speaking aloud so that members can hear. However, if he is drawing on his store of information and is giving his attention primarily to the other, attempting to communicate what he knows to 2 or 0, the act is recorded 1-2 or 1-0 rather than 1-x. In cases where a communication is addressed by one member to another but the interaction refers to a third as the terminal object, especially when some emotional animus of the remark is directed toward the third, score the remark 1-3, omitting the second person. For example, if Person 1 says to Person 2, "I think (Person three's) remarks are stupid," the interaction is scored 1-3 in Category 12. However, if Person 1 adds to Person 2, "Don't you?" an additional score 1-2 in Category 8 is required. In cases where Member 1 whispers or speaks aside to Member 2 when the rest of the group is working on a problem and the observer is unable to determine the content of the act, he scores the act 1-0 in Category 10. If Person 2 answers, he is scored 2-0 in Category 10 also. If in interaction between Person 1 and Person 2, Person 1 makes an emotionally weighted remark about an absent person, the interaction is scored 1-x in the appropriate category, and the fact that the immediate communication is with Person 2 is ignored.

The distribution of acts can be performed more readily if the number assigned to each participant is clearly in view of the observer. A small set of numbers should be kept convenient for this purpose. A key relating this number code to the participants and a crude diagram of the seating positions is frequently desirable.

Resolving classification dilemmas. The present system assumes that a given temporal segment of behavior will be classified in only *one* category. It seems likely that in content analysis generally the frequency with which classification dilemmas arise is in part a function of the fundamental soundness of the underlying rationale from which the dimensions are derived. In the present method the different frames of reference in terms of which interaction categories can be constructed have been reduced to a single level wherein the different frames of reference are equivalent to each other to the maximum degree. It is our hope that even "degrees of intensity" are to some extent taken care of in terms of differences between categories instead of by breakdowns within categories.

Although we believe that many of the common difficulties have been avoided in this way, classification dilemmas do arise. The formal definitions will help in many instances but marginal cases will continue to occur. This marginality arises in terms of the particular function we choose to make the final basis of the classification, and so long as interaction is multi-functional, formal definitions of particular functions will not always solve the problem. For this reason we have established two priority rules which may be employed when other criteria do not provide sufficient basis for decision.

Rule 1. *View each act as a response to the last act of the last other, or as an anticipation of the next act of the next other.*

The question of "depth" or "breadth" of interpretation often hinges on the extensity of the context adopted as the frame of reference. Application of this rule means that the smallest possible context is taken. This applies in several ways:

(a) The immediate, last mentioned, or next anticipated social act of the other takes precedence over the more general social context. If this rule were not followed a client who came into a relief office to ask for funds might be scored in Category 11 every time he spoke. With the less extensive context which is to be used, however, he would be marked in Category 11 only when he actually made an appeal.

(b) The reactive or anticipatory characteristics of the act take precedence over its symptomatic significance as evidence of some more permanent characteristic of personality. If this rule were not followed, a person who stammered would be marked under Category 11 every time he spoke. With the less extensive context which is to be used, however, he would be marked under Category 11 for stammering only if he stammered worse than usual in reaction to what had just happened or what was anticipated.

(c) The meaning of the act for the last or next other (i.e., the way the act would be perceived by the other member to the immediate interaction) takes precedence over its imputed, perhaps unconscious, or depth meaning for the actor. If this rule were not followed, the observer would be obliged to try to "read the mind" or fathom the personality and hidden purposes of the actor in a way which is quite impossible in the scoring situation. The observer tries to operate on the level of a perceptive, knowledgeable, sensitive other, making the kinds of inferences he would make in direct interaction with the actor. A special note is required here: The other usually is another person in the group and often is the last person who spoke or has been mentioned; this, however, is not necessarily true. In therapeutic interviews, the actor often is engaged in a monologue in which he is thinking about and reliving emotionally his relations to others not physically present. In this case, the other to be taken as the context is the other in the monologue, who is present only symbolically because the actor has mentioned him and is now reacting to the symbolic presence.

Rule 2.   *Favor the category more distant from the middle. Classify the act in the category nearer the top or the bottom of the list.*

Thus if one person says, "It's hot today," and the other smiles and responds "Over ninety," the possible dilemma is between classifying in terms of the function of giving information, or in terms of showing agreement, or in terms of showing still more active solidarity. We resolve these competing demands by favoring the category most distant from the middle, and classify in Category 1. The general effect of this rule is to make the observer more sensitive to the "directive" quality of interaction within the task area and to the "active outgoing emotional" quality of interaction within the social-emotional area, and as between the two areas, emphasizes the latter over the former. This rule has another implication relevant to possible hesitation about making classifications in Section D. The observer should not be inhibited about putting down a socially negative score because as a group member he would feel obliged to repress or overlook such an interpretation. In this respect he may feel himself as free as the child who blurts out what he feels intuitively, regardless of its social awkwardness. But such interpretations should be on the same kind of basis which the child presumably uses—an immediate intuition of the actor's emotional state—and not on the basis of a longer, logically tenuous calculation as to what the act must mean on the basis of certain prior premises not obvious in the present situation.

Sample protocol. A very important goal in training operations is the attainment of correspondence between observers. The next chapter shows the way in which a type of training leading toward greater reliability is actually built into the observation procedure under standard conditions. We shall conclude this chapter with a few pages of a scored protocol which may be used in initial training as an independent criterion for checking reliability of scorers. The text can be copied without the scores, then scored independently by trainees. It will be noted that it is not possible to determine with certainty whether the members were speaking to the group or to the therapist.

A group therapy session. The therapist, John Evans, is number 1. Four other persons are present, all veterans who are meeting for their first session in group therapy. They are Paul, 2; Ed, 3; Freddy, 4; and Joe, 5. They have just arrived.

1. Have a seat there any place [(1)1–0]. . . . I guess you can throw your coats there any place [(1)1–0] . . . be comfortable [(1)1–0] . . . these groups are very informal [(1)1–0]. If you want to smoke, why, go right ahead [(1)1–0]. Let's see who we have today [(4)1–0]. I'd like to have each of us sort of introduce ourselves by whatever we're called [(4)1–0], whatever we like to be called by [(1)1–0]. Do you want to start off [(4)1–2]?
2. Paul [(3)2–1].
3. Ed [(3)3–1].
4. Freddy [(3)4–1].
5. Joe [(3)5–1].
1. Well, gentlemen [(6)1–0], we probably have a lot of questions about what we are doing here [(5)1–0]. . . . I imagine you have a lot of questions in mind just what the devil this is [(5)1–0]. Well, what do you think it is [(8)1–0]? Anybody have any ideas as to what in heck this might accomplish [(8)1–0]?
5. Just a little gathering [(5)5–1]? Is that it—a social gatherin' [(7)5–1]?
1. Well, that's one side [(3)1–5]. How about it, do you agree with him [(8)1–0]? Ed, do you agree with him [(8)1–3]?

3. (Ed says something halting and inaudible [(11)3–1].)

5. What are we going to talk about, Mr. Evans [(7)5–1]?

1. Well, now that's something [(6)1–5]. I think that's a good point for discussion [(5)1–0]. I would like to point out one thing [(6)1–0]. It seems to me that every man who comes here comes with a definite purpose in mind [(5)1–0]. He has certain feelings [(5)1–0], symptoms [(6)1–0], or problems [(6)1–0], and I can make a guess that when you came in the door down there, you think, "My God, what in hell am I doing here [(5)1–0]?" And perhaps you have a feeling some guy on the street is going to say, "There goes a nut [(5)1–0]." Still feel that way about it [(8)1–0]? Ever worry about people knowing you're coming here [(8)1–0]?

[Paul looks at the floor [(11)–2–y], Ed wets his lips but says nothing [(11)3–y], Freddy reaches for a cigarette [(11)4–y], Joe shifts uneasily in his chair [(11)5–y].]

1. Of course actually we know that it doesn't mean nuts [(1)1–0] . . . of course a lot of people who got medical discharges from the Service, right away people would say, "Hm, you weren't wounded, were you? Must be nuts [(1)1–0]." Well, these are emotional problems, of course [(5)1–0]; and yet the man on the street, if you say you're psychoneurotic, will rear back and sort of look at you out of one side [(5)1–0] and start getting the hell out of the way [(5)1–0]. Well, all of that, of course, signifies that there's a lot of tension [(5)1–0] . . . you probably recognize it yourself [(5)1–0], the feeling of being keyed up too much [(5)1–0]—perhaps of not being able to sleep [(5)1–0], or if you do sleep, not getting up rested [(5)1–0]—if you're working, being worn out by the work [(5)1–0]; you've got to the point where you probably never think twice about it [(5)1–0]—so what we'd like to do [(5)1–0] . . . this is a treatment [(5)1–0] . . . a little social too [(5)1–0], but it's treatment [(5)1–0]. You've all been with the doctor [(6)1–0], and that's one kind of treatment [(5)1–0]; this is psychological treatment [(5)1–0]. As we go on in the group we will perhaps thresh out the reasons why this treatment has some advantages over the other kind of treatment [(5)1–0], how they fit together [(5)1–0], and how either kind or both fit in with the problems [(5)1–0]. One thing I'd like to do [(6)1–0]

. . . do you agree that you all feel tensed up too often [(8)1–0]?
[Paul and Ed say nothing [(11)2–0] [(11)3–0], Freddy and Joe nod their heads [(3)4–1] [(3)5–1].]

1. I'd like to put in at the beginning of each of our sessions a relaxation exercise [(4)1–0]. It's more or less . . . well, call it a pill [(5)1–0]. It doesn't cure anything [(5)1–0], but it helps to get relaxed a bit [(5)1–0]; and it's not hypnosis [(5)1–0]—it's only purely a relaxation exercise [(5)1–0]. So for this [(6)1–0], if you will [(1)1–0], just take seats over here so you can see the blackboard [(4)1–0]. . . .

(All shift their seats [(3)0–1].)

1. Now are you all in a position where you can see that spot clearly [(1)1–0]? What I want you to do is just sit back on your chair [(4)1–0], get comfortable [(1)1–0], get your arms and everything loosened up so you're sitting just as relaxed as you can get in the chair there [(1)1–0], any position that's comfortable [(1)1–0]. What I want you to do is stare at that spot [(4)1–0], try to focus on it with both eyes [(4)1–0], just thinking only of that spot [(4)1–0]. Keep looking at it with your eyes open until they begin to water [(4)1–0]. When they begin to water, close them [(4)1–0], and continue focusing on that spot [(4)1–0]. If your eyes haven't begun to water after a little while, I'll tell you when to close your eyes [(6)1–0] and keep staring at that spot even after your eyes are closed [(4)1–0], just thinking of that spot, that's all [(4)1–0]. Try to focus both eyes on that spot and keep staring at it [(4)1–0].

(Long pause. All members stare at the spot [(3)0–1].)

1. When your eyes begin to water, just close your eyes [(4)1–0] and continue concentrating on that one spot [(4)1–0].

(Long pause. All members stare at the spot [(3)0–1]. 4 closes his eyes [(3)4–1].)

1. Now close your eyes and continue staring at the spot [(4)1–0].

(Long pause. All members close their eyes [(3)0–1].)

1. Keep thinking about that spot with your eyes closed [(4)1–0].

(Long pause, 5 or 6 minutes [(3)0–1] [(3)0–1] [(3)0–1] [(3)0–1] [(3)0–1].)

[On Continuous Activity: one score per minute]

1. Well [(6)1–0], suppose we move on a little bit now [(4)1–0]. It takes a little practice on that of course [(1)1–0], but I think some of us noticed there was a relaxation that came on with it [(5)1–0]. Did you notice a relaxation as you sat there [7(1–0)]; how did you feel about it, Paul [(8)1–2]?
2. Well, I am just more quiet than I am usually [(5)2–1] . . . that's the only [(11)2–1] . . .

1. How'd you feel about it, Joe [(8)1–5]?
5. I felt a little relaxed [(5)5–1].

1. Freddy [(6)1–4], I thought Freddy there was going sound asleep [(2)1–0].
4. Ha, Ha [(2)4–1]; I was really relaxed [(2)4–0].

1. It really relaxed you, huh [(6)1–4]? How about you, Ed [(8)1–3]?
3. (Ed starts to say something, and laughs a little, apparently embarrassed) [(11)3–1].

1. Well [(6)1–0], Joe asked the question of what we were going to talk about in these sessions [(6)1–0]. In the first place I mentioned that these are emotional problems [(6)1–0], and each individual has a problem [(6)1–0]. Well, these problems are things that we live thru every day [(5)1–0], so we all know the subjects [(5)1–0]. It's a case of connecting it up right [(5)1–0]. So in general, then, I'd say that what we want to talk about in the groups is why the heck do we have symptoms [(4)1–0], why do we feel like we do [(6)1–0]? Of course, there's this about it too [(6)1–0] . . . you may feel, "Sure, that's what I'm interested in, but I don't feel like telling the other guys stuff about my private life [(5)1–0]." Well, the way to get the most out of this treatment [(6)1–0] if somebody says something, and you think he's a stinker and doesn't know what in hell he's talking about, tell him so [(1)1–0]. If you don't like what I say, tell me so [(1)1–0]. So, the more that is put into the pot for discussion the more you will get out of it [(5)1–0]. And there won't be any pressure put on you to come out with anything you feel you don't want to talk about [(1)1–0]. That's up to you [(1)1–0]. Of course it is all to

the good to bring up any of these problems that you may have [(4)1–0]. Well, what about some of these problems [(8)1–0]? What would you suggest as the most immediate problem [(9)1–0]?

2. I'd suggest, from my own point of view, if not from the other fellows' point of view [(8)2–0], this is strictly my own [(11)2–y] . . . I'd suggest something for the relief of pain [(4)2–1].

1. Could you tell us a little more about that [(8)1–2]?

2. Well, I'm [(11)2–0] . . . I'm really not a-scared to discuss mine [(5)2–0] . . . in fact, I'm ready to seek a cure for mine as quick as possible [(5)2–0]. I seem to be bothered with reoccurring symptoms such as pain [(6)2–0] . . . there's always pains [(6)2–0] . . . headaches [(6)2–0], and pains in my left side [(6)2–0] and right side [(6)2–0], and a lot of pulsations [(6)2–0], that's rapid heart beat [(6)2–0] . . . in fact it all has to do with nauseated feelings [(5)2–0], and it's always something [(6)2–0]. For instance [(6)2–0]. If I have a headache now, it may go away in about a couple of weeks [(6)2–0], it lasts for a period of time [(6)2–0]; then the very next day something comes up [(6)2–0], for instance the pain will go to my left side and stay there for about three to six weeks [(6)2–0], and so on and so forth [(6)2–0]. I no sooner get rid of one pain [(6)2–0] . . . it goes from one symptom to the other [(6)2–0]. Now this may not be the trouble with these other fellows here [(5)2–0]. They may have various other symptoms than I [(5)2–0]. That's what's upsetting me at the present time [(6)2–0], and I wish to seek a remedy [(5)2–0], some means of getting rid of them entirely [(5)2–0], to stop this rotating business [(5)2–0]. That's the big problem I present [(6)2–0]. As far as emotional storm [(6)2–0], I'm worried about something that's bothering me [(5)2–0] but as far as family, my work, indebtedness or anything else like that [(6)2–0] I do not present a problem truly [(5)2–0], to speak about myself [(6)2–0]. It's nothing that's causing this [(5)2–0] . . . what, I don't know is causing it [(8)2–y], but as far as things like that [(6)2–0], they're not because I don't present problems like that [(5)2–0], because the things I just mentioned now are all in harmony [(5)2–0] and I have no worries in that category [(5)2–0]. Now there may be something that is causing those pains

[(5)2–0] but as yet I haven't found out what it is [(7)2–y].

1. Let's hear from some of the others [(4)1–0]. How does that sound to you, Éd [(8)1–3]?

3. In nearly every thing I do at home I either break something or nothing's right [(6)3–0] . . . as far as my nerves go [(6)3–0], I want to get cured [(5)3–0]. To my girl I can talk for a half an hour or an hour straight [(6)3–0] I don't seem to lose my voice for about a half hour or an hour [(6)3–0]; as soon as I go to . . . (voice becomes inaudible) . . . [(11)3–y] because I haven't regained my right voice [(6)3–0], the one I lost overseas [(6)3–0].

1. Do you agree with Paul there [(8)1–3], that the cause might be anything, but he's just not sure [(6)1–3]? Have you any idea just what might be causing this [(8)1–3]?

3. (voice inaudible) [(11)3–y].

1. Would you say it might be an infection or something that got in your throat [(8)1–3]?

3. Well, in my case I only actually went to school to learn jiu jitsu [(6)3–0] and I was all right until one night I was attacked by a few Japs [(6)3–0] after I got in the Army of Occupation [(6)3–0]. I was hit in the back of the neck [(6)3–0] and I hadn't lost my voice until about a week after I got hit on the back of the neck [(6)3–0]. I was in the hospital for eight and one half weeks [(6)3–0] and I couldn't talk [(6)3–0]. They gave me treatments for it [(6)3–0]. I came home [(6)3–0] and every now and then I lose it [(6)3–0].

1. So, as far as you know [(8)1–3], that could be caused by some emotional problem too [(5)1–3].

3. Yes [(3)3–1].

1. What do you say about it, Freddy [(8)1–4]? Any connection with your own [(8)1–4]?

4. What bothers me is the headaches coming on and off [(6)4–1].

1. What seems to cause it [(8)1–4]?

4. I don't know [(7)4–y].

1. Well, do you think you have some sort of infection or emotional problem that you could blame it on [(8)1–4]?

4. Well, I had quite a few while I was overseas [(6)4–1]. I had a

good friend who was killed in Germany [(6)4–1]; that same day
I was in an auto accident [(6)4–1]. . . .

1. That might have added to the nervousness of the accident
[(5)1–4], do you think [(8)1–4]? What do you think, Joe
[(8)1–5]?

5. I have trouble not sleeping nights [(6)5–1], temper [(6)5–0]
. . . what the doctor told me [(11)5–0] . . . I hold all my emo-
tions inside [(5)5–1] you know [(7)5–1] I hold things in
[(5)5–0]. It's [(11)5–y] . . . it's on my mind that I'll blow my
top sometime [(11)5–y]. As a matter of fact, I can't take much of
a ribbing [(5)5–0]. I know it's ribbing, but there's not much I can
do to keep myself quiet [(6)5–0], you know [(7)5–1]. I get into
a hell of a lot of trouble [(5)5–0]. When I try to express my emo-
tions I can't talk [(6)5–0]. I get so mad I can't speak [(6)5–0].
I lose control of my voice [(6)5–0]. I stand there and look a little
foolish [(6)5–0]; I might start swinging [(5)5–0], you know
[(7)5–1]. That's all it is [(11)5–0]. . . .

CHAPTER 4

APPRAISING OBSERVER RELIABILITY

Introduction. The existence of variation between the tabulations of observers is a practical reality which has been anticipated in the development of the plan of observation outlined for an actual study. We know from our experience with the method that systematic training does reduce these variations but after a lapse of time, or at the time of a shift to a new situation, retraining will most assuredly be necessary. For this reason we shall outline a procedure which builds the training element into the observation routine. The amount of training is regulated by means of an easily calculated measure of reliability. Acceptable reliability is fixed at an arbitrary level. This is done because data collected for one project are almost invariably found to be of interest from a quite different point of view at a later time. Thus, it is desirable to maintain a relatively high level of reliability at all times instead of fluctuating the reliability level in terms of the anticipated latitude in a particular research design.

It is assumed that the conditions under which reliability is measured will be substantially those which prevail under what we have called the standard conditions of observation. This standard procedure requires three persons. Persons A and B perform interaction recording and Person C obtains an anecdotal record of the meeting and controls the sound recording equipment. There are four basic records generated in the original observation period: the scoring records of A and B; the sound recording; and the anecdotal record of C. In addition to these there are the first-hand recollections of A, B, and C; these will be utilized to reconcile controversies that arise in the interpretation of the sound recording. We shall assume that our study of reliability is restricted to these documents. While still and motion pictures may be used in addition to the above, our preliminary experiments have not indicated that they would contribute substantially to the record generated by the above technique.

The essential notion behind the method we shall propose arises from an analysis of the source of variation between observers into the following factors:

(1) *unitizing*, the division of a period of interaction into acts or separate recorded scores;

(2) *categorizing*, the assignment of acts to interaction categories; and

(3) *attributing*, the designation of an originator and target for an act.

Unfortunately, a matrix which would provide for a simultaneous test between observers of these three characteristics of a protocol would require (n plus 2) (n plus 2) (12 k) cells, where n is the number of persons in the group, k the number of time intervals, and 12 the number of categories. Thus, for 2 persons for ten 10-minute intervals, there would be 1,920 cells in which acts might conceivably be recorded. Since about 10 to 15 acts per minute are scored, the number of possible dispositions of acts usually exceeds the expected number of acts, a fact which would tend to cause many low frequency cells and complicate the computation of reliability scores on this basis. Fortunately, however, the complication can be reduced by considering first the reliability of 1 and 2 above, and subsequently the reliability of 1 and 3. The implications which follow from this division of the problem will be stated more fully in the paragraphs below.

Reliability of categorization. The experimenter may or may not plan to employ mechanical tabulating equipment in the tabulation of his data. For the purpose of this paragraph the technique of tabulating the data is unimportant so long as the basic interaction data of each observer may be reduced to a table of the type shown in Table 1. Let us designate a tabulation of A's data in the form of Table 1 as A_1, and a similar tabulation of B's data as B_1.

One aspect of the problem of reliability concerns the relationship of A_1 to B_1. The ideal of one-to-one correspondence is clearly not to be expected. On the other hand, conventional tests of significance at the .05 level are not applicable, for although the scores will usually represent less than the number of acts that would have been recorded by an omniscient observer, there is no reason to believe they were sampled at random. Acts which occur rapidly are probably under-represented in the score, very dramatic acts are probably over-

Table 1. Paradigm of tabulation employed in appraising reliability of categorization.

Category	k minute intervals						Total
	1	2	.	.	.	k	
1	.	.	.	.	.	.	
2	.	.	.	.	.	.	
.	.	.	.	.	.	.	
.	.	.	.	.	.	.	
12	.	.	.	.	.	.	
Total							

represented, and classification errors derive from states of information and different mental "sets" of the observer which are assuredly not random. In short, there is no question as to whether or not these observers are sampling from the same population. The question is, "Can they score according to the directions?" We recognize below that the correspondence of A's scores with B's scores does not completely establish that "the" standard system is being used. It simply establishes that "a" system common to A and B is being used. Nonetheless, the correspondence between A and B is a legitimate part of our concern. A product-moment correlation coefficient is frequently used as a measure of observer reliability in situations of this type. The acceptance level is usually set in the vicinity of .9. This is not satisfactory for the case at hand, for r tends to be relatively insensitive to variations in values with small densities. It is preponderantly determined by the large values of the distribution. For this reason it is possible to find comparisons between observers which have an r above .9 which do not come within the .05 level when tested by Chi-Square. This latter measure tends to be very much more sensitive to the variations in the pairs of values of smaller magnitude. This characteristic is also in keeping with the probable interpretation of the summaries of interaction materials, for the possible significance of five acts of low over-all density is much greater than the possible significance of five acts of "analyzing the situation" which constitutes a substantial portion of the acts usually recorded. Use of Chi-Square is also indicated because it permits a concomitant test of both categorizing and unitizing, whereas r is insensitive to the number of acts within categories so long as the proportion of acts within categories to the total acts is constant. Chi-Square is more easily extended to situations where there are more than two observers, and is somewhat simpler to compute.

The reader should understand clearly that we are using Chi-Square as an index of goodness of fit which is to be applied to a situation which does *not* represent random sampling. The use of Chi-Square in this sense should be clearly dissociated from the more conventional applications. The significance of this difference becomes particularly evident when we consider the adoption of a value of Chi-Square which may be taken to indicate acceptable agreement between observers. We suggest the use of Chi-Square at the .50 (not .05) probability level. This level is arbitrary; another experimenter may wish to vary it on the basis of his experience.

To determine whether the Chi-Square value for a particular $A_1 B_1$ has a P of .50 or greater and is therefore acceptable, the following conventions are observed:

(1) The total scores of the A_1 and B_1 tabulation are shown by categories for a common interval of interaction:

Categories	A_1	B_1
1	.	.
.	.	.
12	.	.

(2) The average for A_1 B_1 for the category in question is taken as the theoretical value.

(3) Any row in which *either* A_1 or B_1 has a cell with a frequency less than 5 will be collapsed and the sum of the respective A_1 and B_1 values will be accumulated in one row.

(4) r $(c-1)$ degrees of freedom will be used, where r is the number of rows, and c the number of columns.

The method is completely general and may be applied to any interval or combination of intervals the experimenter may choose.

If A_1 and B_1 prove to have a value within the range of acceptance, it is of interest to investigate whether the observers could duplicate their performance again. While the actors cannot be sent through their paces again, it is possible to replay the recording. The recording has the disadvantage of not retaining the minimal gestures and unspoken out-of-field responses that might have been observed in the original scoring. It is quite interesting though, that most observers report very vivid image recall accompanying the replaying of the sound recording of interaction they have previously observed. On the other hand, persons who listen to a disk without having observed the interaction have much greater difficulty in identifying the voices and sensing the feeling tones upon which certain classifications strongly depend. If original observers rescore from a sound recording, they frequently get more scores than originally, probably because the knowledge that derives from their "having been there before" removes the blocks to placement of their scores that perhaps arose from the unanticipated twists of events in the original situation. If the disk is not scored at normal speed but is stopped and replayed, whatever loss of scores that arose in the original situation because of the speed of interaction may be in large part rectified. If nonverbal acts can be recognized from the original record and added to this rescore record, we are provided with a particularly valuable check on the original scoring. We find it desirable to have the observers rescore one half of the original intervals from the sound recording. This is the second phase in the reliability schema presented in Chart 17.

The tabulation of the rescored-from-disk protocol is designated $A_2 B_2$ and provides the possibility of two further Chi-Square measures of reliability: the comparison of the two observers with one another in a manner parallel to the preceding computation, and the comparison of their rescore average with their original average for the same intervals. If these two values have a Chi-Square probability of .50 or higher, the experimenter's confidence in the observation is strengthened.

Chart 17. Proposed reliability schema.

Phase	Persons	Action	Product
1. Original Observation	A & B C	A & B record on interaction recorder. C obtains anecdotal record of issues considered and tenor of meeting; obtains sound recording.	$A_1 B_1$ Anecdotal Report. Sound Recording.
2. Rescore Sound Recording	A & B	Rescore interaction from sound recording immediately after observation.	$A_2 B_2$
3. Preparation of Written Protocol	A, B, & C	Pool understanding of sound recording and prepare written protocol; annotate emotional elements reflected by speed, tone, etc.; add nonverbal elements by reference to $A_1 B_1$ and anecdotal report.	$\overline{A B C}_3$
4. Written Protocol Check	X, Y, Z	Listen to sound recording and check accuracy of transcript; reconcile differences.	$\overline{A B C}_4$
5. Scoring Written Protocol	A, B, C, X, Y, Z	Each individually scores written protocol.	$A_5 B_5 C_5$ $X_5 Y_5 Z_5$
6. Pooling of Scores	A, B, C, X, Y, Z	Meet in conference; pool scores and annotate manual to show new conventions adopted.	Pooled Form.

The final phases of our appraisal of reliability arise from recognition that a team of observers may develop a "private consensus" which may impede communication of results to those who were guided more closely by a standard manual. This tendency toward private interpretation can best be avoided by having the observing team "put down in writing" their mode of operation. To encourage this practice we recommend that the following procedure be followed with a random portion of approximately one tenth of all material scored. Observers A, B, and C jointly prepare a written script for the interval selected. The participation of the anecdotal observer C in the preparation of this script is important for he was oriented to global aspects of the original interaction. The three, by consulting their original protocols can add in parentheses to the verbatim script those statements which best communicate the tenor of the interaction observed, so long as the three can agree concerning the accuracy of the comments in question. This is Phase 3 of the reliability schema.

At this point the written protocol is submitted to three qualified judges who listen to the recording with the written protocol before them. They may listen as many times as they choose in order to satisfy themselves that they have heard the emotional overtones and that the written script reproduces accurately the spoken elements of interaction. Any disputed sections are to be worked out between the judges and the original observers. This is Phase 4 of the reliability schema.

After the written protocol is agreed upon, each of the three judges and the three observers scores the document in the same manner in which the training protocols were scored. We designate the tabulations of the three observers as A_5, B_5 and C_5, and the tabulations of the three judges as X_5, Y_5 and Z_5. While the comparison of these documents may be of great interest, our objective of determining the point by point correspondence cannot be attained with certainty in terms of tabulation totals. For this reason we recommend that the six participants sit down together and go over the document they have scored point by point, discussing differences as they go, and annotating the manual to show the supplementary conventions that were required to enable them to pool their scores. The final pooled score agreed upon for the interval in question is compared by Chi-Square with the original scoring of the interval. This completes Phases 5 and 6 of the reliability schema. We believe that the experimenter need have little concern about the reliability of the original record if the result of this test is consistently above the .50 probability level which is being used as an index for acceptance.

Since the fully allocated cost of each hour's observation under standard conditions may be quite high, an experimenter will probably be reluctant to discard data if the original observation does not come up to the acceptance level. The sound recording provides some insurance against this possibility. For if the A_1 B_1 test is not satisfactory, it is possible to have the rescore operation carried out for the entire period. If this is acceptable, the full written protocol preparation can then be done for one-fifth instead of one-tenth of the time intervals. If the A_2 B_2 test is not acceptable, a written protocol can then be prepared for the full period. The pooled tabulations of observers and judges can then be adopted for the period in question.

There are some intermediate possibilities of acceptable followed by unacceptable and vice versa which can be communicated most easily by the sequential diagram presented in Chart 18. In this reliability control plan, the length of the bar represents the proportion of total time intervals processed under each sequence of possibilities. The hatching refers to the operation performed and the plus and minus refer to "acceptable" and "unacceptable" as previously defined. If the A_1 B_1 scores are acceptable, the average of A_1 B_1 scores is accepted as the criterion for later tests. If A_1 B_1 is not acceptable and A_2 B_2 is, then the average of the intervals of A_2 B_2 for intervals which are subsequently processed through all phases is used in the Chi-Square computation. If neither A_1 B_1 nor A_2 B_2 is acceptably reliable, no test of the final document can be made. We anticipate that the experimenter's final record will be made up of a sum representing the scores derived from the most extensive processing of each interval. For example, if satisfactory reliability were achieved at each step, the final record would be made up of 50% Phase 1, 40% Phase 2, and 10% Phase 6 intervals. At the extreme of unsatisfactory reliability it would be 100% Phase 6. Whatever the degree of processing, the mean score of the observers for the final

Chart 18. The sequence of reliability checks.

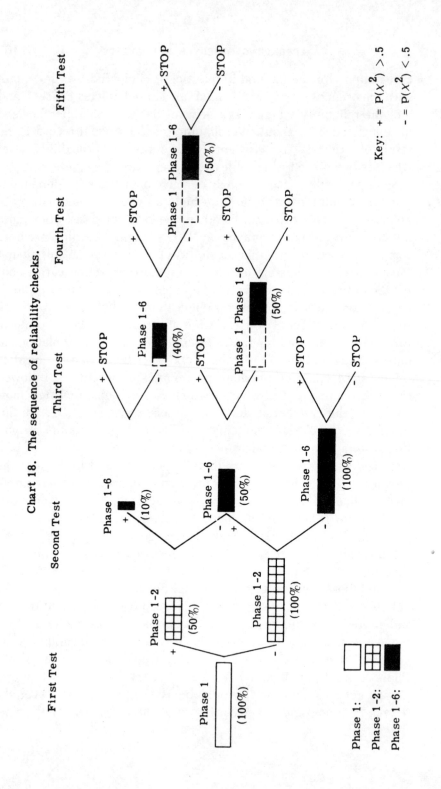

Key: + = P(X^2) > .5
      − = P(X^2) < .5

phase of processing is taken as representative of the interval in question.

The experimenter may feel that since full processing through all six phases may arise in any case, it is preferable to begin with the assumption that a full written protocol will be required and thereby save the time consumed in original observation and intermediate checks. While this is a tenable position, it does not place the reward on accurate on-the-scene scoring that the above system does, and ignores the possible economy and stimulus to research of initially reliable observation. Those who have worked with sound recordings and written protocols are aware that the anticipation of long hours of written transcript preparation has an inhibiting effect on research. Furthermore, the who-to-whom aspect of scoring cannot be reproduced satisfactorily from the sound record in most cases; hence a general confidence in our observers in the original scoring situation is required if we are to use the who-to-whom part of the scoring.

Table 2 illustrates the computation of Chi-Square. The data are the independent scores of two trained observers for a twelve-minute recording of a discussion group criticizing a proposed thesis problem. The computations are carried out in accordance with the conventions previously presented. The probability of a Chi-Square value with seven degrees of freedom greater than the 1.6 observed is approximately .97, well above the .50 acceptance level. For convenience, the crucial acceptance levels are given below:

Degrees of Freedom	Maximum Allowable χ^2 for $P = .50$
3	2.4
4	3.4
5	4.4
6	5.3
7	6.3
8	7.3
9	8.3
10	9.3
11	10.3
12	11.3

Table 2. Determination of observer reliability.

Category	Frequencies		Mean	$\dfrac{(A - \bar{x})^2}{\bar{x}}$
	A	B		
2	17	16	16.5	.02
3	18	17	17.5	.01
5	56	61	58.5	.21
6	86	97	91.5	.33
7	20	22	21.0	.05
10	5	5	0.0	.00
1	4	1		
4	4	4		
8	1 }14	0 }11	12.5	.18
9	1	0		
11	0	5		
12	4	1		
Total	216	229	---	.80 × 2 = 1.60

It may be noted in Table 2 that although the conformity between observers was high, there is a marked difference in Categories 11 and 12. When a difference of this type is noted, it is highly desirable to have the observers discuss the possible ways in which such a disparity may have arisen, and, if possible, to formulate a written convention which can become a part of the formal definition of the categories. To facilitate checks of this type we find it helpful to utilize a graphic method to reveal the significant discrepancies.

To describe the graphic technique, we must first explain the statistical model we are applying. We might describe the situation as follows: the total scores in a given category are of two types—A and non-A, or A and B—and we are testing to determine the reasonableness of the assumption that the P (A) is equal to .5. Stating the problem in this way we have fulfilled the requirements for the conventional binomial paradigm and can therefore approach the graphic solution of our problem with a diagram like the following:

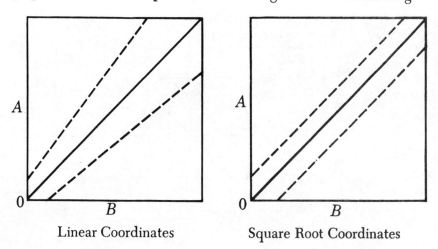

Linear Coordinates   Square Root Coordinates

The diagonal represents the expected and the dotted lines represent the two-standard deviation range plus or minus about the expected. A and B values plotted scatter-gram fashion would be markedly deviant if they did not fall within the dotted lines. By transforming the coordinates to a square root scale it is possible to obtain a two-sigma plus or minus range which appears as two lines parallel to the expected line.

A scale of the latter type facilitates visual comparison of the relative deviance of points. Fortunately a paper which makes the required transformation of data is available commercially.[*] On this paper, two sigma equals approximately one centimeter; therefore the range in which we are interested would be defined between two parallel lines, each 1 cm. from a line drawn from the origin at an angle which represents the 50–50 probability line. (Chart 19 is drawn with square root coordinates as an illustration of the procedure. The data plotted are taken from Table 2.)

We have made the empirical observation that when no point with

[*] Binomial Probability Paper, designed by Frederick Mosteller and John W. Tukey, manufactured by the Codex Book Co., Inc., Norwood, Massachusetts. For details see an article by the designers, "The Uses and Usefulness of Binomial Probability Paper," *Journal of the American Statistical Association*, June 1949, 174–212.

Chart 19. Conformity of scores shown with two-sigma range on square root coordinates.

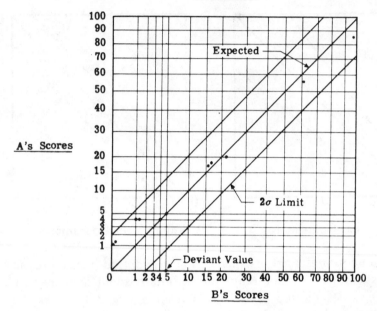

A's Scores

B's Scores

a value greater than 5 falls substantially outside the two-sigma range on either side of the expected line the criterion will be met. The experimenter will soon appreciate the value of this simplified method as a means of maintaining a constant control on the reliability of observers, and as a training aid. As applied in training, the plotting of points highlights the area in which the discrepancy is occurring so that immediate steps may be taken to resolve the differences observed. It motivates the trainees, and brings to the practical training and observing situation an equivalent of quality control as used in modern management.

Reliability of attribution. In the section above we have considered the assignment of an act to a category. In this section we shall consider the designation of the originator and the target of an act. In general, acts may be *originated* by any of the n members of a group, by all of the group, or, on occasion, by some outsider; acts may be *directed to* any particular one of the other members, the self (y), all (0), and the outer situation or out-group other (x), as previously defined in the section on the actor and situation as a frame of reference, p. 44. Thus if acts are arranged in a two-way table with originator on the vertical and target on the horizontal, there will be (n plus 2) (n plus 2) cells. The acts a person directs to himself as a target (y), are placed in the diagonal, as shown in Table 3.

The question of reliability as it applies to attribution refers to the similarity of the distribution of acts within the total matrix by different observers or judges. A matrix of the type shown in Table 3 can be constructed for each time interval, and any combination of time intervals may be summed together for a given group. Various sub-groupings of categories can be distributed in such a matrix for certain purposes of analysis; for example, in appraising the differential distribution of "positive" or "negative" acts. For the present we are interested in the general case of determining the acceptable variation between A's and B's scores when arranged in such a matrix. In the next chapter we shall discuss the possible importance for interaction of variation of cell densities.

From the outset we must recognize that the cell densities will be small and irregular. We must also recognize that the sound recording will not in all cases provide a basis for reconciling differences as unequivocal as it did in the case of categorization. The target of an

Table 3. Paradigm of tabulation employed in appraising reliability of attribution.

Originator	Target						Total
	1	.	.	n	0	x	
1	y						
.		y					
.			y				
n				y			
0					y		
x						y	
Total							

act is often indicated by the eyes of the speaker, and judges cannot determine this from the recording. The similarity of voices is so great in some groups that judges who have not seen the original interaction may have difficulty in distinguishing the individual speaker's voice. Here again, though, the person who scored the original record usually has little difficulty. If we consider simply the row totals which represent the total persons who originated acts, we find that this is highly reliable between observers. This is fortunate for it enables one to analyze with confidence such elements of a tabulation as "who originated the most acts" and "who originated the most acts of particular types." The column totals are less reliable. These totals for the targets of acts also have a much greater range of densities. A very high proportion of all acts of more than two-person groups are directed to "all" and as a result, the column totals of nonleaders are usually very small.

We are helped somewhat in the solution of this problem by the degree of independence that exists between operations. More specifically, categorization is relatively independent of attribution, and the designation of an originator is similarly independent of the designation of a target. This enables the experimenter to use data which meet the acceptance criterion for one operation for whatever conclusions may be drawn from that operation. This is true notwithstanding the fact that some other operation may not have been carried out with acceptable reliability. Unitizing is an exception to the above, for variations between observers in unitizing will affect all three of the above operations. In practice these points are not too important; we find that observers who perform one operation reliably also tend to perform the other operations reliably.

We shall not describe a specific program for the appraisal of the reliability of attribution as we did in the case of categorization. We believe that rescoring and perhaps judging may help in the designation of the originator of an act, and insofar as the target is to a degree determined by the immediately preceding actor, these further steps in the reliability schema may also help to determine the target. But to a very large degree attribution must be done accurately in the on-the-scene observation. For this reason we recommend that Chi-Square with the conventions and acceptance level previously described be used to check both the originator total and the target total. If they are acceptably reliable they may be used in analysis. The joint intercell values should be checked only when these values are to be the basis for a specific part of the subsequent analysis. In this latter case, the same criteria and conventions for collapsing as previously described should be used. No example of these computations seems necessary here, since the procedure is the same as that already illustrated. The reader is again reminded of the time-saving use of binomial probability paper.

CHAPTER 5

ANALYSIS AND INTERPRETATION

Introduction. In the preceding chapters we have tried to build a series of bridges from a body of general theoretical notions to a concrete method of observation which can be applied by different observers in different situations to produce reliable data. The purpose of the present chapter is to share with the reader some of the problems involved in building the bridges back from the data obtained to the more general body of theory again in such a way that what we observe may help us correct and refine our more general hypotheses. Our bridges must work in both directions, and the building of the bridges is the really important part of the job.

"The ground of confidence in any concrete deductive science is not the *a priori* reasoning itself, but the accordance between its results and those of observation *a posteriori*. Either of these processes apart from the other, diminishes in value as the subject increases in complication, and this in so rapid a ratio as soon to become entirely worthless. . . . Bacon has judiciously observed that the *axiomata media* of every science principally constitute its value. The lowest generalizations, until explained by and resolved into the middle principles of which they are the consequences, have only the imperfect accuracy of empirical laws; while the most general laws are *too* general, and include too few circumstances, to give sufficient indication of what happens in individual cases where the circumstances are almost always immensely numerous." °

Our "bridges" are the *axiomata media*, or the middle principles, which tell us, on the one hand, how to give operational content to the referents of our theoretical variables and, on the other, how to give theoretical meaning to the empirical uniformities in our data.

In this chapter we present the essential contents of the two memoranda referred to in the Preface. These two documents constitute a brief statement of the *a priori* reasoning that preceded and provoked the development of the observation method. The implementation of these ideas has only begun. A method has been developed

---

° Mill, John Stuart, *A System of Logic*, from Book VI, "On the Logic of the Moral Sciences," Longmans, Green and Co., New York, 1936, p. 585 and 568.

which promises to give us operational definitions of certain of the variables in certain of their empirical forms. The theoretical hypotheses are much more general in their implication than the present method gives means of testing. The method, however, may hold a peculiarly central position in their testing and refinement, since it is designed to produce simultaneous measures of a system of theoretically relevant variables. Even though the method is only one way of yielding relevant data, it may provide a kind of generally useful pilot test in the problem of getting back and forth from high-level abstractions to lower-level empirical generalizations, and in telling the difference between them.

Some general assumptions about analysis and interpretation. Among the most troublesome and fascinating problems in analysis and interpretation of data is the one we have come to call the "flip-flop" problem. Consider a crude hypothetical example. Suppose in an experiment we need a variation in solidarity, because factor A is said to vary with it, and we wish to determine which of two different types of groups is the more solidary. Can we use some sort of measurement from the interaction categories? Suppose we decide that the group with the higher rate in Category 1, "Shows solidarity, etc.," will be adjudged the more solidary. Let us suppose, then, that to make sure we obtain groups with different degrees of solidarity we choose to take observations on several groups of married couples, on the assumption that they will be highly solidary, and several groups of nursery school children, on the assumption that they will be much less solidary. Suppose we take some base-line observations just to make certain and come out with two types of profiles like those of Chart 10 and Chart 8, as shown in Chapter 1. It turns out that the married couples have a very *low* rate of activity in Category 1, "Shows solidarity, etc.," whereas the children's play groups have very *high* rates. What does the hapless investigator do with this finding? The almost irresistible tendency is to do a "flip-flop" of the original criterion. We maintain our idea that the married couples are more solidary than the children's play groups—in fact, we now believe they are so solidary that they do not need to show it in interaction! Their basic structural solidarity we conclude was not sufficiently threatened while we observed them to cause them to take any special action to restore it. On the other hand, the children's play group was so repeatedly threatened by disagreement and antagonism because of their lack of inhibition and their social ineptitude, we now conclude, that they constantly attempted to restore the balance by activity in Category 1. In fact, we believe our insight has been increased to such an extent that, whereas before we were willing to assume that more solidary groups would show *higher* rates in Category 1 as an "expression" of their basic solidarity, we are now willing to assume that more basically solidary groups will show *lower* rates in Category 1 because they have no special need to express their solidarity.

This is a crude example, but perhaps representative enough to remind the reader of similar dilemmas he has encountered in his own research. In the present case, neither horn of the dilemma is acceptable. Neither the original assumption nor the "flip-flop" assumption is properly stated from a theoretical point of view. What is the fallacy? In the first place, our hypothetical investigator was misled by a similarity of words. He failed to make a distinction between "solidarity" as a concept descriptive of an existing state or structural condition of a social relationship, and "solidarity" as a concept descriptive of certain immediate emotional qualities of interaction. The one is not identical with the other, nor does the presence of one always imply the presence of the other, although we might be led to think that there must be some discoverable connections between them when something else is held constant.

The fallacy is more fundamental than a confusion over words, however. One way of describing the fallacy is to say that it consists in a failure to recognize the necessity of developing and using adequate concepts of structure in order to describe the bounds within which a generalization concerning dynamics may be expected to hold true. In our field there are many problems where it is necessary to make a clear distinction between a more generalized state of being or structural condition of the system with which we are dealing, and a more momentary dynamic movement within that structure. In this kind of theoretical situation, the dilemmas leading to these flip-flop interpretations seem to arise in the process of trying to draw a direct inference from a given state of some single aspect of the structural condition to a conclusion that a given dynamic movement will result; or, conversely, trying to draw an inference from the fact that a certain dynamic movement has appeared, directly back to a conclusion that some single aspect of the structural condition is in a given state.

This problem seems to be particularly acute in comparative analysis, where no actual control groups or empirical norms are available. The only substitute for control groups or empirical norms in these cases is an attempt to fill in the gap by a system of concepts dealing with the structure of the original system. This system of concepts should tell us what kinds of factors we may be overlooking or what factors we must describe and take into account. In short, the system of concepts can be used as a set of "theoretical" controls. The problem is somewhat less acute where numbers of actual control groups provide empirical norms which largely take the place of a theoretical treatment of structure. The problem is still less acute when we can deal with the same system before and after the introduction of an experimental variable. It is least acute when the experimental variable and all the other aspects of the system are continuously variable and are all subject to continuous measurement.

Within this range of kinds of comparison, it may be seen that the example of the children and the married couples is at the very worst end, where the dilemma is most apt to arise. The innocent investigator in our example assumed that from the nature of a single dynamic movement (the rate of activity in Category 1) it was possible to make a direct inference back to a single specific aspect of the structural condition of the system (the basic institutionalized solidarity of the members) without either taking into account theoretically or actually controlling any other aspects of the structural condition. Having made this basic error, the flip-flop conclusion, no matter how plausible and tempting, leaves him in no better position fundamentally than before. Now he is trying to make a direct inference from an (assumed) single aspect of the structural condition of the system (the basic institutionalized solidarity of the members) to the nature of a single dynamic movement (the rate of activity in Category 1), again without either taking into account theoretically or actually controlling any other aspect of the structural condition. Unless our hypothetical investigator improves his procedure, he will be turning another flip-flop with his next observations.

The following points seem to be fundamental assumptions in approaching problems of analyzing and interpreting the data we obtain from our observations: what we observe and what we score is activity—movement—dynamic change. We assume that it is the result of something. We ascribe this activity in the first instance to "present motivation," but this is only the first step. (This is the vantage point, incidentally, from which social psychology as a systematic discipline works.) The next step is to identify the influences in present motivation. Here we have as general classes of structured influences entering into present motivation: (1) the structure of the present outer situation common to all members of the group, (2) the structure of the culture common to all members of the group, (3) the structure of the differential social relationships in the group, and (4) the structure of pre-existing idiosyncratic motivational factors in the personalities. (The formulation of these various classes of structured influence is the task of the various other systematic social sciences into which economics, social anthropology, sociology, and psychology of personality fit in fairly obvious ways. The relation is not simple, however, and this idea of the articulation of the various science fields is a first approximation only.)

We do not observe present motivation, nor do we observe any of these four structured influences. We *infer* them. We have been forced to infer that they are present and real in order to account for similarities and differences in interaction. But it is in a context of attempting to account for similarities and differences that we have been led to make these inferences, and it is only in such a context that scientific questions can be asked. To ask in a vacuum, for example, why for a given group a given rate should be, say .25, is not a reasonable question, or at least not a scientifically framed question. The only answer is a trivial answer. The rate is what it is because the structural context in which it appeared was what it was.

If we take care to ask our questions in a comparative context, as an attempt to account for similarities or differences, then it may be possible to return sensible answers. For example, if it is asked why

it is that for a given group of people, composed of the same personalities, within the same series of meetings dealing with the same
kind of problems, there is a higher rate of activity in Category 2,
"Shows tension release, jokes, laughs, etc." in the first and last ten
minutes of each meeting than in any other periods of the meetings,
then a sensible answer may be returned. The supposition might be
that the difference in activity appeared in response to a difference in
factor (1), the structure of the present outer situation common to all
members of the group which changes as the position of the group in
its problem-solving sequence changes. This answer, in turn, would
then lead to possible deductions which could be tested. This kind of
problem of interpretation is at the opposite end of the series from
the problem of the married couples and the children.

For simplicity in stating the next few points, let us speak within
the context of the latter case. Under these more controlled conditions, when we observe some change in activity from an established
base line or norm (and can assure ourselves that it is not an artifact
of unreliable observation), we conclude that there has been some
change or changes in the underlying structural condition. On the
other hand, if we observe no change in activity, we cannot conclude
that there have been no changes in the underlying structural condition. In some cases, we assume, several changes may occur and cancel
each other out, producing no observable change in activity.

When we observe some change in activity from an established
base line or norm, we cannot assume that the change is necessarily
"proportional" in any simple sense to the change in any particular
element of the underlying structural condition. The relationships of
the underlying factors to each other may be such as to reinforce, reduce, cancel, or reverse the influence on the rate of activity which a
given one of them might have if its effect alone could be observed.

If we wish to determine the influence of changes of single factors
in the underlying structural condition, we attempt to hold all other
conditions constant while we change that one alone. Insofar as one is
willing to assume that he has succeeded in holding all other conditions constant, he may attribute the observed change in activity to
the experimentally induced change in the underlying structure;
he should never forget, however, that the dynamic sequence which

he posits was observed in a *particular* over-all structural condition and does not necessarily hold within others. The range of conditions under which it holds remains to be discovered in the same painstaking way.

Realistic attempts to formulate predictive hypotheses cannot fail to take these limitations into account. Flip-flop dilemmas like the one mentioned above are symptoms of a failure to take these over-all structural conditions into account. This in many instances is a failure which naturally results not from methodological naivete, but from the practical impossibility of having at a given stage in research either a sufficiently articulated theoretical framework for describing the main aspects of the underlying structure or the necessary empirical data to fill it out. To the properly prepared researcher, the flip-flop becomes a critical signal of a missing element in his theoretical approach.

In one sense, many of the most important generalizations in social science probably have already been discovered: they are "obvious," "self-evident," "tautologous." They can be and have been formulated by *a priori* speculation. *A priori* generalizations are not necessarily trivial. The trouble is, literally, that we do not know what they mean. That is, while in many cases they have some unmistakable content which recommends them to the human mind, they are neither rooted nor bounded. On the one hand, the range of concrete referents which will fit the terms of the generalizations is not known. On the other hand, the range of structural conditions within which the generalizations will hold is not determined. Some of the most important advances in our field will come, it may be predicted, not from the discovery of brand new, high level generalizations, but from the discovery of empirical generalizations which are previously unrecognized cases of well known tautologies and from the identification of previously unformulated conditions in which our well-known tautologies turn a flip-flop. Of such undignified misfortunes is scientific progress made.

Since we expect, indeed welcome, some misfortunes of this kind, it is well to be prepared to recognize and take full advantage of them in the generalizations which follow. Certain of the generalizations have been stated roughly in this form: "If X (one specified change) occurs, then a strain is created toward Y (another specified change)." This does not mean that Y always appears, but that Y is an effective solution apparently within a fairly wide range of underlying structural conditions, and as such, with some undetermined regularity, it is adopted. However, unique properties of (1) the structure of the present outer situation common to all members of the group, (2) the structure of the culture common to all members of the group, (3) the structure of differential social relationships in the group, and (4) the structure of pre-existing idiosyncratic factors in the personalities may enter in to modify the reaction from "Y" to some other type of reaction. These unique properties may be either systematically operative and explainable, or historically determined by factors which are too rare to be formulated systematically. However, when one of the generalizations, once made concrete by the development of an operational procedure, fails to predict as it should or indeed turns a complete flip-flop, it is a signal to start a search for the difficulty, and if possible to incorporate the insight systematically either into the theory or the operational definition.

In order that those cases where prediction fails shall not be simply trivial oversights, let us assume the best possible control of the factors mentioned above. Let us assume that the generalizations are meant to apply within the context of an experimental framework like that described in Chapter 1, in some standard type of situation such as that provided by a series of chess problems as described there, and, except where otherwise specified or implied, within the same group of members, within a reasonable time span, so that the factors of situation, culture, social organization, and personality may vary as little as possible simply through lack of control.

The hypotheses are presented in three sections: first, dynamic tendencies of the interaction process (distribution of activities without regard to persons); second, dynamic tendencies of role structure (distribution of activities between persons); and third, dynamic tendencies of ideological structure (the expression of sentiments concerning institutionalized aspects of the interaction process and role structure). Wherever possible, the hypotheses will be given suggestive implementation in terms of data produced by the present method of interaction process analysis.

Criteria for criticism of hypotheses. The tentative nature of the material in the following section cannot be overemphasized. It is much too early to form any well founded judgments on the promise of the method as a means of testing the various hypotheses contained in this chapter. As to the hypotheses themselves, it would be possible to use them as a point of departure for the marshaling of experimental and observational work reported in the literature. As they stand, however, they are not the product of any such systematic marshaling of existing evidence. They do represent a general simplified abstract of the author's understanding of the nature of social systems, which squares with his feeling for the evidence, but this is a very different thing. Without a systematic testing of the "bridges" it is impossible in many cases to tell whether a hypothesis seems "right" because it connects properly with a body of empirical uniformities as well as with a body of theory or because it simply has some logical, syntactical, or sentimental association with other high order abstractions which we like for one reason or another.

Since we are not prepared at this writing to give a critical appraisal of the hypotheses and yet feel that they are an organic part of the method which should be known to those who use the method, perhaps it would be proper to suggest a list of the kinds of questions which the author thinks should be asked about the hypotheses. These questions we might call criteria for criticism. They constitute nothing more than a particular statement of the methodological questions we usually ask of hypotheses in our field:

1. Are the terms of the generalization empirically specific? That is, do the concepts or variables in terms of which the generalization is made, refer either directly or indirectly to designated or classified aspects of activity or situation which can be observed and separately distinguished from each other in all kinds of concrete cases?

2. Is the relationship which is asserted to exist between the variables an empirically verifiable type of relationship? That is, does it specify or imply some kind of operation in terms of which the results of observation can be related to each other to yield a judgment of true or false? Or is the relationship asserted a matter of verbal definition, i.e., a syntactical or a tautological statement?

3. If the variables are empirically specific and the relationship

asserted to exist between variables is empirically verifiable, is there any evidence, either from common experience or from technical studies, that the generalization is either true, partially true, or false?

4. If no evidence or insufficient evidence exists, would it be possible to design an appropriate observational or experimental study to produce evidence one way or the other?

5. Are the variables "context bound," that is, meaningful and empirically specific in one or more restricted types of empirical system (such as a play group or gang) but non-meaningful or inappropriate when applied to other systems (such as a family or work group) sufficiently similar in some abstract way to justify the supposition that generalizations can be made which will hold for all?

6. Are the generalizations "culture bound," that is, true in one or more restricted types of cultural context (among Americans and British, for example) but false or qualified when applied to other cultures (among the Navajo or Zuñi, for example)?

7. Are the generalizations insufficiently qualified, that is, true, all things being equal perhaps, but actually applying to variables so much a part of a larger system that the assumption that all other things might be equal is never justified?

8. If, under certain conditions, other relevant factors can be treated as being equal, that is, not changing sufficiently as to require simultaneous treatment of all variables for the application of the particular generalization, are these other relevant factors specified or enumerated in such a way that the observers can make sure whether or not they have actually changed during the period of observation necessary to test the generalization?

9. Is the generalization a part of a more inclusive system of assumptions, definitions, syntactical statements, and other empirical generalizations, such that the particular generalization can be derived logically by a process of deduction as well as verified empirically by a process of observation and experiment?

10. Does the system of assumptions, definitions, syntactical statements, empirical generalizations, and techniques of observation and experiment render the empirical system of phenomena with which it deals sufficiently clear to understanding as to make prediction

possible, and does it articulate the variables involved far enough to indicate where, in concrete situations, changes might be introduced to bring the system within the range of control?

Dynamic tendencies of the interaction process. In this section we are concerned with tendencies or uniformities that may occur in the distribution of interaction over time within a given group, without reference to the particular persons who initiate it or toward whom it is addressed. In Chapter 1 several alternative ways of conceiving the process of interaction as a problem-solving sequence were outlined briefly and in Chapter 2 were considerably expanded. There is little new material to be added here on the theoretical side. Our main task will be to suggest ways of attacking the problem empirically.

One important point seems to emerge from a series of attempts to conceptualize the problem-solving process. The problem-solving process cannot be formulated successfully in a way which ignores either of two fundamental properties: (1) it is distributed in time, and (2) it is distributed between persons. In observing group discussion, for example, this duality of distribution is obvious. What is not obvious is that the distinction cannot be disposed of even in the most abstract formulation. This is very inconvenient theoretically, since one of its consequences is that we are left with two only slightly different modes of conceptualization which overlap in extremely subtle and multifarious ways and yet can never be entirely resolved into each other.

One way of describing the two modes of conceptualization is to say that one mode is functional, the other structural. Another pair of terms expressing the distinction is "dynamic" and "static." Always, it seems, this duality is present. "No matter how thin you slice it, it always has two dimensions." One may simplify down to two major dichotomies, subject-object and past-future, but it is still impossible to get down to a single dichotomy. To take another example, the concepts of four different major types of functional problems in interaction—instrumental, expressive, adaptive, and integrative—have been a long standing source of theoretical difficulty in the author's thinking. In the original memorandum the relation was stated in the following fashion:

It is one of the basic assumptions made here that the social structure and culture of groups can be understood primarily as a system of institutionalized solutions to various functional problems which arise in the course of action. Similarly, changes in the social structure and culture are to be understood primarily as reactions to changes in the content or state of solution of these functional problems. For present purposes the main classes of functional problems can be indicated by an overlapping fourfold classification:

1. The implementing of needs and desires which for any reason are active in the members as organized personalities and as biological organisms. This instrumental process of activity, once initiated in a situation, immediately involves the second class of functional problems:
2. The adaptation of activities to the situation external to the social system. In turn, this process of modification, once initiated, immediately involves the third class of functional problems:
3. The integration of activities within the social system itself. In turn, this process of modification, once initiated, immediately involves the fourth class of functional problems:
4. The expression of emotional tensions created within the personality by changes in the situation, the social system, and its culture. This expression, in turn, once initiated, immediately re-involves the class of instrumental problems expressed as "1" above.

These four classes of functional problems are so intimately intertwined in the actual process that they can be distinguished only by a deliberate and difficult act of abstraction, which involves, among other things, a distortion of the actual time perspective, and a shift of the empirical referents of the concepts so rapid and subtle that it can only be followed with the greatest difficulty. In practice, it is impossible to speak of one of these classes of functional problems without assuming the others. Hence no exposition based upon them can be started in other than an arbitrary way.

Obviously there is a shifting and indeterminate area of overlap, which creates a desire in the theorist to get things straightened out and solidified. At various times it has seemed to be possible to eliminate one or the other of these concepts or to resolve it into another. Each of the concepts has been a candidate for extinction; each of them, however, has proved to be somehow indispensable, and in spite of the unhappy overlap, the four remain. It now appears that this is simply another case of the fundamental property of interaction systems mentioned above. The two concepts "instrumental" and "expressive" relate to the extension of the interaction system in time and its orientation forward and backward, whereas the two concepts "adaptive" and "integrative" relate to the extension of the interaction system in a structurally differentiated outer and inner dimension.

If this point of view can be grasped, it will be apparent that the various formulations suggested in Chapters 1 and 2 are simply variations on a theme, some emphasizing the temporal extension a little more in the connotation of the terms, others the structural extension, but all in one way or another assuming both at once.

In terms of operations, as well as in terms of theoretical formulations, there are several ways of attacking the problem. One may be concerned with single categories of action, with more inclusive groups of categories, or with more complicated derived relationships of rates. For any of these one may be concerned with microscopic act-to-act sequences, with more molar changes in emphasis through sequences of longer time periods, or with concomitant variation of rates and more complicated derived relationships of rates by time periods. We have only a few preliminary explorations to report here.

Table 4 shows the frequency of various category-to-category sequences. This tabulation puts together data from three of the groups for which profiles are shown in Chapter 1. The individual tabulations show very great similarities. In the table, for each category the most frequent subsequent category of activity is encircled. From this pattern it is easy to see certain "tendencies" (if this term may be permitted). First there is a tendency toward repetition. For categories of prior acts 2, 4, 5, 6, and possibly 9, a repetition in the same category is the most frequent subsequent act. Second there is a tendency for acts of high general frequency to appear frequently as subsequent acts for all categories considered as prior acts. For example, for Categories 1 (possibly), 3, 7, 8, 10, 11, 12, considered as prior acts, Category 5 or 6 is the most frequent subsequent act. Thus for each of the twelve categories considered as prior acts, the most frequent subsequent act is either a repetition in the same category or a reversion to the two most frequently used categories. We will return to this in a moment. Ignoring repetitions, we see a number of expected tendencies according to pairs of categories. Category 7 leads most frequently to its answering category, 6. Category 8 leads most frequently to its answer, 5. Similarly, Category 9 leads most frequently to its answer, 4. Categories 10, 11, and 12 seem to lead to their opposite categories, 1, 2, and 3, with less than their expected frequency.

When we begin to speak of "expected frequency," however, we run into difficulties. The frequency of repetitions and the frequency of overall occurrence are very prominent factors but they are not of much theoretical interest in the present context. It becomes evident that if we are to explore other characteristic sequences we will have to find some way of eliminating within-category sequences and putting between-category sequences on some comparative basis.

Table 5 has been constructed as an attempt to do this. Here the categories are grouped according to the sections: C, Questions; B, Attempted Answers; A, Positive Reactions; and D, Negative Re-

Table 4. Frequency of sequences between categories for three selected groups. *

Section	Category of prior act	Category of subsequent act												
		A			B			C			D			
		1	2	3	4	5	6	7	8	9	10	11	12	Tot.
A	1 Shows solidarity, raises other's status, gives help, reward:	2	1	1	1	.	4	4	.	.	1	1	.	15
	2 Shows tension release, jokes, laughs, shows satisfaction:	2	75	7	4	37	33	7	4	1	6	1	2	179
	3 Agrees, shows passive acceptance, understands, concurs, complies:	2	16	20	9	110	48	11	18	6	8	4	1	253
B	4 Gives suggestion, direction, implying autonomy for other:	4	5	17	32	29	15	3	4	5	4	1	1	120
	5 Gives opinion, evaluation, analysis, expresses feeling, wish:	1	34	114	32	399	114	35	27	7	46	19	7	835
	6 Gives orientation, information, repeats, clarifies, confirms:	3	29	58	23	136	346	48	30	8	15	15	1	712
C	7 Asks for orientation, information, repetition, confirmation:	.	3	5	.	21	89	11	3	2	4	4	1	143
	8 Asks for opinion, evaluation, analysis, expression of feeling:	.	2	13	2	44	27	6	15	2	3	2	.	116
	9 Asks for suggestion, direction, possible ways of action:	.	1	6	9	8	4	3	3	9	.	.	.	43
D	10 Disagrees, shows passive rejection, formality, withholds help:	.	5	9	5	36	15	4	5	.	17	3	5	104
	11 Shows tension, asks for help, withdraws out of field:	.	3	6	2	14	12	6	5	1	1	7	.	57
	12 Shows antagonism, deflates other's status, defends or asserts self:	.	5	2	1	10	10	.	3	.	3	1	4	39
	Total	14	179	258	120	844	717	138	117	41	108	58	22	2616

* GM, ND4, and D3 combined.

Table 5. Index of observed to expected sequences between sections, excluding sequences within sections.*

Category section of prior act	Basis of calcula- tion	Category section of subsequent act				Total observed
		A	B	C	D	
A	Observed: Expected: Difference: $\frac{D}{E}$		246 189 +57 +.30	51 82 -31 -.38	24 50 -26 -.52	321
B	Observed: Expected: Difference: $\frac{D}{E}$	265 247 +18 +.07		167 183 -16 -.09	109 111 -2 -.02	541
C	Observed: Expected: Difference: $\frac{D}{E}$	30 78 -48 -.62	204 134 +70 +.52		14 36 -22 -.61	248
D	Observed: Expected: Difference: $\frac{D}{E}$	30 46 -16 -.35	105 79 +26 +.33	24 34 -10 -.29		159
Total observed		325	555	242	147	

*Data from groups GM, ND4, and D3 combined. Observations in the diagonal are omitted. Expected frequency calculated by distributing row total by column totals excluding in each case total of column containing diagonal.

actions. For each of the types of sequences between sections, the observations may be tabulated from the preceding table. Our first step is to eliminate the diagonal, since we are not interested in within-section sequences. For those types of sequences which remain, an index has been computed which represents the difference between the expected and observed as a percentage of the expected. When a particular section of prior acts leads to a given section of subsequent acts in direct proportion to their prominence in the total number of all acts, then the index value is zero. Thus we are provided, in crude form, with a basis for appraising the degree to which outgoing acts in a given section deviate from exact proportionality in the sections to which they lead. Again for convenience we shall speak of these deviations as positive and negative tendencies.

From Table 5 it may be seen that our general expectations regarding the nature of the sequences by sections, as formulated in Chapters 1 and 2, are roughly confirmed by these data. The strongest positive tendency revealed is for prior acts in Section C, so-called Questions or Initial Acts, to be followed by subsequent acts in Section B, called Attempted Answers or Medial Acts. From Section B, the three tendencies, back to Section C or on to Section A or D, are about evenly balanced. From Section A, Positive Reactions, the strongest positive tendency is back to B, and this is also true for Section D, Negative Reactions. Both of these types of Terminal Acts tend to return to Medial Acts, but neither has a positive tendency to return to Initial Acts. Positive Reactions and Negative Reactions seem to be more or less mutually exclusive. Neither one tends to lead directly to the other, and this is in line with our general impressions about interaction. Insofar as the two central sections C and B can properly be designated as primarily concerned with Instrumental-Adaptive functions, whereas the two terminal sections can be said to be concerned with Integrative-Expressive functions, the tendency toward alternation between these two types of functions (rather than indefinitely protracted sequences which stay within one area or the other) may be said to appear even on the act-to-act level. It is not known how representative the results suggested by these data may be, but the expectation is that this sort of finding may be quite general and may hold within a fairly wide range of conditions.

A more interesting and strategic conception of the problem-solving sequence is in terms of the pairs of categories as described in Chapters 1 and 2. According to the theoretical rationale, each of the pairs of categories is concerned with the solution or lack of solution of a particular functional problem encountered in interaction systems. Furthermore it was posited that the pairs, taken in order from the center line outward, were interrelated in a peculiar way: roughly speaking, a "nested hierarchy" was held to exist. According to this view, the interrelation was such that the solution of each type of problem in turn depended on the solution of the preceding and was a functional prerequisite to the solution of the next. That is, the solution of Problems of Communication, represented by Categories 7 and 6, was a functional prerequisite to the solution of Problems of Evaluation represented by Categories 8 and 5, which in turn was a functional prerequisite to the solution of Problems of Control, and so on. It was also suggested in Chapter 1 that in some cases this order of functional problems might appear on a larger scale than act-to-act sequences or, in other words, that it might appear as a kind of order of "agenda topics" within a complete meeting.

The series of Charts from 20 to 25 shows indices of pairs of categories as they vary in emphasis in the course of a single meeting. The meeting represented is the meeting of the "Group Mind," the total profile of which is shown in Chapter 1. The curves were obtained in the following way: the meeting was originally scored for another purpose from sound recordings. The total period had been arbitrarily divided in the original recording into sides of phonograph records about twelve minutes each. There were sixteen sides in all, or a little over three hours. In scoring, the tabulation for each side of each record was kept separate as a matter of convenience for the job at hand. From these tabulations the curves were later obtained. This, incidentally, is an excellent example of the kind of advantage we hope may accrue from a standard method of observation, where the data may later be used for unforeseen purposes.

The tabulations were combined into eight sequential periods of about twenty-four minutes each by adding each successive two sides together. Then for each period so obtained, a profile of rates, similar to the total profile shown in Chapter 1 as Chart 11, was calculated. The total profile gives the mean rate for each category for the total period. The rates of the categories for each sub-period were then combined into pairs: 7 plus 6, 8 plus 5, 9 plus 4, 10 plus 3, 11 plus 2, and 12 plus 1. This procedure gave rates for *pairs* of categories by sub-periods. The rate of each such pair was then compared with its mean rate for the total period, and the plus or minus difference was

Chart 20. Percentage deviation of Categories 7 plus 6 from meeting mean, by subperiods, Group GM.

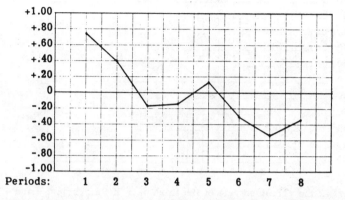

On Chart 20 the combined rate of the first pair of Categories, 7 and 6, concerned with Problems of Communication (nearest the center line on the observation form) shows its greatest preponderance in the first period of the meeting and thereafter shows a declining trend.

Chart 21. Percentage deviation of Categories 8 plus 5 from meeting mean, by subperiods, Group GM.

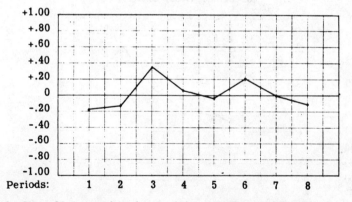

On Chart 21 the combined rate of the second pair of Categories, 8 and 5, concerned with Problems of Evaluation, shows its greatest preponderance in the third period of the meeting. (No pair was at its peak during the second period, but the the first pair was still high.)

Chart 22. Percentage deviation of Categories 9 plus 4 from meeting mean, by subperiods, Group GM.

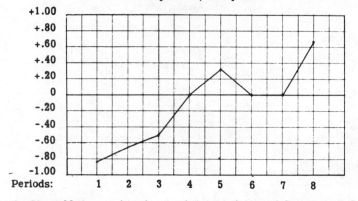

On Chart 22 the combined rate of the third pair of Categories, 9 and 4, concerned with Problems of Control, shows a prominent peak, but not its highest, in Period Five. (No pair was at its peak during Period Four, but the second pair was still above its mean.)

Chart 23. Percentage deviation of Categories 10 and 3 from meeting mean, by subperiods, Group GM.

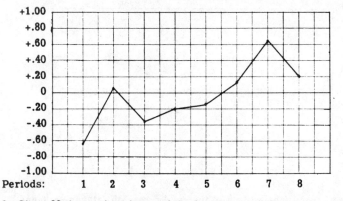

On Chart 23 the combined rate of the fourth pair of Categories, 10 and 3, concerned with Problems of Decision, shows its highest peak in the seventh period of the meeting. (No pair was at its peak during Period Six, but a secondary peak of Evaluation was prominent during this period.)

Chart 24. Percentage deviation of Categories 11 and 2 from meeting mean, by subperiods, Group GM.

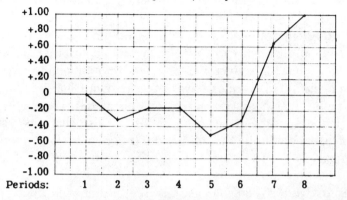

On Chart 24 the combined rate of the fifth pair of Categories, 11 and 2, concerned with Problems of Tension Reduction, shows its highest peak in the last period of the meeting. In the previous period also this rate was high.

Chart 25. Percentage deviation of Categories 12 and 1 from meeting mean, by subperiods, Group GM.

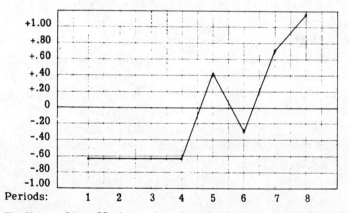

Finally, on Chart 25, the combined rate of the sixth pair of Categories 12 and 1, concerned with Problems of Reintegration, shows its highest peak also in the last period of the meeting. It also had a preliminary rise during Period Five, when Problems of Control were at their peak. This rise was primarily on the antagonistic side, while the final peak was primarily on the solidary side.

determined. This difference was then divided by the mean rate for
the pair. These indices are called percentage deviations from the
mean, and they are plotted by successive sub-periods as shown in
Charts 20 through 25. The index tells us nothing about the total
importance of the pair of categories as compared to other pairs. It
tells us simply that for a given sub-period within a meeting a given
pair of categories had more or fewer than its own usual number of
scores. To give the theoretical interpretation, it tells us whether a
given functional problem received more or less than its usual
amount of attention during the sub-period. It does not tell us whether
the functional problem was successfully solved; indeed, it specifically
masks this information out.

The results were striking—at least to the author, who had been
working for approximately three years to produce a system of categories and an arrangement of them which would produce patterned
empirical results approximately like this. It was felt from the first
that if the system of categories and method of observation were
adjusted at the proper level of abstraction, and if data were analyzed
properly, uniformities would appear in the observations which, by
their *a priori* reasonableness, would provide a kind of criterion of
validity.

The essential empirical uniformity revealed by the curves is that
for this group, with minor exceptions, the peak rate of each pair of
categories appears within the meeting in the same order in which
the pairs of categories are arranged on the observation list (Chart
16), which in turn is an order suggested by *a priori* assumptions about
the hierarchical nesting relations of the various functional problems
involved in interaction systems.

In short, we have an example of an actual meeting following
pretty closely the conceptually simplified order of events as described in Chapter 1. These data fit so beautifully into the rationale
which underlies the arrangement of categories according to pairs
that one is almost inclined to suspect that "something must be
wrong." There is something wrong. Fortunately or unfortunately, our
theory does not say that interaction always goes this way or that
"this is *the* problem-solving sequence." The theory postulates that
under certain unknown conditions, perhaps quite rare, groups *may*

proceed in this way, since it is an economical order in that problems are attacked in the order in which their solutions are functionally prerequisite to each other. However, in actual process, all kinds of "accidents" may impinge upon the system from the outer situation, while particular features of personalities, social organization, and culture of the group may prevent the solution of any of these problems anywhere along the line. Any of these likely events would destroy any hypothesis of this degree of complication which is not highly qualified as to the structural conditions within which it is expected to hold.

We suspect, in other words, that as an empirical predictive hypothesis it is quite fragile, that is, it is highly dependent upon particular structural conditions which we cannot specify, although of great strategic significance for the leader and participants in group process as a way of thinking about their process and perhaps trying to regulate it. Although we have not had the opportunity to explore this lead further, we suspect that the order of events discovered in this group was a "lucky find" under optimum conditions of some kind. This finding, in short, gives us greatly increased confidence about the essential soundness of the rationale underlying the categories and their arrangement, without increasing our confidence very much that substantial numbers of other groups would show a similar pattern.

What we really need, perhaps, is a way of stating our hypotheses about the importance of solution of preliminary functional problems *lower* in the nesting hierarchy to the solution of terminal functional problems *higher* in the nesting hierarchy, a statement which will take into account more "accidents" or structural variations in conditions. There may possibly be ways of doing this in terms of the system of categories itself, without going outside the system for data. Theoretically this would seem to require that we be able to use certain of our categories to infer certain critical things about the momentary structural condition of the system, and that we then be able to treat certain other categories as the dynamic response to that implied structural condition. The hypotheses would then be stated in the general form: if no X, then no Y. The original memoranda contained a series of hypotheses which suggested how this might be done. These hypotheses (in some cases slightly modified) and their possible implementation in terms of indices derived from the categories are discussed below. (I) is concerned with communication, (II) with evaluation, (III) with control over the outer situation, and (IV) with control of activity within the system. Taken together, they lead to an empirical prediction of a composite sort.

I. Unless the members of a group are able to establish adequate, continuing perception of the situation and communication with each other, they are unable to cooperate, and hence are subjected to insecurity (i.e., to the various threats of isolation, confusion, conflict, frustration, deprivation) and will react to remove this insecurity by adaptive-instrumental activity. Insofar as this is successful, the solution will tend to be institutionalized. Insofar as these attempts are incomplete, inadequate, or unsuccessful, the persisting insecurity will result in expressive-malintegrative behavior.

In small groups which continue over a long time period there are a number of common developments which tend to help solve this series of problems of perception and communication. These developments include the establishment of a common language, often a specialized argot which is more or less peculiar to the group; the growth of a body of common definitions or ideas about the situations they frequently encounter; the arrangement of the affairs, schedules, and physical location of the members so that frequent association with each other is possible; the development both in session and between sessions of regularized and expected channels of communication between particular members; the development of specialized procedures for gathering facts and making reconnaissance of activities completed; the emergence of special times and procedures for disseminating information to the members; the emergence of specialized fact-finding, recording, and reporting roles or sub-organizations within the group; and so on.

Any or all of these types of development may in part be initiated in an instrumental attempt to solve problems of perception and communication and they may tend to become institutionalized. The general tendency for these features to develop in many small groups may be taken, perhaps, as a kind of rough *ad hoc verification* of the first part of the hypothesis. However, the verification is rough and has little predictive value, since we are unable to specify just what we mean by "adequacy of communication," and since the conditions under which the adaptive-integrative alternative will appear rather than the expressive-malintegrative alternative, are not specified.

As to the second part of the hypothesis, we know of a great many variations of expressive-malintegrative behavior as it occurs in groups. Some of these variations seem to be fairly closely connected with breakdown in perception and communication, or involve various manipulations and distortions of it. A very broad and tentative indication of these various types of reactive patterns would include symbolic manipulation directed toward anxiety reduction or palliative satisfaction of tensions, such as magic, ritual, fantasy, rumor, compulsions, obsessions, or the like; actual or symbolic withdrawal or escape from the situation; active or passive aggressive attacks of various kinds on the situation, other persons, or the self: all of these either individually or collectively. It is clear that reactions of these types, while they may be perfectly "natural" and understandable in the scientific sense and may have a definite immediate function in expressing and perhaps reducing tensions in a short term sense, tend in the long run to set up circular developments ("vicious circles") which may interfere with the adaptation of the group to the outer situation, or with the integration of personalities and activities within the group. When any activity tends to serve only expressive or instrumental functions and sets up ulterior circular processes which interfere with the adaptation or integration of the group, the activity may be called "pathological" from the point of view of that group.

It would be possible to specify in considerable detail the pathologies of small groups and to trace out a number of fascinating ways in which they seem to be tied up with various failures to solve the problems of communication. This kind of analysis would be taken, perhaps, as a rough *ad hoc* verification of the second part of the hypothesis. Here again, however, the verification would be rough and would have little predictive value, since the dilemma is the same as before. We are unable in general to specify either what we mean by adequacy, or what constitutes the conditions under which the expressive-malintegrative alternative will appear rather than the adaptive-instrumental alternative.

It should be apparent that the hypothesis as stated has something to recommend it—and that it is much broader in implication than the present method gives means of testing—but that it suffers from the typical defect of abstract, *a priori* generalizations: we do not know what it means. We do not know the range of referents or their complete concrete content nor do we know the structural conditions within which it will or will not hold. The usual and very sound recommendation in such situations is the experimental approach. Experimental verification and refinement seem quite possible, though in many ways difficult and necessarily piecemeal. There are various ways of interfering with or facilitating the process of communication: by the original selection of members to make up an experimental group; by manipulation of the conditions under which perception of the situation or communication between members must take place; by indoctrination, briefing, or training of the members and then noting the results in terms of changes in the rates of particular types of interaction; or by other means.

Of the various experimental approaches, those which take a before and after design may be distinguished from those in which there is possible a continuous measurement of variables. Since the present method can produce something like the latter for a limited number of variables, let us see whether from the measurements we take we can construct a miniature reproduction of the hypothesis stated so broadly above, a miniature reproduction simply in terms of the variables of our restricted system.

The rate of activity in Category 6 may be taken as an index of the amount of interaction which the group actually devotes to attempted solutions to the problems of perception and communication. This rate in itself, however, in absolute terms, does not give any indication as to whether the communication is "adequate," since the amount required would be expected to vary with many conditions. Possible exceptions to this might be highly restricted situations where dependable norms have been established.

The rate of activity in Category 7 may be taken as an index of amount of interaction which the group actually devotes to indicating to each other that problems of perception or communication exist. This rate again, however, does not give the required index as to adequacy of perception and communication.

However, the ratio of the two categories may give an approximation of the index of adequacy or the lack of it that we require. If we assume that for a given group under given conditions there is a kind of normal balance between the number of interactions in Category 7 (asking for orientation, information, etc.) and the number of Category 6 interactions in answer to these indicated needs, or in anticipation of these needs, the changes in this ratio from period to period of interaction may indicate a favorable or an unfavorable imbalance for any given period. In general we would assume that when requests for orientation in Category 7 build up *without a comparable increase* in Category 6 which provides the answers, the imbalance is for the moment unfavorable. The initial conditions for the hypothesis stated above thus might be satisfied. As a first approximation, then, an Index of Difficulty of Communication might be written in this fashion:

$$\text{Index of Difficulty of Communication} = \frac{7}{7+6}$$

The numbers in this formula are the numbers of the categories, and stand for the raw number of scores in the designated category for the given period of tabulation. The numerator category is also included in the denominator in order to stabilize the index and insure that all values will be percentages falling between 0 and 100. As the percentage increases, we will assume that difficulty of communication is increasing, and vice versa. The absolute level of the index will have no meaning apart from some kind of empirically established norm. This is not a critical problem, however, when it is desired simply to compare the difficulty in one period of a meeting with the difficulty in another part, since the index for the series as a whole serves the purpose of a norm about which component periods fluctuate.

Now for the second element of the hypothesis, which states that as adaptive-instrumental attempts to solve the problem of communication are incomplete, inadequate, or unsuccessful, the persisting insecurity will result in expressive-malintegrative behavior. The Index of Difficulty of Communication has been accepted as an evidence of the relative, momentary failure or inadequacy of communication. Our system of categories provides a series of categories from which an index of expressive-malintegrative behavior can be derived. Categories 10, 11, and 12 added together may be taken as a reasonable indicator of this class of behavior insofar as it can be grasped by the present method. A still better indicator possibly would be the balance between Categories 10, 11, 12 on the one hand, and Categories 1, 2, and 3 on the other. For the same reasons of convenience as above, the Index of Expressive-Malintegrative Behavior may be written as follows:

$$\text{Index of Expressive-Malintegrative Behavior} = \frac{(10 + 11 + 12)}{(10 + 11 + 12) + (1 + 2 + 3)}$$

Now, since we wish to say that as the Index of Difficulty of Communication increases, the Index of Expressive-Malintegrative Behavior will also tend to increase (though we do not know just how rigid or linear the correlation will be), we can write:

$$\frac{7}{7 + 6} = f\left(\frac{(10 + 11 + 12)}{(10 + 11 + 12) + (1 + 2 + 3)}\right)$$

We thus have a tentative operational equivalent of the hypothesis stated earlier in broad verbal terms, insofar as we can reproduce its meaning in terms of the present method of observation.

It would be possible at this point to test this hypothesis with observations from any group one might have happened to observe. We would not expect the correlation to be very high or dependable, however, since our theory tells us that in the underlying structural condition of the group there are some other very important factors which have a bearing on the Index of Expressive-Malintegrative Behavior. Perhaps if the influence of these factors can be taken into account also by a "composition of causes," to use Mill's term, we can arrive at a better empirical prediction.

II. Unless the members of a group are able to establish adequate, continuing evaluation and inference as to what they consider valuable, desirable, right, proper, moral, beneficial, and likely about the situation and about their activities as addressed both to the situation and to each other as persons and as solidary sub-groups, they are unable to cooperate and hence are subjected to insecurity (i.e., to the various threats of isolation, confusion, conflict, frustration, deprivation) and will react to remove this insecurity by adaptive-instrumental activity. Insofar as this is successful, the solution will tend to be institutionalized. Insofar as these attempts are incomplete, inadequate, or unsuccessful, the persisting insecurity will result in expressive-malintegrative behavior.

It is not necessary to illustrate again, as for the preceding hypothesis, the exceedingly broad character of this hypothesis, the difficulties with it from the point of view of prediction, etc. It will probably be clear without further comment that our second pair of categories, concerned with Problems of Evaluation (and Inference) can be made to yield an Index of Difficulty of Evaluation, which is constructed in exactly the same way and on exactly the same type of reasoning as before, thus:

$$\text{Index of Difficulty of Evaluation} = \frac{8}{8+5}$$

This index is assumed to be connected with the Index of Expressive-Malintegrative Behavior in a way similar to that of the preceding Index. That is:

$$\frac{8}{8+5} = f\left(\frac{(10+11+12)}{(10+11+12)+(1+2+3)}\right)$$

We are now ready for the next element in the "composition of causes" which we hope will enable us to predict the balance of negative social-emotional behavior in group interaction.

III. Unless the individuals in a group are able to apply their efforts and skills to a degree and in a way which is actually effective in producing changes in the situation, and to the degree that their efforts are not so efficient as they would like, or feel that they should be, they will be subjected to frustration or deprivation in varying degrees, and will react to remove this insecurity by adaptive-instrumental activity. Insofar as this is successful, the solution will tend to be institutionalized. Insofar as these attempts are incomplete, inadequate, or unsuccessful, the persisting insecurity will result in expressive-malintegrative behavior.

The reasoning here is exactly parallel to that which has gone before. Hence, we may write an Index of Difficulty of Control over Situation as follows:

$$\text{Index of Difficulty of Control over Situation} = \frac{9}{9+4}$$

This index is assumed to be connected with the Index of Expressive-Malintegrative Behavior in the same way:

$$\frac{9}{9+4} = f\left(\frac{(10+11+12)}{(10+11+12)+(1+2+3)}\right)$$

However, control over the situation also requires control over the action process directed toward the situation and hence, potentially, control of certain persons over others. At this point in the action process, where decision is about to be taken on the plan of action, the realistic constraints of the situation begin to be felt more stringently and to impose more constraint over action. Until reward is actually achieved, this constraint is felt as a partial frustration or increase in tension. This is probably true even though the constraint is "self-imposed" (i.e., demanded by the nature of the situation rather than by another person). When the control is suggested, imposed, or demanded by another person, problems of status, authority, and ego-defense also become involved (see next section) and tend to increase the tension and frustration threat. Hence we expect that as the action process becomes more directive or potentially constraining as to the free choice of alternatives, e.g., as the point of decision approaches, tension tends to increase and malintegrative social behavior is more likely to occur. (Note in comparing Chart 22 with Chart 25 that there seems to be a fairly close relation between rises in rates of Categories 9 plus 4, asking for and giving suggestions, and rises in rates of Categories 1 plus 12, showing solidarity and antagonism. The first peak in each comes in period 5; they both fall off and then rise rapidly toward the end of the session.) This trend of thinking about the tension-producing effects of control also fits in quite closely with what we know about the effects of "autocratic leadership" from the classical study of Lippitt and White and about the effects of non-directive versus more directive therapy and counseling from the work of Rogers and his school. Our hypothesis with regard to the control of persons over each other may be stated as follows:

IV. Unless individuals in a group are able to exercise control over their cooperative efforts in an integrated way on the one hand, and on the other, unless they are able to maintain a delicate limitation as to the degree and circumstances under which particular members or sub-groups exert their potential power over each other through suggestion, persuasion, relative prestige, fraud, coercion, or physical force, they will be unable to cooperate successfully or to satisfy their own needs individually, and hence are subjected to insecurity (to the various threats of conflict, frustration, deprivation), and will react to remove this insecurity by adaptive-instrumental activity. Insofar as this is successful, the solution will tend to be institutionalized. Insofar as these attempts are incomplete, inadequate, or unsuccessful, the persisting insecurity will result in expressive-malintegrative behavior.

We make the assumption that of the three types of activity included in Categories 6, 5, and 4, activity in Category 6 is the least directive or the most non-directive. Activity in Category 5 is more directive than that in Category 6, and is closer to the point of decision. Finally, activity in Category 4 is more directive than that in Category 5, and is still closer to the point of decision. (We include actual autocratic control of one person over another in Category 12 and hence omit it from our predictive index.) We thus propose an Index of Directiveness of Control for the total action stream, based on the preponderance of 4 and 5 in the total process as compared to 6. (This index may also be used to characterize the role of a single individual, when based on his interaction alone.) The index may be formed as follows, and may be divided by two if it is desired to make it vary from zero to 100 as the preceding indices do:

$$\text{Index of Directiveness of Control} = \frac{4}{4+6} + \frac{5}{5+6}$$

The relationship of this index to the Index of Expressive-Malintegrative Behavior is conceived to be the same as in the previous cases, hence we can write:

$$\frac{4}{4+6} + \frac{5}{5+6} = f\left(\frac{(10+11+12)}{(10+11+12)+(1+2+3)}\right)$$

We have now completed a series of derived indices from the central portion of our system of categories, 4, 5, 6, 7, 8, and 9, or as we have called it, the task area. These indices, we assume, may give us a series of running indications as to how far along in the problem-solving sequence the group is within any given period and as to the difficulty that is being experienced in solving the several problems of communication, evaluation, and control. The solutions to these problems are regarded as functional prerequisites to the solution of the problems of decision, tension reduction, and reintegration about which we are trying to predict. Or to put the matter in a slightly different way: we are trying, from measures as to the rates of certain activities in the task area, to form an inference as to the immediate structural condition of the system, from which structural condition we can infer in turn certain other things about the functioning of the system in the social-emotional area.

In order to get the best prediction, we should like to know how much weight should be assigned to each of the indices we have constructed. At this point, however, there is no basis for making any complicated estimate. Consequently for a first trial it is decided to weight all equally and to combine them simply by adding. With this decision we can state the prediction we want to test as follows:

For a series of sub-periods (of undetermined optimum length, say eight in number) within a complete meeting, the following relationship between raw scores in the designated categories will hold (the numbers refer to the categories):

$$\left(\frac{7}{7+6}\right)+\left(\frac{8}{8+5}\right)+\left(\frac{9}{9+4}\right)+\left(\frac{4}{4+6}\right)+\left(\frac{5}{5+6}\right) = f\left(\frac{(10+11+12)}{(10+11+12)+(1+2+3)}\right)$$

Chart 26 shows the result of the application of this prediction to the data of one meeting (the meeting of group D3, the profile of which is shown in Chapter 1). The eight sub-periods are shown along the horizontal. The fluctuation of the predictive index—the left side of the above formula—is shown as the solid line. The fluctuation of the predicted index—the right side of the above formula—is shown as the dotted line. In order to prepare this visual comparison each series was converted into t scores. The correlation of these two series for this meeting is + .81.

This is a very encouraging finding. Data for two other meetings, GM and ND4, are not so encouraging. The correlation of the two

Chart 26. Predicted and observed Index on Expressive-Malintegrative Behavior, by subperiods, Group D3.

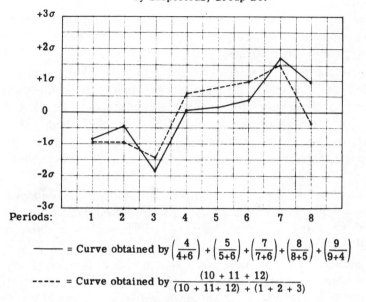

$$\text{———} = \text{Curve obtained by} \left(\frac{4}{4+6}\right) + \left(\frac{5}{5+6}\right) + \left(\frac{7}{7+6}\right) + \left(\frac{8}{8+5}\right) + \left(\frac{9}{9+4}\right)$$

$$\text{-----} = \text{Curve obtained by} \frac{(10 + 11 + 12)}{(10 + 11 + 12) + (1 + 2 + 3)}$$

series for GM is + .43, and for ND4 is + .29. It should be remembered that this is a first trial, with the very crudest kind of weighting. There is a chance that proper weighting and rational modification, as well as empirically suggested changes, may give better results. It is particularly relevant to our general methodological interest to emphasize that this hypothesis was actually derived deductively on *a priori* grounds practically in the form presented in exposition here before it was subjected to the test. Thus, whether or not this particular hypothesis holds up in empirical test, it may serve as an illustrative model of the type of theoretical approach leading to an "accordance between the results of *a priori* reasoning and the results of observation *a posteriori*" which we hope may be achieved with the present method.

Dynamic tendencies of role structure. The purpose of this section is to present an approach to the "social structure" of the group and its tendencies to change, insofar as that structure is expressed by or may be a result of the distribution of interaction between persons.

At the beginning of the previous section we suggested that one can-not consider this problem without considering also the temporal extension of the interaction process. A social relationship is a relationship existing in time, as well as in space, but neither time nor space as such is usually regarded as its essence. Nor is it so regarded here.

Nevertheless, there is a sense in which the distribution of (acts of) individuals within the *functional span* of the problem-solving *sequence* is of significance for their social relationships. In short, we may suppose, it is an expression of a difference or "it makes a difference" whether in an interaction system a given person is one who repeatedly asks Questions, or is one who repeatedly is asked. It makes a difference whether he comes into the sequences repeatedly as one who gives the Attempted Answers or as one to whom they are given, and whether he is typically asked before he gives or gives the Answers before he is asked. It makes a difference whether his Attempted Answers are typically met with Positive Reactions or with Negative Reactions. It makes a difference whether he is a person who typically reacts in a positive fashion or a negative fashion, and toward whom. These kinds of differences and their implications are the concern of this section.

As an approach to the problem of the present method as an indicator of social relationships, it may be interesting to look at a series of profiles of the individual members of a group. This will help to give a sense of the ways in which they differ and the possible implications of these differences for their social relationships. Chart 27 shows the total profile of a chess problem-solving group under the experimental conditions described in Chapter 1. The group is made up of five persons who are designated by the numbers they had in the actual session. These numbers were assigned according to the order in which they seated themselves, from left to right. The setting was highly similar to that shown in Illustration 1, page 2, except that there was one more male member at the right. As in the illustration, member 1 was a male, 2 a female, 3 a male, 4 a female, and 5 a male.

First, it is of interest to note that the total profile is a regular, conventionally patterned profile, highly similar to the other chess problem-solving profiles shown in Chapter 1, with certain differences which may be related to differences in group size. The pro-

Chart 27. Interaction profile, Total Group, standard chess situation, Case 4, five persons

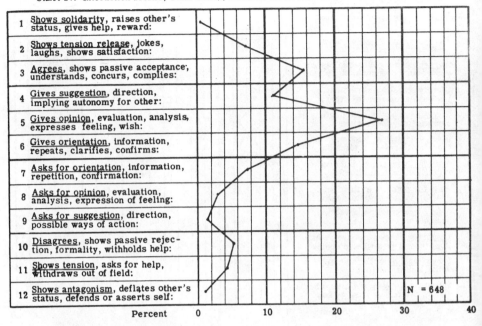

Chart 28. Interaction profile, Member 1, standard chess situation, Case 4, five persons.

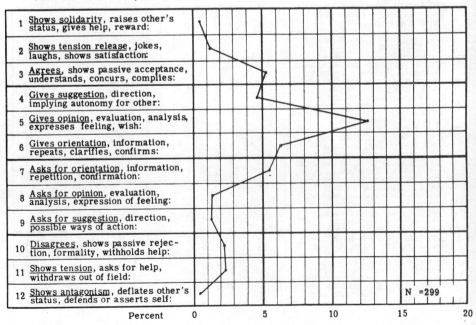

Chart 29. Interaction profile, Member 2, standard chess situation, Case 4, five persons.

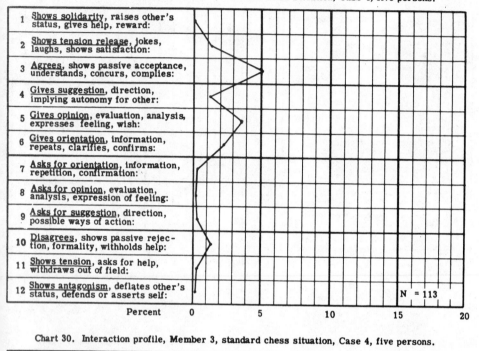

1 **Shows solidarity**, raises other's status, gives help, reward:

2 **Shows tension release**, jokes, laughs, shows satisfaction:

3 **Agrees**, shows passive acceptance, understands, concurs, complies:

4 **Gives suggestion**, direction, implying autonomy for other:

5 **Gives opinion**, evaluation, analysis, expresses feeling, wish:

6 **Gives orientation**, information, repeats, clarifies, confirms:

7 **Asks for orientation**, information, repetition, confirmation:

8 **Asks for opinion**, evaluation, analysis, expression of feeling:

9 **Asks for suggestion**, direction, possible ways of action:

10 **Disagrees**, shows passive rejection, formality, withholds help:

11 **Shows tension**, asks for help, withdraws out of field:

12 **Shows antagonism**, deflates other's status, defends or asserts self:

N = 113

Percent   0   5   10   15   20

Chart 30. Interaction profile, Member 3, standard chess situation, Case 4, five persons.

1 **Shows solidarity**, raises other's status, gives help, reward:

2 **Shows tension release**, jokes, laughs, shows satisfaction:

3 **Agrees**, shows passive acceptance, understands, concurs, complies:

4 **Gives suggestion**, direction, implying autonomy for other:

5 **Gives opinion**, evaluation, analysis, expresses feeling, wish:

6 **Gives orientation**, information, repeats, clarifies, confirms:

7 **Asks for orientation**, information, repetition, confirmation:

8 **Asks for opinion**, evaluation, analysis, expression of feeling:

9 **Asks for suggestion**, direction, possible ways of action:

10 **Disagrees**, shows passive rejection, formality, withholds help:

11 **Shows tension**, asks for help, withdraws out of field:

12 **Shows antagonism**, deflates other's status, defends or asserts self:

N = 149

Percent   0   5   10   15   20

Chart 31. Interaction profile, Member 4, standard chess situation, Case 4, five persons.

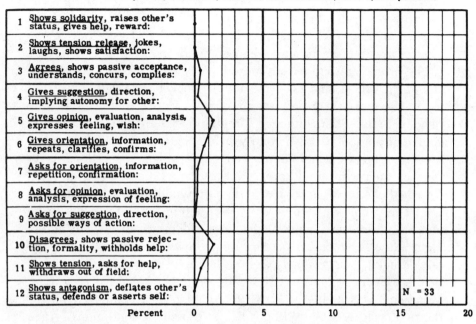

| | | Percent | 0 | 5 | 10 | 15 | 20 |

Chart 32. Interaction profile, Member 5, standard chess situation, Case 4, five persons.

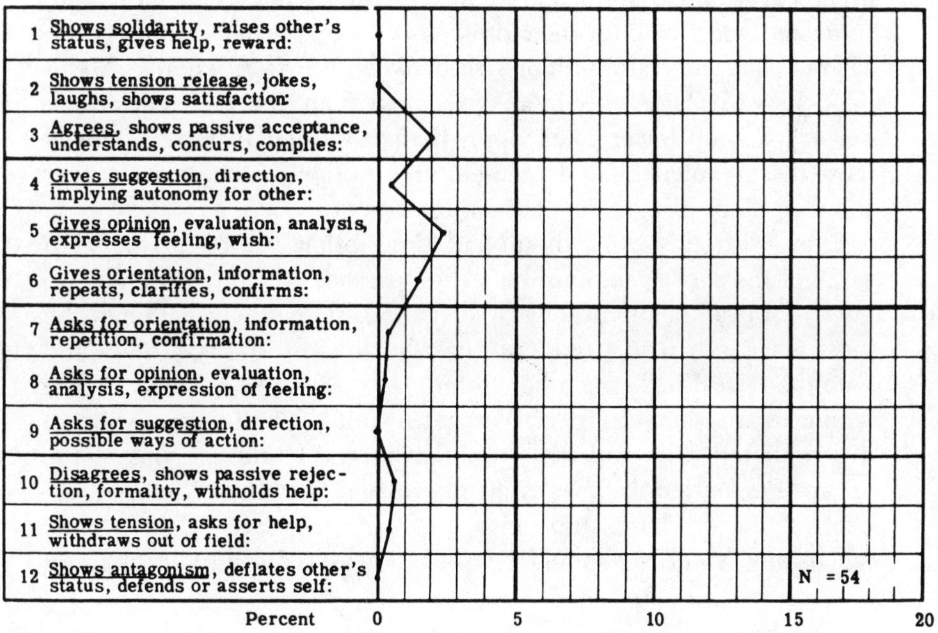

files of the individual members, however, constitute a highly differentiated series. (It should be noted that the scale for the individual
profiles in Charts 28 to 32 has been enlarged to twice that of the
total profile in order to make their comparison easier.)

The profile of Member 1 is more like the total profile than that of
any of the others, and his gross activity makes up about 46% of the
total. He was, according to all our subjective impressions, the
"leader" of the group, although Member 3 at the beginning strode in
confidently and sat down solidly in the middle chair. There were
several instances when Member 3 made major suggestions as to
the way the group should proceed; these suggestions, however, were
"brushed off" by Member 1 who then drowned them with a flood of
talk. The profile of Member 3 is very interesting. He seems to be
unusually high on giving suggestions and relatively low in agreement. No other member of the group shows a profile in which the
rate of making suggestions exceeds the rate of agreement. In spite of
this, however, he does not show high rates of Negative Reactions.
Member 2 was highly attentive to Member 1. Her highest rate is
the rate of agreement. Without her to provide a continuous "green
light," Member 1 might have been slowed down considerably.
Members 4 and 5 were almost lost in the shuffle. The most conspicuous aspect of both their profiles is the small number of scores.
There is one interesting difference between the two: whereas Member 5 shows considerably more agreement than disagreement, Member 4, who had fewer total scores than any other member, showed
more disagreement than agreement and, in fact, is the only member
showing more disagreement than agreement.

Even with this brief thumbnail description we begin to get a
sense of the social relationships of the persons. We might be able to
guess, for example, who suggested the most moves and who had the
most accepted, who would receive the highest status ratings and
who the lowest if the members rated each other, who would choose
whom on a sociometric test. We get a quite definite impression of
differentiated roles and structural "positions" of the persons in the
group. Furthermore, there is an impression that these different aspects of social relationships are connected with each other in some
molar way which we should be able to grasp conceptually without

too much difficulty. The series of hypotheses below is an attempt to state our conception of these interconnections in the most general way possible, for all sorts of small groups:

As particular functional problems (instrumental, adaptive, integrative, or expressive) become more acute, pressing, or continuous, more demanding in time and effort, strains are created toward the definition of specific social roles, differentiated in terms of particular persons, who are given the implicit or explicit responsibility of meeting and solving the specific functional problems as they arise in the group. Furthermore:

As the felt importance of the specific function performed by a particular person increases, strains are created toward an increase in his generalized social status. Conversely, as the felt importance of the particular function decreases, strains are created toward a decrease in his generalized social status.

As the functional social roles in a group become more specific, differentiated, and formal, more demanding in time and effort of the particular individuals performing the roles, strains are created toward a more individualistic and inequalitarian distribution of access to resources and rewards, both in terms of access to the instrumentalities involved in the performance of the function and in terms of some reward or compensation for the loss of time and effort and the value rendered to the group. Furthermore:

As the felt advantage of a particular person in the distribution of access to resources increases, strains are created toward an increase in his generalized social status. Conversely, as the advantage of the particular person decreases, strains are created toward a decrease in his generalized social status.

As the functional social roles in a group become more specific, differentiated, and formal, strains are created toward a more differentiated and centralized exercise of directive control in order to coordinate and regulate these special functions. Furthermore:

As the directive control of a given person increases, strains are created toward an increase in his generalized social status. Conversely, as his directive control decreases, strains are created toward a decrease in his generalized social status.

Moreover, to point up the significance of the foregoing tendencies, as status differences between persons increase, strains are created toward a less solid (more neutral, indifferent, or antagonistic) relation between them. Thus, to conclude, as the functional roles performed by persons in a group become more specific, differentiated, and formal, strains are created toward a less solidary relation between them.

This is a conception of a series of changes in social relationships "set off" by changes in the functional problems which the group faces in its problem-solving process. It is a somewhat more abstract statement of the kinds of relationships we tend to find in larger social systems between the occupational system and the institutions of property, authority, social stratification, and solidarity, each of which finds its more abstract statement in the series of hypotheses above.

The phenomena in one way or another associated with this series of changes in the larger social system are extremely varied and interesting. This is not the place to attempt to present a convincing analysis, but they would include, as we view it, the institutionalization of a certain "indifference," "impersonality," "impartiality," or "emotional neutrality" as an explicit obligation in the performance of certain roles, such as those of the judge, the doctor, the administrator, the foreman, etc.; compulsive tendencies toward absenteeism, migration, isolation, refusal to communicate; the formation of sects, schisms, minority sub-groups, etc. In another direction they may include the practice of black magic, witchcraft, and sorcery; compulsive striving for and retention of symbols of achievement, wealth, power, authority, and prestige; compulsive striving for symbols of love, acceptance, solidarity; ritual and symbolic attempts to increase the solidarity of the whole group; fantasy about and romanticization of desired symbols of security, such as symbols of achievement, wealth, power, authority, prestige, love, acceptance, solidarity; etc. In still another direction, the phenomena may include active attacks on or modifications of the existing division of labor, and the existing system of property and authority; compulsive competitiveness and rebelliousness; passive resistance and non-cooperation; the designation of specific targets for aggression, such as scapegoats within or outside the group; the permission of aggressive displays in certain contexts, such as in drinking, warfare, or punishment of transgressors; the prohibition and inhibition of aggressive tendencies such as complaining, agitating, "conniving," and meeting in secret; the establishment of certain modes of self-aggression, such as mutilation, flagellation, asceticism; etc.

Before discussing whether these general ideas may be translated into hypotheses which might be tested in terms of the data produced by the present method, it seems desirable to present the other side of the coin. The series of hypotheses above have to do with certain changes which are "set off," as it were, by changes in the division of labor which, in turn, is closely related to the task demands facing the group. There is a complementary or contrary series of changes, we hypothesize, which are "set off" by changes in the state of solidarity of the group. The general terminal effect of the first chain of events is to produce strains toward a lesser solidarity. One of the possible reactions to this strain is a reactive, compulsive attempt to secure and retain symbols of love, acceptance, solidarity, and the initiation of rituals and fantasies on this theme, as mentioned above. However, this reaction may go so far as to create difficulties in its own right. From the point of view of the overall functioning of social systems in terms of the various kinds of flexibilities they need to have, *either* marked uncontrolled antagonism or marked uncontrolled solidarity has its "dangers." In general, both tend to be regulated and controlled as to when, toward whom, and to what degree they may be expressed in action or institutionalized in a social relationship. A very strong relationship of solidarity (as well as a marked antagonism) between persons or within sub-groups or even of the group as a whole, may interfere with the adaptation and integration of the whole group by the following "chain of events":

As solidarity between persons of different status increases, strains are created toward a merging, or equalization of their status, both as they view the relation and as others view the relation. In general, members of solidary groups tend to be classed together in the scale of stratification, and individual mobility in the scale of stratification involves some loosening or breaking of former ties of solidarity. Solidarity and status differences are in certain respects incompatible. However:

The adaptation of the social system to its outer situation requires a certain degree of neutrality, mobility, and recognition of status differences in certain social relationships since:

As solidarity between persons performing specific, differentiated and formal roles increases, strains are created toward a more diffuse, less differentiated, and less formalized performance of functional social roles, which in turn may be accompanied by a loss of efficiency and responsibility, a loss of the inducement of increased status, a perversion of function from group ends to the individual ends of the persons immediately involved, and so may threaten the adaptation and integration of the group as a whole. (Nepotism, favoritism, particularism, etc.)

Similarly:

As solidarity between persons having different advantages in the distribution of property rights increases, strains are created toward a more "communal," "equalitarian" distribution of property rights, which may tend to interfere with the adaptation and integration of the whole group by the dissociation of reward from functionally specific tasks, and consequent reduction of motivation to the efficient performance of explicit functions on behalf of the group.

Similarly:

As solidarity increases between those in authority and those subjected to control, strains are created toward a more diffuse, less differentiated, and less formal exercise of authority, which in turn may interfere with the adaptation and integration of the whole group by making it difficult or impossible for the persons in authority to require or demand that which is necessary but unpleasant, difficult, or dangerous.

Thus, to sum up, as sub-group or interpersonal solidarity increases in the contexts mentioned above (i.e., in functionally specific, differentiated, and formal contexts), strains are created toward insecurity through the threat of a less effective adaptation of the system as a whole to the outer situation, and various reactive attempts to remove or express this insecurity may be expected. In larger social systems there are various interesting phenomena which are apparently associated with this series of strains. Again, simply to give some examples, we would include: limitation of contact, by avoidance or physical segregation; institutionalization of "impersonality" or "impartiality," as mentioned above; prohibition (in functionally specific contexts where they might be disruptive) of certain activities which symbolize or tend to create solidarity, such as sexual approach (note incest taboos), performance of personal favors, eating together (note food taboos), drinking together, marrying, loaning of money or other articles, similarity in dress, speech, etc. In another direction, the damaging effects of over-strong sub-solidarities may be counteracted to some extent by communal rituals directed toward the maintenance and creation of sentiments which will (1) secure the allegiance and obligation of individuals and sub-groups to the group as a whole, (2) make for a conscientious performance of specialized function, and (3) justify the existing differentiation of property, authority, and status, in terms of a more general over-arching system of major values and hierarchical sub-values. In still another direction, the damaging effects of malintegrative sub-solidarities may be combatted by creating an emphasis on some threat to the group as a whole and by making an aggressive attack on personal or impersonal aspects of the outer situation in such a way as to increase the over-all solidarity at the expense of sub-group solidarities.

Now, to sum up the argument to this point, we have an idea of two "chains of events" or "series of strains" starting from opposite poles and proceeding in opposite directions, tending to cancel each other out, and each in its terminal effects tending to set off the opposite chain of events. One chain of events has its starting point in the necessities of adaptation to the outer situation and proceeds in its series of strains through changes in the division of labor, changes in the distribution of property, authority, and status and has its malintegrative terminal effects in the disturbance of the existing state of solidarity. The other chain of events has its starting point in the necessities of integration or reintegration of the social system itself and proceeds in its series of strains through a reactive (or perhaps aboriginal) emphasis on solidarity which exerts a dissolving, undermining, equalizing or curbing effect on the differential distribution of status, on differences in authority, differences in distribution of property, and differences in functional roles in the division of labor, with an ultimate terminal effect that may be maladaptive. The social system in its organization, we postulate, tends to swing or falter indeterminately back and forth between these two theoretical poles: optimum adaptation to the outer situation at the cost of internal malintegration, or optimum internal integration at the cost of maladaptation to the outer situation.

If this is an even partly adequate conception of the dynamic forces at work in social systems, the actual attempt to predict the structural condition of the system by a "composition of causes" appears to be a very difficult job indeed. It may be possible, however, that a rough kind of hypothesis can be formed as to the final common result of these various forces, as they would be in a kind of "middling" position. Let us attempt such a hypothesis:

As a result of these various strains and reactive patterns, the system as a whole probably tends toward a sort of balance or equilibrium in which indifference, neutrality, or impartiality, ranging on into antagonism is stronger:

   a. Between persons and sub-groups performing more different and functionally specific social roles than between persons and sub-groups performing more similar or functionally diffuse social roles.
   b. Between persons having more unequal advantages in access to resources than between persons having more equal advantages.
   c. Between persons having more unequal advantages in the hierarchy of control than between persons having more equal advantages.
   d. Between persons having more unequal status in the hierarchy of generalized social status than between persons having more equal status or belonging to the same stratum.

We are not, at the present time, in a position to attempt a systematic translation of these general *a priori* hypotheses into a series of hypotheses or a combined master hypothesis in terms of the observations produced by the method. We have, however, been working with the development of a series of summary indices of the way in which the various types of activity are distributed between persons and this may provide what we need for such a translation.

In this series of indices we encounter again the same duality of the functional emphasis and the structural emphasis that has been commented upon repeatedly. In theoretical terms, these two emphases appear in the concepts of functional aspects of role and structural aspects of role. In terms of the tabulation and manipulation of data, these two aspects appear in terms of "profiles" and "matrices."

The profiles of the five members of the chess problem-solving group which we shall take as our illustrative example have already been shown. In a sense, perhaps, any one of these profiles might be said to represent the functional role of the particular individual in the group, i.e., what he did in terms of its relevance to the problem-solving sequence. They represent, however, only the activity which he *initiated* and we should also like to know the nature of the activity which was directed to him by others. Surely this too can be considered a part of his role. Part of what he "did" is to provide a target for certain kinds of activity. Furthermore, the activities which other people addressed to him must indicate something about their "expectations" with regard to him, and this too, we find, is an aspect of our general *a priori* ideas as to what we ought to mean by "role." We cannot attempt at this writing to work out in detail the relations of this particular empirical model to our general terminology concerning role. We shall simply indicate the hope that one of the contributions of the present method will be the untangling of some of our terminological problems by providing a concrete model we can talk about.

If we simply decide at this point to use the phrase "role of the individual in the group" to designate *both* the qualitative distribution of his total *outgoing* behavior as compared to that of others *and* the qualitative distribution of the total behavior *addressed specifically to* him, we can construct a number of indices which will describe different aspects of his role. Table 6 shows a type of matrix designed to hold the data for one group during its total meeting period in this form. The twelve interaction categories are shown on the vertical dimension and the five different group members are shown on the horizontal dimension. For each individual on the horizontal dimension we include two columns, one for the activity which he initiates and one for the activity which he receives. The matrix is then filled in, from the original tabulation of observations, to show the total raw scores in each box.

The original tabulations consist of a series of pairs of tables like those for Member 1 shown in Table 7 and Table 8. For the five-man chess group plus 0 and x ("all" and "outside sources"), seven such pairs of tabulations would be required. In obtaining the data to go into Table 6 for Member 1, we simply transfer the totals from Tables 7 and 8, and this we do also for the other members up through Member 5.

Table 6. Number of interactions initiated and received by persons, by categories, five-man chess problem-solving group, Case 4.*

| Section | Cate-gory | Person | | | | | | | | | | Total Σ Σ | |
| | | 1 | | 2 | | 3 | | 4 | | 5 | | | |
		I	R	I	R	I	R	I	R	I	R	I	R
A	1	3	-	-	-	1	-	-	-	-	2	4	2
	2	9	13	10	2	7	4	-	-	-	-	26	19
	3	35	44	35	14	19	28	2	4	14	7	105	97
B	4	33	17	8	6	30	13	1	-	4	3	76	39
	5	86	37	25	11	45	41	10	1	17	8	183	98
	6	43	29	16	3	17	15	5	3	10	5	91	55
C	7	38	7	3	5	9	15	1	5	2	5	53	37
	8	9	7	1	2	9	5	1	-	1	-	21	14
	9	8	2	2	-	2	3	-	-	-	-	12	5
D	10	15	8	9	2	3	15	9	5	4	6	40	36
	11	16	1	3	-	4	-	4	-	2	-	29	1
	12	4	1	1	1	3	2	-	-	-	1	8	5
Total		299	166	113	46	149	141	33	18	54	37	648	408

*O, x, and y not counted as persons.

Now one thing we may wish to know for a given individual is whether, taking into account the number of people in the group, he initiated or received more than would have been expected. For purposes of this discussion, let us agree to regard a deviation of one sigma as significant. We can then apply the qualitative designations "over," "even," and "under" to describe the deviation of a given individual from our expectancy. For the expectancy, let us

Table 7. Acts, by category, from Person #1 to others. Five-man chess problem-solving group, Case 4.

Category	Target of act							Total
	Self	2	3	4	5	0	x	
1					2	1		3
2			1			8		9
3		9	15		4	7		35
4		2	9		2	20		33
5		5	24		5	52		86
6		2	9	1	4	24	3	43
7		4	12	4	4	13	1	38
8		1	4			4		9
9			2			6		8
10		1	8	2	2	2		15
11						16		16
12			2		1	1		4
Total		24	86	7	24	154	4	299

Table 8. Acts, by category, to Person #1 from others. Five-man chess problem-solving group, Case 4.

Category	Initiator of act							Total
	Self	2	3	4	5	0	x	
1								
2		2				11		13
3		24	14		6			44
4		2	13	1	1			17
5		10	17	4	6			37
6		7	12	4	4	1	1	29
7		1	5		1			7
8			6	1				7
9		1	1					2
10		1	3	2	2			8
11			1					1
12		1						1
Total		49	72	12	20	12	1	166

apply a chance error paradigm and assume that each person's share will be $\frac{1}{n}$, where n is the number of members in the group. In other words, we make the binomial assumption that each person is equally likely to speak or equally likely to receive acts (whether of the total or of a given category). Then the designation "even" simply means that the number of acts actually allocated to a given person falls within the 68% probability interval about the theoretical mean; "over" and "under" means that the number of acts actually allocated to the person fall above or below the 68% probability interval. (We recognize that a multinominal assumption is probably more appropriate for the case at hand, but is somewhat less convenient.) The intervals can be computed by the use of the binomial probability paper described on page 111, footnote.

The illustrative case under consideration involves the interaction of five persons. Hence the mean expected would be 1/5 or .2. Thus, we are interested to see which individuals either received or initiated significantly more or less than the theoretical .2. The margins about this value differ with the number of observations involved but, as we have explained in Chapter 4, this is taken into consideration by the binomial probability paper. Thus, in Table 6, for the 105 acts originated by the whole group in Category 3, any particular individual would have been expected to initiate .2 × 105, or 21 acts. By plotting the point 21 on the ordinate and the remainder (105 minus 21, or 84) on the abscissa of the binomial paper and drawing a circle of approximately .5 cm. in diameter about this point, we determine the locus of all values within the 68 percent probability range. Thus we find that the values of Table 6, i.e., 35, 35, 19, 14, and 2, are distributed as follows with respect to our criterion:

> 35 "Over"
> 35 "Over"
> ———————
> 19 "Even"
> ———————
> 14 "Under"
> 2 "Under"

In Table 9 all of the numbers in Table 6 have been converted into such designations, with O, E, and U standing respectively for Over,

Table 9. "Over," "even," and "under" designations applied to interactions initiated and received by each member by Categories,
chess problem-solving group, Case 4.

Category	1 I	1 R	2 I	2 R	3 I	3 R	4 I	4 R	5 I	5 R
1	O	U	U	U	E	U	U	U	U	O
2	O	O	O	U	E	E	U	U	U	U
3	O	O	O	U	E	O	U	U	U	U
4	O	O	U	E	O	O	U	U	U	U
5	O	O	U	U	O	O	U	U	U	U
6	O	O	E	U	E	O	U	U	U	U
7	O	E	U	U	E	O	U	U	U	U
8	O	O	U	E	O	O	U	U	U	U
9	O	E	E	U	E	O	U	U	U	U
10	O	E	E	U	U	O	E	E	U	E
11	O	O	U	U	E	U	E	U	U	U
12	O	E	E	E	O	E	U	U	U	E
Total	E=0	E=4	E=4	E=3	E=7	E=2	E=2	E=1	E=0	E=2

Table 10. Selected acts, initiated and received, by person and section. Five-
man chess problem-solving group, Case 4.

Section	Person #1 I	#1 R	#2 I	#2 R	#3 I	#3 R	#4 I	#4 R	#5 I	#5 R	Total Initiated	Total Received
A	47	57	45	16	27	32	2	4	14	9	135	118
B	162	83	49	20	92	69	16	4	31	16	350	192
C	55	16	6	7	20	23	2	5	3	5	86	56
D	35	10	13	3	10	17	13	5	6	7	77	42
Total	299	166	113	46	149	141	33	18	54	37	648	408

Even, and Under. From Table 9 it is simpler to make a qualitative description of the roles of individuals than in terms of either numbers or profiles. We can say, for example, that Member 1 was Over on every category of acts initiated and was Under in only one category of acts received. This mode of description is probably preferable to either numbers or graphic profiles for feedback to participants.

A table of this sort can provide us with a measure of differentiation on any given category or a summary measure of total differentiation within the group, which may be useful for some theoretical purposes. If there were no differentiation of roles within the group, that is, if each category of activity were originated equally by each member of the group and were directed equally to each other, all of the designations in the table would be "E." Insofar as either "O" or "U" appears, it may be taken as an indication of a degree of differentiation between persons. Thus for the group as a whole, during the period as a whole, an index may be formed as follows:

$$\text{Index of Total Differentiation} = 1 - \frac{\Sigma E}{2n \times 12} = 1 - \frac{25}{120} = .79$$

In this formula, ΣE represents the total number of boxes in Table 9 in which individuals are Even, and n represents the number of members in the group.

We now become interested in a series of indices which attempt to express certain critical aspects of the "position" of the individual in problem-solving sequences. Theoretically, the indices we are aiming at are indices of Access to Resources, Degree of Control, and Generalized Status. Empirically, we hope that indices which describe certain relationships between the interaction addressed to a person and the interaction which he addresses to others may provide suitable translations. In order to explain how these indices are derived, it is advantageous to summarize the data in Table 6 now in terms of the four sections of the system of categories:

> A   Positive Reactions
> B   Attempted Answers
> C   Questions
> D   Negative Reactions

The result appears as Table 10.

In the formulas which follow, describing the way in which the indices are derived, these conventions will be employed:

a_i represents the total number of acts in Section A *initiated* by the *i*th individual.

$\bar{a}_i$ represents the total number of acts in Section A *received* by the *i*th individual.

A represents the sum of the acts of type A *initiated* by all of the *n* individuals.

$\bar{A}$ represents the sum of the acts of type A *received* by all of the *n* individuals.

Thus:
$$A = \sum_{i=1}^{n} a_i \quad \text{and} \quad \bar{A} = \sum_{i=1}^{n} \bar{a}_i$$

To illustrate, referring to Table 10: $a_1 = 47$, $\bar{a}_1 = 57$, $A = 135$, and $\bar{A} = 118$. Parallel conventions are adopted for data from Section B, C, and D.

One of the things we should like to summarize is the degree to which a given individual is asked for information, or for his opinion, or for his suggestion as to what should be done. We should like to compare him with all the other individuals in the group with regard to this characteristic of his role. Now, a particular person in a group may be asked questions for many different reasons—perhaps because he will not otherwise participate, or because he expresses himself so poorly that the rest of the group is forced to keep asking questions to determine what he means—but in many instances it would seem to be an indication that the given individual is regarded by others as having command of the resources needed in discussion. That is, it may be an indication that they think he has the information or the orientation they need; they may think he has some special ability at analysis, or some right to make evaluations or to suggest and decide about what course of action the group shall take. In these latter cases, we may say that he is regarded as having direct access to resources to which others have access only through him. It is desirable to distinguish clearly between the more general theoretical interpretation that may be put on a derived index and the more specific operational designation of how the index was derived. Hence, although for some purposes we may wish to regard the following index as an Index of Direct Access to Resources, we shall designate it simply as the "CR" Index, meaning the index of actions received in section C. For this summarizing measure we propose the following:

$$CR \text{ Index} = \frac{\bar{c}_i}{C} \times 100$$

This index thus yields a number somewhere between 0 and 100 which will answer the question: Of all acts in Section C received by all individuals, what proportion did Individual "i" receive? It should be clear that this measure will not be comparable for groups of different sizes.

Individual "i" is also a person who asks questions of others, either because he doesn't know, or because he thinks it will be better for the other person to give the answers, or for any number of reasons we may or may not be able to infer from looking at his profile. Whatever his reason, it is interesting to know whether, in terms of the amount of asking he did, he received a proportionate number of answers, whether he was "more than answered," or whether others "held out" on him. In general, the degree to which implied or actual requests of the given individual for needed information, inference, or suggestions are answered might legitimately be called an Index of Indirect Access to Resources ("indirect," because although he gets what he needs, he gets it through other persons who have direct access to it). In accordance with the suggestion above, a neutral designation is applied: the "BR" Index, meaning the index of actions received in Section B, with the understanding that this is in terms of the number of requests made in C.

$$BR \text{ Index} = \left(\frac{\bar{b}_i}{\bar{b}_i + c_i} \right) \times \left(\frac{\bar{b}_i}{B} \right) \times 100$$

This index yields a number somewhere between 0 and 100 which will answer the question which might be phrased: To what extent were the questions of Individual "i" answered, as compared to others in the group?

So-called Attempted Answers in Section B are attempted answers to the instrumental-adaptive problems facing the group. So far as the social relationships of the members are concerned, however, the activities in this section may be regarded as Attempted Control. This is quite clear in the case of Category 4 in many cases but, in the broader sense, all the categories in Section B may be said to constitute cases in which the individual is "taking the part of the demands of the situation" and relaying them on to the other members. If nothing more, he is mediating a control or constraint which has its source in the structure of the situation. Especially if the gross amount of activity in this Section becomes large for Individual "i," we will feel there is some justification in regarding this increase as involving attempts to control. So regarded, it is of great interest to ask to what degree the attempts are answered by positive reactions on the part of others, rather than by negative reactions. Theoretically, we are interested in deriving an Index of Degree of Control. As a neutral designation we propose the ADR Index, meaning the index of actions received in Section A compared to the actions received in Section D, with the understanding that this is in terms of Attempts made in Section B.

$$ADR \text{ Index} = \left(\frac{b_i}{B}\right) \times \left(\frac{\bar{a}_i}{\bar{a}_i + \bar{d}_i}\right) \times 100$$

This index yields a number somewhere between 0 and 100 which will answer the question: To what extent were the attempts of Individual "i" answered positively instead of negatively, as compared to others in the group?

Now for a measure of status. Our general assumption is that status does have some kind of phenomenal reality for the participants in the group, at least in the larger social system, which is not identical with the symbols usually taken to stand for it—property, occupation, authority, identification with a particular solidary sub-group, and other lesser indicators. We believe, however, that the generalized global meaning is closely related to the more particular aspects or symbols of it. For present purposes we propose to treat status as a kind of common denominator into which both differences in degree of access to resources and differences in degree of control tend to be generalized. Status, we think, is "something more," but that something more we do not for the moment think we can capture any more closely with the present method than with the indices already mentioned. Hence we do not propose a direct index of status, but an indirect index based upon the three preceding components. Some more complicated weighting might be superior, but as a first approximation we propose to weight the three components equally and write the index as follows:

$$\text{Generalized Status Index} = \frac{CR \text{ Index} + BR \text{ Index} + ADR \text{ Index}}{3}$$

This index yields a number somewhere between 0 and 100 which is based upon our former estimates of the access of the individual to resources, both direct and indirect, and upon the control which he exercises. It may be thought of as a kind of answer to the question: Just in general, how does the status or prestige of Individual "i" compare with that of other members of the group? It should be remembered that so long as we retain this method of deriving status, we cannot in terms of the present method alone make any statements about the relation of status to these other variables which are not simply a matter of definition. We use status as a concept to link certain observations to other observations; we do not have an independent measure of it.

Finally, to come to the problem of solidarity, it is possible to form indices comparable to those above. These might be called AI or DI Indices, meaning the amount of activity in Section A initiated by a given individual, or the amount in Section D initiated by a given individual; but at this point it becomes of greater interest to ask specifically "toward whom, in particular" rather than just "how much in general." Another way of viewing this point is to say that whereas the preceding indices, theoretically referring to Access to Resources, Degree of Control, and Generalized Status, are best stated with a functional focus and indeed are expressions of the way the given individual "fits into the problem-solving process regarded as a *sequence*," the present index, theoretically referring to solidarity, is best stated with a structural focus, as an expression of the way the given individual "fits into the problem-solving process regarded as a *unified group of persons*."

Consequently we propose a different sort of matrix representation for the relationships of the persons in terms of solidarity. This matrix

Chart 33. Indices of Interindividual Solidarity, chess problem-solving group, Case 4.

Persons as initiators	Persons as targets					Total
	1	2	3	4	5	
1		90	62	0	66	57
2	93		66	33	100	78
3	78	84		0	100	73
4	0	0	50		20	13
5	75	100	66	66		70

In a matrix of this sort can be placed various types of raw scores or derived indices. In the present case we show a matrix of indices, each of which consists of:

$$\text{Index of Interindividual Solidarity} = \frac{a_{ij}}{a_{ij} + d_{ij}} \times 100.$$

This represents the acts of types A and D originated by the i th individual and directed toward the j th individual.

is constructed simply, as in Chart 33. Along the vertical is shown each of the persons in the group as the initiator of acts; along the horizontal the same persons are shown as the targets. Thus the relationship of each person with each other person in each direction is represented by an appropriate box.

One of the obvious difficulties with this kind of index is the instability arising from small numbers of scores in some of the cells. This difficulty is relieved for longer periods to some extent, but not entirely. It may be that the person-to-person distribution of all scores without distinction as to category will prove to be of more general use than any of the specific indices described. From such a matrix, as shown in Chart 34, it is possible to form an immediate idea of the total number of scores initiated by each person, and the total number received by him; the proposed Index of Generalized Status in many cases is probably not far removed from some simple combination or

Chart 34. Distribution of total interaction by persons as initiators and as targets, chess problem-solving group, Case 4.

Persons as initiators	Persons as targets							
	1	2	3	4	5	0	x	Tot.
1		24	86	7	24	154	4	299
2	49		38	4	2	20		113
3	72	17		1	5	54		149
4	12	1	4		6	10		33
5	20	3	10	5		15	1	54
0	12	1	3	1		13		30
x	1					5		6
Tot.	166	46	141	18	37	271	5	684

mean of these two. In addition, one sees which channels of communication were most used, and there is probably some fairly close empirical connection between channel frequency and solidarity. It should be noted that the numbers in such a matrix easily can be converted into "Over-Even-Under" designations, as described previously, for qualitative analysis.

In Chart 35 we show the various indices described above computed for the five members of the chess problem-solving group. The reader will recall the thumbnail sketch presented above, and can compare it with the indices on this chart. Here it is of interest to note that although Member 1 shows the highest index of Control, Member 3 shows the highest index of Direct Access to Resources. Roughly translated, this means that while Member 1 "carried the ball," he directed a good many questions to Member 3, and Member 3 held a certain amount of power by "veto," as it were. As to generalized status, they came out very close together, although this status was based upon different components in each case. Members 4 and 5 came out low on all the indices, with 4 holding the lowest status in the group.

Chart 35. Indices of major aspects of role, by member, by type, chess problem-solving group, Case 4.

Index	Member				
	1	2	3	4	5
CR Index (direct access to resources)	29	13	41	9	9
BR Index (indirect access to resources)	26	8	28	1	7
ADR Index (degree of control)	39	12	17	2	5
Generalized Status Index	31	11	29	4	7

According to Chart 33, freely interpreted, we note that Member 1 and Member 2 show a warm friendly relationship—more so, apparently, than Member 1 and Member 3. Member 4 neither gives nor receives much positive activity and appears to be a peripheral member of the group in terms both of status and of solidarity. By contrast, Member 5, who also had a low generalized status, both gives and receives a high proportion of positive activity.

It may be interesting to compare the results of the computation of these various indices from the interaction with certain other information obtained by different methods. In general, the correspondence is very close to expectation based on the interaction indices. Member 1 suggested the greatest number of moves (21, as compared with the others in order, 7, 13, 5, and 3). Member 1 also had the largest number of his suggested moves accepted by group decision (6, as compared with the others in order, 1, 0, 0, and 1). After the meeting the members were asked to rate each other on the "*value* of each member to the group . . . by value to the group we mean: How much did the group gain by his presence, either in solving the problem or keeping the group coordinated and working harmoniously?" A five-point scale was provided. Member 1 received the highest average rating (4.25, as compared with the others in order, 2.5, 3.75, 2.75, and 3.0). The members were also asked to give a sociometric choice in terms of answers to the question: "Are there any of the members

of this group with whom you would like to establish a closer friendship if you should meet them again?" Member 1 received the highest
number of positive choices (4, as compared with the others in order,
1, 2, 0, and 1). To cap the climax with a wry result: Member 1 did
not have the highest chess aptitude, as measured by our pre-test.
His score was a minus 5, as compared with the others in order, plus
25, minus 7, plus 32, and plus 36.

Very little work has been done with the indices as yet. They were
developed subsequent to the last modification of the categories, of
course, and have only an *a priori* validity to recommend them. However, as the illustration above shows, it should be possible to obtain
independent validation of them. It is not yet clear to what extent
these indices or others similar to them can be linked with the verbal
hypotheses (stated earlier in this chapter) out of which in part they
grew. It is hoped that an inclusive systematic approach, similar to
that foreshadowed at the end of the last section, can be developed.

Dynamic tendencies of ideological structure. The description of
the major kinds of analysis that can be done with the present method
of interaction process analysis, as we now see it, has been completed.
There is, however, a level of content "just above" the present method
with which it links closely: the ideology the members have about the
structure and dynamics of small groups. Various ideologies about
these matters are generally present in our culture, of course, and are
brought into any particular small group as a part of its culture base.
However, the ideology which becomes institutionalized in a particular group of members at a particular time is in part a result of
their interaction with each other. The analysis of ideology is closely
linked with the present approach because the topical content of
ideology is a body of ideas and sentiments the members of the group
have about the same aspects of structure and dynamics we are attempting to describe. Furthermore, as a part of our general theory
about the changes in group organization and strains toward changes,
we postulate that there is a series of concomitant changes in ideological emphasis among the members of the group. Without any
attempt to round out the ideas, and simply as a kind of memorandum
for the future, we present the following hypotheses:

In general, depending upon more or less independently variable strains introduced by changes in the outer situation, the culture of the group, and the personalities involved, small groups as social systems probably tend to show a sort of nonperiodic but cyclical fluctuation about a moving "equilibrium" or balance of structural features, such that:

1. There is a fluctuation about an unstable balance between tendencies toward functional diffuseness and tendencies toward functional specificity of social roles.

   a. The tendency toward functional diffuseness will manifest itself in sentiments which might be paraphrased: "We are all alike. When there is something to be done, we all pitch in and do it. Everybody does his share. Each one does what is needed when he sees it needs doing. We all work together. We all help each other."

   b. The tendency toward functional specificity will manifest itself in sentiments which might be paraphrased: "Everybody should have a specific job to do which is best fitted to his abilities, and then he should be held responsible for it. It's more efficient that way. When everybody is responsible, nobody is responsible. The job is too big and complicated to leave things to chance."

2. There is a fluctuation about an unstable balance between tendencies toward a communal and equitable distribution of property rights and tendencies toward an individualistic and inequitable distribution of property rights.

   a. The tendency toward a communal and equitable distribution of property rights will manifest itself in sentiments which might be paraphrased: "We share and share alike. Each one gets what he needs. The things we have belong to all of us. Each of us has the right to ask for what he needs. 'From each according to his ability; to each according to his needs.' All for one and one for all."

   b. The tendency toward an individualistic and inequitable distribution of property rights will manifest itself in sentiments which might be paraphrased: "Each one should be given what he needs to do his job. He should receive a share proportionate to what he has done. He should be rewarded according to the importance of his work; otherwise, why should he try to do better? It is only right that those who have contributed more should receive more."

3. There is a fluctuation about an unstable balance between tendencies toward an informal authority of diffuse scope and limited control and the tendency toward a formal authority of more specific scope and greater control.

   a. The tendency toward an informal authority of diffuse scope and limited control will manifest itself in sentiments which might be paraphrased: "We have no real leaders. Everybody has an equal say. We are democratic. We talk things over and decide what should be done unanimously."

   b. The tendency toward a formal authority of specific scope and greater control will manifest itself in sentiments which might be paraphrased: "You've got to have somebody in charge to get things done. It's better to choose somebody to take charge and run things and then hold him responsible, even if he does some things we don't like."

4. There is a fluctuation about an unstable balance between the tendency to make generalized social status contingent only upon solidarity and loyalty to group norms and the tendency to make generalized social status contingent upon composite criteria which include the excellence of performance of specific function, the relative advantage in the distribution of property rights, and the relative degree of authority in such a way that the various criteria of status roughly coincide with each other as applied to given individuals or solidary sub-groups.

   a. The tendency to make generalized social status contingent only upon solidarity and loyalty to group norms will manifest itself in sentiments which might be paraphrased: "We are all members of the same group. Nobody is any better than anybody else. There are no distinctions of rank. Everybody here is equal. Everybody has an equal chance and an equal say. We are all on the same level."

   b. The tendency to make generalized social status contingent upon the composite criteria mentioned is manifested in sentiments which might be paraphrased: "It is only right that those who do the more important jobs should receive more recognition. One must respect merit and achievement. Some people are just naturally more efficient than others and efficiency ought to be rewarded."

5. There is a fluctuation about an unstable balance between the tendency for solidarity to grow up spontaneously within sub-groups on the basis of particularly close association and continued communication and the tendency for overall solidarity to take precedence over sub-group solidarity in the face of outer crises.

   a. The tendency for sub-group solidarity to take precedence over obligation to the whole group will manifest itself in sentiments which might be paraphrased: "We all belong to the larger group, but it is only natural that a man should be more loyal to certain particular people: his friends and relatives. We (the sub-group) understand each other, like to associate with each other, and cooperate with each other. We are bound together by strong ties of love and respect."

   b. The tendency for overall solidarity to take precedence over sub-group solidarity in the face of outer crises will manifest itself in sentiments which might be paraphrased: "We are all members of the same group and we are all in the same boat. We are one. There are no special attachments; we are all equally close. We have a specific job to do and if we do not hang together we shall all hang separately. We should all work together to accomplish our purpose. We cannot get the job done without cooperation from everybody."

In general, this balance of conflicting tendencies, fluctuating according to more or less temporary changes in the relative urgency of functional problems of instrumentation, adaptation, integration, and emotional expression probably shows a trend toward a greater specificity of functional social roles, a greater differentiation of property rights, a greater formality of authority, a greater differentiation of strata, and a lesser overall solidarity, under the following conditions:

1. As the group grows older.
2. As the size of the group increases.
3. As the members of the group change, so that some are new and some are old.
4. As the group members become more heterogeneous as to age, sex, ethnic and physical characteristics, personal background and qualities, etc.
5. As the complexity and degree of difficulty of adaptation to the external situation increases.

APPENDIX: DEFINITIONS OF THE CATEGORIES

1. Shows solidarity, raises other's status, gives help, reward:

    a. *Initial and responsive acts of active solidarity and affection:* Includes hailing the other, waving, drawing near him in order to speak, greeting him by saying "hello" or in some other friendly manner, approaching, touching, shaking hands, placing a hand on the shoulder or clapping the other on the back, putting the arm around the other, or linking arms, welcoming the other, extending an invitation to him to be one of the in-group, treating him to food or drink, or some other symbol of solidarity and acceptance. Includes acts in return to a friendly gesture, such as accepting a treat, accepting an offer of help or assistance, thanking the other, accompanying or escorting him, saying or waving "goodbye." Includes any indication of mannerly consideration for the other, any indication of good will, any gesture that indicates that the actor is friendly, congenial, sociable, affiliative, cordial, or informal. A friendly comment on the weather or some other matter of common interest to "break the ice" and start a conversation would belong here. Any act of befriending the other, of showing hospitality, of being neighborly, comradely, is included. The expression of sympathy—"I can see how you feel"—is included. Any indication in the course of interaction that the relationship is becoming more intimate or familiar, as when the actor begins to use the other's first name, or a nickname, or the term "we" where it has not been used before is recorded in this category. Any indication that the actor identifies himself with the other, or confides in him, or entrusts the self to him is included. Any act of adherence where the actor chooses to be a fellow member with the other, any act of making a covenant, or of forming an alliance, any act of adhering to the other or becoming a partisan on his behalf, is included. Any indication that the actor is attracted to the other, all demonstrations of affection, love, and sexuality, such as acts of courting, flirting, coquetry, embracing, fondling, petting, caressing, kissing, are included.

    b. *Initial and responsive status-raising acts:* Includes all acts which have the specific aim or effect of raising or enhancing the other's status, whether the initial status of the actor is assumed to be higher than that of the other, equal to it, or inferior to it. In situations in which the status of the actor is assumed to be higher, included are praising, rewarding, boosting the other, giving approval or encouragement, or any statement, question, or comment in which the intent is to sustain, reassure, or bolster the status of the other. Examples: "That's fine," "You've done a good job," "Swell," "You've covered a lot of ground today." With regard to situations in which the actor and the other are presumed to be of equal status, included are complimenting, congratulating, showing approval of the other, giving credit to the other, showing enthusiasm for his views, applauding or cheering him. In situations where the actor is assumed to be of inferior status to the other, included are expressing gratitude or appreciation, showing admiration, esteem, or respect, wonder, awe, or reverence. Any act which indicates that the actor is attempting to imitate or emulate an admired superior is included. Includes praising, honoring, eulogizing a superior; lauding, acclaiming, extolling, idealizing, paying homage, deifying, adoring, or worshiping the other. The range is thus very great, from comparatively minor degrees of raising the other's status to very extreme recognitions of the other's superior status.

c. *In response to Category 11:* Includes any behavior in which the actor offers assistance to the other, volunteers, assumes a task or duty on behalf of the other or the group, offers to undertake a job which is indicated by a group decision, offers his services, assists, offers to contribute time, energy, money, or any other resource. Any act of sharing, of distributing something to the other, any giving out of materials, goods, or resources of activity, any attempts to make sure that the other is supplied with what he needs, invitations to the other to participate in some satisfaction or reward are included. More neutral or deliberate exchanges of one satisfaction for another, such as trading, paying, or loaning are included. The manifestation of any attitude the observer would interpret as altruistic, liberal, generous, self-denying, or self-sacrificing is included. Any act of bequeathing something or giving a gift to the other is included. Any behavior in which the actor defends the other, protects him, acts as a guardian for him, represents or advances his interests, vouches for him, certifies his integrity, speaks for him, advocates his cause, assists him when he is in need is included. Giving support, reassurance, comfort, consolation, encouragement, the showing of sympathy, pity, compassion, tenderness, expressing condolence and commiseration are included. Attempts to calm the other or assuage some hurt, by feeding him, nursing, healing, gratifying needs of any kind are included. The manifestation of any attitude which the observer interprets as nurturant, gentle, maternal, paternal, benevolent, humanitarian, merciful, charitable is included.

d. *In response to Categories 10 and 12:* Includes acts which may appear after a situation of difficulty or during a situation of estrangement, such as interceding or mediating, conciliating or moderating in a difficulty between two or more others. Acts of pacification, as when the actor mollifies the other, any attempt to allay opposition, to be discreet, tactful, diplomatic, to avoid wounding the other is included. Any act where the actor urges unity or harmony, agreement, cooperation, mutual obligation or expresses other values of solidarity is included. In cases of disagreement or antagonism between two or more others, the suggesting of a compromise, by some addition or amendment, expansion or modification of the suggested procedure is included.

2. Shows tension release, jokes, laughs, shows satisfaction:

a. *Spontaneous indications of relief:* Includes expressions of feeling better after a period of tension, any manifestation of cheerfulness, buoyance, satisfaction, gratification, contentment, enjoyment, relish, zest, enthusiasm, pleasure, delight, joy, happiness. Positive responses to a compliment, appearing to be charmed, beaming are included. Includes the manifestation of any psychological state which the observer interprets as a diffuse expression of positive affect, any indication that the actor is thrilled, elated, ecstatic, euphoric.

b. *Joking:* Includes the making of friendly jokes, trying to amuse or entertain; any jovial, jocular, humorous, funny, frivolous, "silly," nonsensical remark, whether spontaneous or in an attempt to smooth over some tension situation. Clowning, bantering, "kidding" the other in a friendly fashion are included. More active "horseplay" or "rough-housing," so long as the element of aggression is not too obviously present, are included. If the element of aggression is present, as it often is, it must be lower than the element of friendliness in the opinion of the observer in order to be marked in this category. If the element of aggression is stronger than the element of friendliness, the act should be scored in Category 12. Similarly, the attempt must indicate some sensitivity to the readiness of others to laugh, otherwise the observer concludes that the actor is excessively ego-involved and places the abortive attempt in Category 11, as an indication of anxiety, or in Category 12, as an indication of status seeking, according to his judgment.

c. *Laughing:* Positive responses to joking, such as smiling, grinning, giggling, chortling, chuckling, or laughing are included. With regard to laughs in response to jokes, an arbitrary convention is adopted that each new "wave" of laughter—essentially each time the person or the group "takes a new breath" and starts laughing again—a new score is entered. In cases where the group as a whole indulges in a general laugh, the score is entered 0–0, even though one or two may not be laughing. These one or two, if noticed, are scored as showing rejection, Category 10.

3. Agrees, shows passive acceptance, understands, concurs, complies:

a. *In response to Category 1 or 2:* Includes any indication to the observer that the actor is modest, humble, respectful, unassertive, retiring.

b. *In response to preceding acts of decision in the same category (3):* Includes the kind of final confirmation by repetition or affirmation which one sometimes notices at the end of a difficult process of thinking or discussion, when the actor (or actor and other) appears to come to a decision, to make up his mind, to crystallize his intention, to adopt a plan of action or resolution, and accepts a responsibility to carry it on into overt action. Examples: "Yes, that's it." "That's what I'll do." "Then I guess we're all agreed on that."

c. *In response to Category 4:* Includes any concurrence in a proposed course of action or assent to a suggestion the other has made. Examples: "I second the motion." "Let's do that." Includes any act (not already classified in Categories 4, 5, and 6) in which the actor either verbally or overtly complies with a request or suggestion, obliges the other, conforms with some direction or desire of the other, cooperates with an order, or does as he has been requested. The carrying out of any activity which has been decided by the group or the other is included. Yielding, obeying, following, or desisting from some activity when requested are included.

d. *In response to Category 5:* Includes agreement with an observation or report, analysis, or diagnosis which the other has made; that is, belief, confirmation, conviction, or accord about facts, inferences, and hypotheses. Examples: "That's the way I see it too." "I think you are right about that." "Yes, that's true." "Precisely." Similarly includes agreement, approval, or endorsement of an expression of value, feeling, or sentiment. Examples: "I feel the same way you do." "I hope so too." "Those are my sentiments exactly." "That's right."

e. *In response to Category 6:* Includes giving any sign of recognition, interest, receptiveness, readiness, responsiveness, such as looking at the speaker, sitting erect, or getting into a position to see or hear. Includes giving specific signs of attention to what the other is saying as he goes along, as a means of encouraging him to say what he wishes, by nodding the head, saying "I see," "Yes," "M-hmn"; completing by adding a word the other searches for or is hesitant to say, or otherwise aiding and facilitating communication. Includes showing comprehension, understanding, or insight, after a period of puzzlement and subsequent explanation by the other. Examples: "Oh." "I see." "Yes." "Sure, now I get it."

f. *In response to Category 10:* Includes admitting an error or oversight, admitting that some objection or disapproval of the other is valid, conceding a point to the other, giving way, withdrawing politely, asking the other's pardon. Includes introductory phrases which anticipate disagreement of the other and attempt to forestall it by admitting the point in advance. Examples: "Now I may be wrong about this. . . ." "This is not an important point perhaps. . . ."

g. *In response to Category 11:* Includes any indication of a permissive attitude, where the other is led to understand that he is accepted "as he is," so that the incorrectness of his solution to any problem or the quality of his performance does not adversely affect his status, so that he can "make mistakes without blame," and is reassured that he does not need to feel anxious. With regard to the permitting of activity on request of the other, includes all acts in which the actor gives the other freedom to do something, consents to a request, condones, countenances, or legalizes some activity of the other; in which he grants a privilege, abrogates or sets aside a custom or requirement for the other, excuses, forgives, pardons, or exonerates the other from the blame of some misdeed. Includes the manifestation of any attitude which the observer interprets as benign, kind, genial, good-natured, indulgent, lenient, forbearing, or tolerant. Includes the giving of approval of required work, as in situations where the other must have approval of his work at a given stage before going on to the next stage.

h. *In response to Category 12:* Includes acts which indicate that the actor is submissive, acquiescent, pliant, meek, in response to aggression directed toward him. Includes allowing the self to be talked down, surrendering, giving in, acknowledging defeat, renouncing a goal or object in favor of the other who demands it, standing aside, taking a back seat, letting the other push by aggressively and have the best. Includes any act in which the actor submits passively, allows himself to be bullied, dispossessed of objects, where he accepts coercion, domination, injury, blame, criticism, censure, punishment, without retaliation, rebuttal, rebellion, or complaint.

4. Gives suggestion, direction, implying autonomy for other:

a. *The process of cooperative action itself in its conative-instrumental aspect:* Includes all acts which suggest concrete ways of attaining a desired goal by attacking or modifying the outer situation, or by adapting activity to it, proposing a solution, indicating or suggesting where to start, what to do, how to cope with a problem in terms of action in the near future time perspective.

b. *The desired action of the other as the object of conative-instrumental effort:* Includes cases where suggestive orientation is given to the other as to what kind of activity is expected of him in the immediate future under some given conditions, as when a client comes into a counseling situation, or in a situation of instruction or briefing preliminary to cooperative activity, such as the setting up of a hypothetical example or situation for exploration or demonstration (such as a role-playing situation) where the actor proposes or suggests how the situation is to be defined, the purpose and nature of the roles to be taken, gives instructions or makes proposals about the task, showing where, when, how, why, something is to be done. Examples: "We will have to stop at the end of the hour." "Consider for a moment what would happen if. . . ." "Suppose we set up the following situation. . . ." "The foreman in this situation approaches the workman. . . ." "John, will you take the role of the foreman?" "Go right ahead." Includes direct attempts to guide or to counsel the other regarding some activity, to prevail upon him, persuade him, exhort him, urge, enjoin, or inspire him to some action. Includes the exercise of routine or established and accepted control, or control which is exercised in such a way that it is clear that the right of request rests ultimately on the free consent of the other, and the other retains the residual right to protest or modify the request so that his own autonomy is not severely threatened. Includes acts in which a recognized leader requests other(s) to do things as a part of the routine mechanics of group management, or as administrative short-cuts to leader determined goals or group determined goals. The leader's requests may be unsolicited by the other and yet anticipate conformance on the part of the other, on the assumption that the leader is acting as a legitimate agent and instrument of the group. Routine signals for control of some detail of procedure in the opening or closing of some group activity are included such as calling the meeting to order or pronouncing that it is adjourned. The assignment of tasks, the appointment of persons to committees, where the chairman or leader has been given the authority to do so, the giving or imputing of a role to another; that is, a request by the leader to another individual to play a certain role in a group discussion, such as acting as a recorder or observer, selecting the other for some activity on the basis of the other's interest or consent, are included. Includes delegation of authority or initiative. Where leadership is not implied, small emotionally neutral requests of the actor to the other are included, such as "Would you hand me the ash tray please?" (Emotionally toned requests for help, however, are classified in Category 11.)

5. Gives opinion, evaluation, analysis, expresses feeling, wish:

a. *The process of action itself in its inferential and optative aspects:* Includes all indications of thought-in-process leading to an understanding or dawning insight, such as introspection, reasoning, reckoning, calculating, thinking, musing, cogitating, or concentrating. The actual statement of the hypothesis or expression of understanding or insight is included. Further logical elaboration, exploration, or testing of the hypothesis or diagnosis is included, whether by example, analogy, analysis of cause and effect relations, symbolic or categorical labeling, or by any sort of logical, intuitive, or conjectural process. The inferential and evaluative element distinguishes acts in the present category from acts in Category 6. Includes acts of expressing or enunciating feelings or sentiments in the optative mood. Includes any expression of desire, want, liking, wishing, or hoping, any expression of sentiment or moral obligation, any affirmation of major values, any statement of policy, intention, or guiding principles, or law, referring to a broad and indefinite future time perspective, as yet unimplemented as to ways and means. Examples: "I wish we could fix it so that. . . ." "I think we ought to be fair about this." "I hope we

can do something about that." "That seems to be the right thing to do."
Any expression on the part of the actor of a need to achieve, any expression of ambition or aspiration, of determination or courage, is included.
Manifestations of attitudes which would be called earnest, grave, reverent,
serious, or prayerful are included insofar as they involve a kind of expression of a major value or intention. Certain parts of prayer or performance
of ceremonial or ritual acts are included, insofar as they are expressions
and intensifications of intention, value, or desire.

b. *The self and own motivation as object of inference and evaluation:*
Includes activity in which the actor attempts, by inference or reasoning,
in a primarily objective way, to understand, diagnose, or interpret his
own motivation or the "why" of his own behavior. In a practical problem
situation, any assessment or evaluation of the effectiveness or efficiency of
one's past action is included, as when the actor reflectively examines a
plan he has just tried out, or when he examines his own rehearsal or role-
playing of future action. In a training, therapeutic, or counseling situation, any statement or indication that the trainee, patient, or client sees
patterns and relationships in his own motivation, conduct, or verbal production is included so long as it indicates to the observer an attempt at
a logical and reasoned explanation rather than a self-defensive rationalization of conduct. Examples: "I must have been so mad at him that I didn't
see he was trying to help me." "Probably I don't realize how nervous I
am in situations like that." "I can see now that I totally misjudged the
situation." (Statements which are considered to be largely self-defensive
rationalizations are classified under Category 12. Statements considered
to be largely negatively toned evaluations of self or conduct are classified under Category 11. Statements which involve only simple recall or
reporting about one's experience, without inference, are classified in
Category 6.)

c. *The other, his motivation, or the group as a whole as the object of
inference and evaluation:* Includes activity in which the actor attempts,
by inference or reasoning, in a primarily objective way, to understand,
diagnose, or interpret the other, his motivation or activity, the group, its
structure, dynamics, or past action. In counseling situations, includes all
responses in which the counselor makes inferences or diagnoses, or points
out patterns and relationships in the material presented by the client, of
which the client has not yet expressed awareness, interpretations where
causation is implied or indicated. Example: "You do this because all authority figures remind you of your father." An example from group discussion in an evaluation period: "Maybe we got off the track because some
of us were more anxious to show what we knew than we were to solve the
problem at hand." Activity in the present category is distinguished from
activity in Category 6 in that it involves inference or interpretation rather

than a simple report, reflection, or rephrasing. In group activity this kind of interaction is likely to occur in cases of self-evaluation and feedback, where the aim is to arrive at new insights about the motives, feelings, or problems of the other or group members generally, the relations of members to each other, or features of group procedure. (Statements considered to be motivated largely by a desire to expose the other, or deflate his status, or which have this effect, are placed in Category 12. Statements which involve only simple report or recall about the other or group, without inference or diagnosis, are placed in Category 6.)

d. *The outer situation as the object of inference and evaluation:* Includes all statements about the nature of the outer situation facing the group as a whole, which are essentially inferential, hypothetical, a matter of opinion or plausible interpretation—not immediately observable. Examples: "It seems to me that the patient we have just seen is more introverted than the last time we saw him." "He has not been doing well." "According to my calculations it must be about three miles." "Well, let's see. Two times the square root of this second term is. . . ." "It's the same as. . . ." (This sub variety of Category 5 is the most frequent type of interaction for many groups, if not most.)

6. Gives orientation, information, repeats, clarifies, confirms:

a. *The process of activity or communication itself as the object of cognition:* Includes all acts which are intended to secure or focus the attention of the other or to insure his readiness for a series of communications to follow, such as calling his name, clearing the throat, engaging the eyes of the other, holding up the hand, mentioning a problem to be discussed, calling attention to what one is going to say, or pointing out the relevance of what one is saying or doing, any reference back to an agenda, the giving of any routine signal that one is beginning a new phase of activity or a new focus of effort, or signifying the end of a phase. Examples: "Ah . . . ," "Say John . . . ," "There are two points I'd like to make." "In the first place . . . ," "Now with regard to our problem of . . . ," "Going back for a moment . . . ," "What I am about to say relates to . . . ," "That seems to finish our agenda." Interaction in this category may occur when a new individual comes into a situation or interaction process with which the other(s) are familiar, as when a new person arrives in the middle of a group discussion. Examples: "We were just discussing . . . ," "I might bring you up to date on what we've been doing." Efforts to prevent or repair breaks in the flow of communication include repeating, clarifying confusion about something said, explaining, enlarging, summarizing, restating, not with the purpose of convincing or carrying the argument further, but simply with the purpose of making communication and orientation to process more adequate. Includes any reflective looking back on past activity of the group, such as the reading of a report or minutes, or any preparatory looking forward, as in the reviewing of items on an agenda which have already been decided.

b. *The self and own motivation as the object of cognition:* Includes activity in which the actor simply reports without inference or tells about some past thought, feeling, action, or experience of his own, either spontaneously, or in response to questions as in Category 7. Includes any account of one's own private experience, where the actor tells what he felt, what was done, how it was done, the position he took on some issue, what happened, or where he gives information of a more public nature about himself, or how others regard the self. Examples: "I felt pretty downhearted about that time." "They all thought I was crazy." "This secretly pleased me." "I was actually on their side." "I am twenty-one years old." "I have lived here all my life." "I'll never forget the time I. . . ." In counseling or therapeutic interviews a great deal of activity falls in this category as the actor reports about the feelings he has, dreams he had, as he states facts about his past history, and as he reports about symptoms of difficulties which he faces. Only statements about the self which are essentially non-inferential, however, and comparatively neutral in emotional tone are included here. (Whenever emotion or affect is apparent in the report as a present psychological state, the act is classified in an appropriate category above or below, even though the emotion or affect is not connected with or directed toward the other to whom the actor is talking. In this case, the interaction is scored by placing the number of the actor, as usual, followed by an "x" rather than by the number of the other spoken to. Example: If, in a therapeutic interview, the client expresses aggression against the father, mother, or some other person not present, the act would be classified under Category 12 below, and would be marked as directed to "x" rather than to the therapeutist.)

c. *The other, his motivation, or the group as a whole as the object of cognition:* Includes showing an understanding of the other or something the other has said by restating, reporting the essential content of what he has said, reflecting the content or feeling back to him, rephrasing, accepting and clarifying the feeling involved, without, however, resorting to inference or interpretation beyond that given by the subject himself. It includes putting the ideas, feelings, or affective tone in somewhat clearer or more recognizable form, with the intent of aiding the other in the formulation or reformulation of his problem, but the inference, if present, must be minimal. This type of activity is the non-directive technique par excellence, and probably appears more frequently in this type of counseling than in most other types of interaction. Example: (The client has been talking about his mother and says,) "Oh she means well enough, I guess, but she just keeps bringing it up and bringing it up. Sometimes I wish she'd just forget the whole thing." Counselor: "Her intentions are good, but when she keeps harping on it, you get irritated." (The client has not said he was irritated, but irritation shows in his voice and manner.) In problem-solving groups interaction of essentially the same kind may appear, either spontaneously or in the process of group self-evaluation or in the process of a more formal feedback, where certain observations about the characteristics of the group taken by observer(s) are reported to the group, without interpretation, in order to make it possible for them to make an analysis of their own organization and procedure. Example: "Three of the members indicate dissatisfaction with the meetings."

d. *The outer situation as the object of cognition:* Includes statements of fact about the nature of the outer situation facing the group which are essentially objective, straightforward, non-inferential, non-emotionally toned, descriptive observations or empirical generalizations which are recognized as generally established or easily confirmed by observation. Includes factual information given gratuitously, as in a lecture or in tutoring, in the process of conveying knowledge where there is the implication that the other wants to know or needs to know something the actor can tell him. The implication is that the information given will be accepted, if understood. Examples: "We have just two days left." "The phone is out of operation." "It would take three days to reach him by mail."

7. Asks for orientation, information, repetition, and confirmation:

a. *The process of action as the object of cognitive effort:* Includes acts which indicate or express a lack of knowledge sufficient to support action: confusion or uncertainty about the position of the group with regard to its goals, the course of the discussion to the present point, about what has been said or is going on, about the meaning of a word or phrase, even though the actor has been present and has been paying attention. Includes the appearance of any attitude the observer would describe as puzzled, bewildered, baffled, stumped, fuddled, or obfuscated. Verbal examples: "What?" "What was that?" "I didn't quite understand you." "Would you repeat that?" "I don't quite get what you mean." More deliberate attempts to get the group to assess and clarify its position in the problem-solving process are also included, whether or not the actor is actually confused or disoriented himself. Examples: "Where are we?" "Where do we stand now?"

b. *Self, other, or group, or outer situation as the object of cognitive effort:* Includes direct or outright questions which require the giving of a factual rather than an inferential answer; i.e., an answer which can be judged as true or false on the basis of simple observation, or which is generally accepted as a matter of convention. Also includes less focalized, or more indefinite expressions of a lack of knowledge or cognitive clarity sufficient to support action; i.e., instances in which the requesting or asking is only implicit. Examples: "I don't know about this." "(I have looked,) but I can't make it out." "It isn't clear to me." "It may be true, or it may not be." The questions or requests, whether explicit or only implicit, can be about the outer situation facing the group, about the group itself, its structure or organization, about another person, or about the self (rare). Examples: "What day of the month is it?" "I'm not sure of the exact date." "Who is in charge of the arrangements for the next meeting?" "I have forgotten whom we appointed." "How long have you lived here?" "Let's see, how old was I at that time?" (to self). (This category does not include interrogative statements which are designed to redefine, clarify, or redescribe a feeling, such as: "You mean you don't really like him?" A remark of this kind would be classified under Category 5 or 6, according to the degree of inference or interpretation involved.)

8. Asks for opinion, evaluation, analysis, expression of feeling:

a. *The process of action itself as the object of inferential or evaluative effort:* Includes open-ended, non-directive leads and questions aimed at the exploration or intensification-through-expression of the other's feelings, values, intentions, and inclinations. Includes any kind of question which attempts to encourage a statement or reaction on the part of the other without limiting the nature of the response except in a very general way, with the implication that the other has freedom to express interest or disinterest, where he is not put under pressure to agree or disagree, or to come out with any predetermined answers, type of answer, or attitude. Good examples may be found in non-directive counseling: "How do you feel today?" "Tell me more about it." "Just feel perfectly free to talk about anything you like." This kind of behavior occurs in group interaction where there is a desire and attempt on the part of the leader or group member to sound the other's feelings on a problem before discussion has begun or at any point in the process where evaluation may come into play. Examples: "I wonder how you feel about that?" "What do you think (i.e., feel)?" "Could we have an expression of feeling on this point?" "What is the sense of the meeting?" "What should our policy be?" "What do you think we ought to aim at?"

B. *Self, other, group, or outer situation as the object of inferential or evaluative effort:* Includes questions, statements, or responses which seek an inferential interpretation, hypothesis, diagnosis, or further analysis of some idea from the other, his definition of the situation or opinion on some topic in a non-threatening or objective manner. Also includes less focalized, or more indefinite expressions of an inability to make satisfactory inferences or value resolutions sufficient to support or lead on into overt action, i.e., emotional conflict, ambivalence. In these cases the requesting or asking is only implicit, perhaps, but is scored in the present category unless the emotional tone is marked enough to justify its inclusion under Category 11 (shows tension, anxiety, etc.). The inference or evaluation requested, either explicitly or implicitly, may refer to the outer situation facing the group, to the group itself, its structure or organization, to the other person, or to the self. The actor may wish to get the other's interpretation or opinion as an aid where there is no known answer and only conjecture is possible, or it may be to help the other to see implications of something he has said, to see action possibilities toward a solution of his problem, to facilitate his choosing a course of action, or to explore his motivation. Examples: "How long do you suppose it will be?" "I can't figure out how long it would take." "I wonder what changes that would involve?" "I don't know whether it would require changes or not." "I wonder if there are any other possibilities?" "I wonder if we are proceeding in the most effective way?" "Why do you think you feel that way?" "I don't know how I really feel." (So-called "significant pauses" may be scored in this category.)

9. Asks for suggestion, direction, possible ways of action:

a. *The process of action itself, the self, other, or outer situation as the object of active modification:* Includes all questions or requests, explicit or implicit, for suggestions as to how action shall proceed through the utilization of concrete ways and means to goals in the immediate future time perspective. The request of a chairman for a motion from the floor is a pure example of this category of activity in explicit form, but more indefinite requests for suggestions as to what should be done in terms of finding ways, means, and solutions, requests for suggestions as to where to start, what to do next, what to decide, which are meant to begin a crystallization of a concrete plan of action are also included. Examples: "Is there a motion on this point?" "I wonder what we can do about this?" "I don't know what to do." "What do you suggest?" This kind of activity might appear in counseling where the counselor asks, "What shall we talk about today?" (Appeals for suggestions which have an emotional undertone of dependence, or of a need for help, an inability to take responsibility for direction rather than a sharing of the right to determine direction, should be classified in Category 11. Whether dependency is indicated or not, if the emotional tone becomes marked, the activity should be classified under Category 11. Example: "Gosh! What do I do now?" or Category 12. Example: "Well, what do *you* suggest then?"

10. Disagrees, shows passive rejection, formality, withholds resources:

a. *In response to Categories 1, 2, and 3:* Includes any indication of an attitude which the observer considers over-cool, frigid, inexpansive, unsmiling. Any situation in which an emotional response would be expected, where the actor refuses to give applause, or is unappreciative, unacknowledging, ungrateful, unallured, "hard to please," "hard to get," is included. Includes passive forms of rejection, such as remaining immobile, rigid, restrained, silent, close-mouthed, uncommunicative, inexpressive, impassive, imperturbable, reticent, responseless, in the face of overtures of the other. Includes any passive withholding of love or friendship, any indication that the actor is psychically insulated, detached, isolated, indifferent, disinterested, impersonal, aloof, formal, distant, unsocial, reserved, secluded, unapproachable, exclusive, or forbidding. Refraining from intimacies and confidences where the other appears to be seeking this kind of response is included. All undetermined member-to-member contacts, that is, asides, whispering, winks, etc., while the main discussion is going on between others are classified in this category as rejections by both participants of the rest of the group. Working at something other than the problem with which the group is concerned, when there is an expectation that all will be attending or actively participating is included. Speaking or paying attention to outsiders, such as observers, when the group as a whole is working on another problem is included. (More positive and aggressively toned acts of rejection, such as actually excluding the other, abandoning him, deserting him, dropping, rebuffing, repulsing, jilting, are marked in Category 12.)

b. *In response to Category 4:* Includes demurral with regard to suggestions made, any act in which the actor appears to be skeptical, dubious, cautious about accepting the proposal, hesitant, critical, suspicious, or distrustful. (More positive and aggressively toned acts of demurral are scored in Category 12.)

c. *In response to Categories 5 and 6:* Includes the milder degrees of disagreement, disbelief, astonishment, amazement, or incredulity regarding reports and observations, inferences or diagnoses or interpretations made by the other. More marked forms of strictly ideational disagreement are also included, as when the actor amends or corrects another's description of the situation, his interpretation or diagnosis, contradicts something the other has said. (Includes disapproval of an expression of value or feeling *only* if very mild and confined to the actual expression or suggestion, and it is made plain by some means that the disapproval does *not* extend to the other as a "person." Very usually, when moral judgments or disapproval are applied to expressions of feeling or suggestions, they reflect so strongly on the person making them that they should be scored under Category 12.)

d. *In response to Categories 7, 8, 9, 11, 12:* Includes failing to pay attention when the other is speaking, failing to give a requested repetition, disregarding the other, ignoring a request of any kind or a complaint, by direct evasion, postponement of answer without expressed reason or consideration for the other, equivocation, delay, noncommittal hedging. More generally, includes any refusal to act which frustrates the other, thwarts, balks, blocks, obstructs, or puts barriers in the way, any behavior which restrains, hinders, limits the ongoing activity of the other, confines, constrains, or stands in his way, or which renders his efforts vain, upsets his plans, forestalls, contravenes, foils, or checkmates him. Includes any act of withholding resources, the manifestation of any attitude which the observer interprets as possessive, retentive, retractive, or secretive. Any act in which the other is denied something requested, in which the actor disappoints the other, refuses to let the other participate in some satisfaction or have access to some resource may be included here, if the aggressive tone is comparatively low. (As the active, outgoing aggressive element increases, the activity should be scored in Category 12.)

e. *In response to previous acts in Category 10:* If the actor has made a suggestion, and someone else in the meantime has disagreed with him, when the actor returns to defend or restate his original definition of the situation or proposal, his return is marked in this category as disagreement. (In general, only the *initial* reaction of disagreement is marked in the present category, when the disagreement is essentially ideational. The arguments which follow, in the form of statements about the situation, analyses of the facts, alternative suggestions, rhetorical questions, etc. are scored in their respective categories. Example: "I don't think so. It seems to me that there were more than that. In fact, I remember seeing at least five." In the foregoing statement only "I don't think so," would be scored in the present category. The argument which follows in support is broken up and scored in the categories above as usual.)

11. Shows tension: asks for help, withdraws out of field:

a. *Diffuse tension:* Includes all sorts of non-focal manifestations of impatience, indications that the subject feels strained, on edge, restless, restive, keyed-up, agitated. The appearance of various "nervous habits"—doodling, self-grooming, fiddling, biting the nails, playing with some object—are included. Where the behavior is constant, a new score is entered once each minute. In machine scoring, a signal light is provided which flashes once each minute, at which time the observer scans the group rapidly and enters any indicated scores in this category.

b. *Diffuse anxiety:* Includes any manifestation or indication to the observer that the actor is startled, disconcerted, alarmed, dismayed, perturbed, concerned, qualmish, or has misgivings about something he has done or intends to do. Any show of anxious emotionality, such as hesitation, speechlessness, any indication of flurry, fluster, trembling, blenching, blushing, flushing, stammering, verbal disjunctivity, sweating, "blocking up," gulping, swallowing, or wetting the lips persistently is included. Includes any verbal or motor expression of fear, apprehension, worry, dread, fright, terror, or panic. Includes the manifestation of any attitude which the observer would interpret as overcautious, overwary, where the actor is overhesitant about undertaking some action, hangs back, shuns, evades, or shrinks from a perilous situation, or refrains from action because of fear of failure. Any behavior which the observer interprets as overprudent, careful, vigilant, tense, abashed, timid, shy, self-distrustful, self-effacing, self-conscious, shrinking, or infavoidant, is included. Wherever the actor seems to be overanxious, inhibited, fearful of blame, sensitive about, or concerned about the good opinion of others, is overcareful to do nothing that will annoy, antagonize, or alienate the affections of others, these indications are scored in this category. Includes the manifestation of any attitude which the observer would interpret as overscrupulous, unobjectionable, conscientious, conventional, dutiful, apparently because of fear of provoking opposition or hostility.

c. *Shame and guilt:* Includes responses to accusations in which the actor acknowledges, confesses, admits responsibility for some act of his which has been inconvenient, unjust, or unfair to another, or any act in which he admits his own ignorance or incapacity. Laughing alone, giggling nervously or apologetically is marked here. Appearing to be embarrassed, fussed, sheepish, chagrined, chapfallen, crestfallen, chastened, at a loss, mortified, are included in this category. Moaning or cringing, covering the face with the hands, any act which indicates a consciousness of guilt, or any indication that the subject is furtive, ashamed, morose, depressed, or remorseful is included. Following this, any acts of atonement, in which the actor does something to balance a wrong, to expiate guilt, or humiliates himself, any action which shows that he is apologetic, contrite, penitent, is included. Passing on to more extreme forms, blaming, belittling, and mutilating the self are included. Any act which could be described as self-dissatisfied, -critical, -depreciating, -accusing, -exposing, -convicting, -condemning, -dispraising, -disparaging, -reproving, -reproachful, -upbraiding, -scornful, -degrading, -humiliating, -contemptuous, or self-destroying is included.

d. *Frustration:* Includes any indication on the part of the actor that his effort has failed, that some problems confronting him in his earlier efforts still remain, expressions of feeling frustrated, thwarted, or deprived are included in this category, unless they are expressed in some more specifically socially oriented way as formulated in other categories. (For example, frustration tension may be expressed in a more socially oriented way by showing antagonism against the other, Category 12.) Wherever the observer interprets that the actor is dissatisfied, discontented, disappointed, displeased, and these feelings are expressed only in a diffuse way, with no special social object, the indications are scored here. Includes expressions of unhappiness, any indication that the actor is discouraged, disheartened, disconsolate, downcast, downhearted, resigned, desolate, despairing, miserable. Includes any appearance of brooding, any indication of distress, disturbance, discomfort, fatigue, pain, or injury.

e. *Asking for help, permission:* Requests for permission or help which carry a noticeable undertone of emotionality are included. (More neutral requests may be scored above in a variety of categories, i.e., 4, 7, 8, 9, according to their form.) Any act which the observer interprets as an attempt to place the responsibility for the solution of one's own problems on the other or on the group is included, such as asking for aid, advice, support, asking for or appealing to the other's good nature, mercy, forbearance. Includes acts in which the actor flatters, cajoles, or attempts to appease the other, where he insincerely abases himself, cowers, curries favor, fawns, footlicks, bootlicks, or is servile with the purpose of obtaining ulterior ends, where he attempts to shame the other into some kind of desired behavior by acting as if injured, hurt, martyred, or put upon, but in the judgment of the observer does not actually feel the emotion which he pretends to display. Includes any act in which the actor petitions, pleads, begs or beseeches the other for some favor. The telling of misfortunes, hardships, accidents, failures, with the intention of arousing sympathy is included. Bewailing, whining, weeping, adopting a pathetic or tragic attitude, holding out the arms, extending the hands for help, exhibiting one's wounds, attempting to move the other to pity are included. Attempts to exaggerate an injury, illness, or symptom of any kind, complaints of being miserable, depressed, sad, worried, tired, are included. The manifestation of any attitude which the observer interprets as forlorn, forsaken, insecure, grieving, tragic, despairing, helpless, lonesome, tearful, sniffling, self-pitying, plaintive, suppliant, succorant, or dependent is included. Showing any kind of need to be supported, nursed, sustained, protected, loved, advised, guided, indulged, forgiven, consoled, is included. Any manifestation of a craving for affection or tenderness is included.

f. *Withdrawal out of field:* Includes any behavior which indicates to the observer that the actor is unattentive, bored, or psychologically withdrawn from the problem at hand; slouching, yawning, closing the eyes, daydreaming, looking away from the others in the group, looking away from the work, letting the eyes wander, are included. Includes the manifestation of any attitude the observer would interpret as listless, languid, bemused, absorbed, abstracted, adream, unaware, oblivious to others. More definite and overt withdrawal, such as giving notice, leaving, resigning, deserting, striking, quitting, retreating from humiliation, retiring, going home, are included. More extreme forms of autistic, subjective, or socially irrelevant behavior or response which indicate a lack of contact with what is going on are included, such as talking to the self, or mumbling. Any indication of excessive inaction, non-responsiveness or reclusiveness may be classified in this category. Any indication to the observer that the actor is psychologically shut-in, indisposed, apathetic, resigned, despondent, numbed, stunned, stupefied, or inarticulate is included.

12. Shows antagonism, deflates other's status, defends or asserts self:

a. *Autocratic control:* Includes attempts to control, regulate, govern, direct, or supervise in a manner which the observer interprets as arbitrary or autocratic, in which freedom of choice or consent for the other person is either greatly limited or nonexistent, with the implication that the other has no right to protest or modify the demand but is expected to follow the directive immediately without argument. Includes the arbitrary assignment of a role, the location or relocation of the other, a defining or restricting of the other's powers by fiat, demands or commands such as "Come here!" "Stop that!" "Hurry up!" "Get out!" Any act in which the actor peremptorily beckons, points, pushes, pulls, or otherwise directly controls or attempts to control the activity of the other is included. More extreme acts of dismissal or expulsion, where the actor evicts, discharges, cashiers, banishes the other are included. Includes any act in which the observer interprets the attitude of the actor to be overbearing, dogmatic, assertive, imperious, inconsiderate, or severe. Includes arbitrary attempts to lay down principles of conduct, standards, or laws, arbitrary attempts to judge or settle an argument, to give a decision, to force, compel, coerce, subdue, subject, tame, master, dominate. Includes acts in which the actor prohibits the other from doing something, represses the other, proscribes some activity, interdicts, taboos, gives warnings, threats.

b. *Autonomy:* Includes any response to an attempt at control in which the actor shows active autonomy, is noncompliant, unwilling, or disobliging, where he resists some effort or imagined effort of a superior other to take some satisfaction from him. Includes any act in which the actor rejects, refuses, or purposefully ignores directions, commands, demands, or authoritative requests. Includes any behavior in which the actor defies authority, is negativistic, stubborn, resistant, obstinate, refractory, contrary, sulky, or sullen. Includes shrugging the shoulders, avoiding or quitting activities prescribed by authority, resisting coercion and restriction, trying in any manner to shake off restraint or get free. Includes any behavior which works against or circumvents authority, in which the actor shows independence, nonsubmissiveness, nonconformity, is disobedient, insubordinate, rebellious, irresponsible, willful, obstreperous, unrestrained, disorderly. Includes aggressive acts against authority, such as carping, harping, griping, nagging, badgering, harassing, annoying, perturbing, disturbing, or pestering the other. Includes the manifestation of any attitude which the observer interprets as disrespectful, discourteous, impudent, bold, saucy, flippant, impervious, unashamed, or unrepentant when justly accused.

c. *Status deflating:* On the milder side includes conspicuous attempts to override the other in conversation, interrupting the other, interfering with his speaking, gratuitously finishing his sentence for him when the other does not want help, insisting on finishing, warding off interruption. With regard to active attacks or deflation of the other's status, any implication of inferiority or incompetence on the part of the other is included, such as appraising the other contemptuously, belittling, depreciating, disparaging, ridiculing, minimizing the other, reducing his remarks to absurdity, making fun of him. Includes any acts in which the actor would be described as maliciously sarcastic, satirical, ironical, in which the actor lampoons, caricatures, burlesques the other, or becomes unduly and insultingly familiar. Includes teasing, taunting, heckling, gloating, crowing, jeering, scoffing, mocking, sneering, bedeviling, goading, baiting, or provoking the other to say something indiscreet or damaging. Includes damning the other, finding fault with him, complaining, criticizing him; any act that would be interpreted as abusive, accusatory, acrimonious. Includes making charges against the other, imputing unworthy motives to him, blaming him, denouncing him, excoriating, berating, prosecuting, ill-treating, or browbeating him. Includes any act of gossip, any libel, slander, smirching of the other's character, branding him with undesirable characteristics, demeaning him, tattling against him, informing against him, exposing him, or undermining his position, maligning, or discrediting him, placing him at a disadvantage or oppugning him. Includes tricking, hoaxing, duping, fleecing, hazing, humiliating the other or rendering him conspicuous. With regard to disapproval, includes acts ranging from mild forms of disapproval, such as reprimanding the other, blaming him, scolding him, admonishing or reminding him of his duty, on to more extreme forms, such as indications that the actor is shocked, indignant, appalled, scandalized at something the other has done, and shows horror or disgust. Includes any indication that the actor is indignant, offended, insulted, affronted. Includes indications of moral indignation, such as a grim appearance, appearing incensed, irate, outraged, infuriated. Includes any act of showing ascendance, any act that would be described as pompous, pontifical, ceremonious, self-opinionated, self-important, self-righteous, self-satisfied, self-complacent, or smug. Includes any act which would be regarded as haughty, proud, vain, arrogant, "uppish," snobbish, self-admiring, self-conceited, presumptuous, condescending, or disdainful.

d. *Status defending:* Includes any act in which the actor suppresses, conceals, hides, fails to mention, or justifies something which is considered discreditable, such as ineptitude, ignorance, a defect, some misdeed, failure, or humiliation. Includes the manifestation of any attitude which the observer would regard as indicating that the actor is "on his guard," has a "chip on his shoulder," such as interpreting a harmless remark as a slur, bristling when criticized, protesting, asserting one's own claims. Includes any act of defending or protecting the self, one's sentiments, or theories against assault, criticism, or blame, in an ego-involved way. Includes any act of self-vindication or exculpation, such as explaining, excusing, justifying, offering extenuations for or rationalization of inferiority, guilt, or failure, giving alibis, any act of disavowal, disacknowledging guilt, any disclaiming, denial, or refusal to admit guilt, inferiority, or weakness.

e. *Status seeking:* Includes any act in which the actor is self-assertive from a position which has the implication of lower status, in which he tries to impress the other with his importance, tries to be seen or heard, in which he pushes himself forward, dramatizes himself, poses as a unique, mysterious, incalculable person. Includes any behavior which the observer regards as exhibitionistic, spectacular, or conspicuous. Includes attempts to excite, amaze, fascinate, entertain, shock, intrigue, or amuse the other(s) as a means of raising one's own status. Includes any behavior in which the observer regards the subject as "acting," showing off, seeking applause or approbation, playing the clown, especially the making of jokes which fall flat or do not provoke a general laugh. Includes attempts to attract attention by mannerisms, expressive gestures, emphatic or extravagant speech, posturing, posing for effect, displaying the self, seeking the limelight, bragging, boasting, strutting, blustering. Includes praising the self, glorifying, exalting, applauding, approving, or advertising the self. Includes any act in which the actor tries to outdo the other, shows rivalry.

f. *Diffuse aggression:* Includes any manifestation of an emotional reaction to another which the observer would interpret as cranky, uncongenial, touchy, tiffish, testy, surly, irritable, ill-tempered, irascible, contumacious. Includes the manifestation of any attitude the observer would interpret as aggressive, combative, belligerent, pugnacious, quarrelsome, or argumentative. Includes any behavior in which the actor appears to be provoked, in which he shows annoyance, irritation, heat, anger, rage, or has a temper tantrum. Includes any indication of intolerance, malevolence, such as glaring, frowning, cursing, fuming, hissing, jostling, pushing, having a fit of rage, screaming, kicking, scratching. Includes moving or speaking in a threatening manner, challenging, defying, attacking, assailing, assaulting, hitting, striking, beating, fighting the other. Includes the manifestation of any attitude which the observer would interpret as destructive, cruel, or ruthless, or any act the observer interprets as resentful, vengeful, vindictive, or retaliative. Includes any indication of envy, jealousy, covetousness, cupidity, avarice, acquisitiveness at the expense of the other, or attempts to take something away from the other.

BIBLIOGRAPHY

(1) Allport, Gordon W., and Odbert, Henry S., "Trait Names, a Psycho-lexical Study," *Psychological Monographs,* Vol. XLVII, No. 1, 1936.

(2) Anderson, Harold H., and associates, *Applied Psychology Monographs,* Numbers 6, 8, and 11, Stanford University Press, 1945–1946. (See also Anderson, Harold H., "Domination and Social Integration in the Behavior of Kindergarten Children and Teachers," *Genetic Psychology Monographs,* Vol. XXI, No. 3, Clark University Press, Worcester.)

(3) Back, Kurt, "Interpersonal Relations in a Discussion Group," *Journal of Social Issues,* Vol. IV, pp. 61–65, 1948.

(4) Bales, Robert F., "Interaction Content Analysis," *Preliminary Report of the First National Training Laboratory on Group Development,* National Education Association and Research Center for Group Dynamics, M.I.T., 1947, obtainable from National Education Association, Washington, D. C.

(5) Bales, Robert F., and Gerbrands, Henry, "The 'Interaction Recorder,' an Apparatus and Check List for Sequential Content Analysis of Social Interaction," *Human Relations,* Vol. 1, No. 4, 1948.

(6) Benne, Kenneth D., and Sheats, Paul, "Functional Roles of Group Members," *Journal of Social Issues,* Vol. LV, No. 2, pp. 41–49, Spring, 1948.

(7) Carr, Lowell J., "Experimental Sociology: A Preliminary Note on Theory and Method," *Social Forces,* Vol. VIII, No. 1, pp. 63–74, Sept., 1929.

(8) Chapple, E. D., "Measuring Human Relations: An Introduction to the Study of Interaction of Individuals," *Genetic Psychology Monographs,* February, 1940.

(9) Covner, B. J., "Studies in Phonographic Recordings of Verbal Materials: III, The Completeness and Accuracy of Counseling Interview Reports," *Journal of General Psychology,* Vol. 30, pp. 181–203, 1944.

(10) Curran, Charles A., *Personality Factors in Counseling* (published doctoral dissertation, Ohio State University), Grune and Stratton, New York, 1945.

(11) Deutche, Morton, unpublished manuscript, Research Center for Group Dynamics, University of Michigan.

(12) Frank, Jerome D., and associates, "Preliminary Report for the National Research Council, Group Therapy Research Project," mimeographed report, The Washington School of Psychiatry, Room 1108, Veterans Administration Regional Office, 1825 H Street, N. W., Washington, D. C.

(13) French, J. R. P., "Organized and Unorganized Groups under Fear and Frustration," *Studies in Topological and Vector Psychology,* University of Iowa Press, 1944.

(14) Guetzkow, Harold, and associates, mimeographed materials prepared in connection with *Experimental Research on the Administrative Conference,* University of Michigan, Ann Arbor, Michigan, 1948.

(15) Hader, John J., and Lindeman, Eduard C., *Dynamic Social Research,* Harcourt, Brace and Company, New York, 1933.

(16) Joël, Walther, and Shapiro, David, "A Genotypical Approach to the Analysis of Personal Interaction," *The Journal of Psychology,* No. 28, pp. 9–17, 1949.

(17) Lewis, Virginia W., "Changing the Behavior of Adolescent Girls," *Archives of Psychology*, Columbia University, New York, 1943. (See Curran (10) above for discussion.)

(18) Lippitt, Ronald, "An Experimental Study of Authoritarian and Democratic Group Atmospheres," *Studies in Topological and Vector Psychology*, Vol. XVI, No. 3, University of Iowa Studies in Child Welfare, University of Iowa, Iowa City, 1940.

(19) Murray, Henry A., and associates, *Explorations in Personality*, Oxford University Press, New York, pp. 36–242, 1938.

(20) Norfleet, Barbara, "Interpersonal Relations and Group Productivity," *Journal of Social Issues*, Vol. IV, pp. 66–70, 1948.

(21) Porter, E. H., *The Development and Evaluation of a Measure of Counseling Interview Procedures*, unpublished thesis. (See Curran above (10) and Rogers below (23) for descriptions.)

(22) Raimy, Victor Charles, "The Self-concept as a Factor in Counseling and Personality Organization," Ph.D thesis, Ohio State University, Columbus, Ohio, 1943. (See Curran above (10) for discussion.)

(23) Rogers, Carl R., *Counseling and Psychotherapy, New Concepts in Practice*, Houghton Mifflin Co., Boston, 1942.

(24) Royer, Anne Elizabeth, "An Analysis of Counseling Procedures in a Nondirective Approach," M.A. thesis, Ohio State University, Columbus, Ohio, 1942. (See Curran above (10) for discussion.)

(25) Snyder, William U. (ed.), *Casebook of Nondirective Counseling*, Houghton Mifflin Co., Boston, 1947.

(26) Steinzor, Bernard, "The Development and Evaluation of a Measure of Social Interaction," *Human Relations*, Vol. II, No. 2, 1949, pp. 103–121.

(27) Thelen, Herbert, "Report of the Conference on the Scientific Problems of Utilization of Sound Recordings for Research," Department of Education, University of Chicago, August 22–24, 1947 (including multigraphed material sent out in preparation for the conference).

(28) Thomas, Dorothy Swain, and associates, *Some New Techniques for Studying Social Behavior*, Bureau of Publications, Teacher's College, Columbia University, New York, 1929.

(29) von Wiese, Leopold, *Systematic Sociology, On the Basis of Beziehungslehre and Gebildelehre*, "Frame of Reference for the Systematics of Action Patterns," adapted and amplified by Howard Becker, John Wiley and Sons, Inc., New York, Table 2, pp. 717–730, 1932.

(30) Withall, John G., "Resume of Study Entitled: 'The Development of a Technique for the Measurement of Social-Emotional Climate in Classrooms,'" mimeographed, Department of Education, University of Chicago. See also: Herbert Thelen and John Withall, "Three Frames of Reference: A Description of Climate," *Human Relations*, Vol. II, No. 2, 1949, pp. 159–176.

(31) Zander, Alvin F., "The W. P. Club: An Objective Case Study of a Group," *Human Relations*, Vol. 1, No. 3, pp. 321–332. (See also Hendry, C. E. (ed.), "A Guide for Observing a Scout Troop in Action," *Scouting for Facts*, Special Research Supplement No. 6, Research and Statistical Service, Boy Scouts of America, 2 Park Avenue, New York, Sept., 1944.)

INDEX

A

Acculturation of observer, 40

Action, forward and backward reference of, 49–50

internal complexity of, 49, 60

as referent of observation, 31

Action process, distribution of, between members, 58

in time, 58

Activity, concomitant variation of types, 16

coordination of, 76

Actor, as executive agent, 47

as part of frame of reference, 42

as related to time dimension, 45

symbol for, 48

Adaptive-instrumental significance of interaction, 10

Adaptive problems in interaction, 126

ADR index, 167

Affective mode of orientation, 51

social dimension of, 60

surpluses, 52

AI index, 168

Anecdotal recording, 100

A priori generalizations, 140

Attributing scores, 101, 112

Authority, structure of, 76, 154

informal, 174

Axiomata media, 116

B

Basic language of interaction, 69

Binomial probability paper, 111

BR index, 166

C

Categories, arrangement of, 63

chart of, 9, 59

companion pairs of, 10, 132

as agenda topics, 11

comprehensiveness of, 35, 63

context, as a, 63

hypotheses, as a set of, 64

modifications of, 88, 89

sections of, 8, 55, 131

sequences of, 128–9

simplifications of, 69

Chi square, acceptance levels, 109

as a measure of reliability, 102

computation, illustration of, 108

conventions of calculation by, 103

Classification, conflicts in, 36

inference of, 6, 35

resolving dilemmas of, 90–91

Cognitive orientation, 51, 60

Communication, as a functional problem, 11, 54, 79, 138

channels of, 79, 170

Comparative analysis, 33–34, 119

Conative orientation, 51, 60

Concepts, and empirical generalizations, 31

for experimental controls, 119

instability of referents of, 46–47

Content, ideosyncratic, 34

interaction, 33

limitations on kind, 35

of motivation, 80

topical, 34, 48

Context, as involved in classification, 36, 91